Samsung Electronics and the Struggle for Leadership of the Electronics Industry

ANTHONY MICHELL

WILEY

John Wiley & Sons (Asia) Pte. Ltd.

Other Wiley Editorial Offices

John Wiley & Sons, 111 River Street, Hoboken, NJ07030, USA

John Wiley & Sons, The Atrium, Southern Gate, Chichester, West Sussex, P019
8SQ, United Kingdom

John Wiley & Sons (Canada) Ltd., 5353 Dundas Street West, Suite 400, Toronto,
Ontario, M9B 6HB, Canada

John Wiley &Sons Australia Ltd., 42 McDougall Street, Milton, Queensland
4064, Australia

Wiley-VCH, Boschstrasse 12, D-69469 Weinheim, Germany

Library of Congress Cataloging-in-Publication Data
ISBN 978-0-470-82266-1

Typeset in Janson Text 11pt by Macmillan Publication Solutions
Printed in Singapore by Saik Wah Press Pte. Ltd.
10 9 8 7 6 5 4 3 2 1

Contents

Acknowledgments   vii

Note on the Romanization of Korean names   ix

Introduction   The problem of sustained business success   1

Chapter 1   The life cycle of Samsung Electronics   17

Chapter 2   Samsung Electronics and the Samsung Group: The burden of the Korean system   47

Chapter 3   Samsung and Sony compared: The tale of two life cycles   71

Chapter 4   Branding Samsung Electronics   93

Chapter 5   Making the "Samsung Man"   121

Chapter 6   Mobile phones   151

Chapter 7   Sleeping with the enemy: S-LCD   167

Chapter 8   Retaining creativity and avoiding bureaucracy   185

Chapter 9   The crisis of Samsung Electronics: The descent into bureaucracy   201

Chapter 10   Samsung's crisis and the global crisis, 2008–09   221

Appendix 1   237

Appendix 2   239

Index   243

Acknowledgments

This book was written at the invitation of Mr. Park Haeng-ung of the Korean Publishers Association in collaboration with the late Mr. Son Sang-mok of Indebook. The book was to have been published in time for the 2005 Frankfurt Book Fair. However, the complexity of the subject meant that the original deadline could not be met. These two gentlemen are responsible for making this book a reality. Equally, a chance encounter with C. J. Hwu of John Wiley over lunch in Singapore gave the book traction at the end of 2005.

But my real debts are much older. I owe two key people: Professor Charles Wilson of Cambridge University and Dr. Kim Jae-ik, both of whom changed my life. Charles Wilson took a shy undergraduate under his wings and set an avuncular role as thesis supervisor. Professor Wilson was also a source of inspiration with his *A History of Unilever*, one of the best business and economic historical accounts of the nineteenth and twentieth centuries written.

I am equally indebted to Dr. Kim Jae-ik, director general of the Economic Planning Bureau (EPB) who, in 1978, saw something in me of value to Korea. He persuaded me to work with him at EPB for one and a half years. Sadly, Dr. Kim, who was by 1983 Blue House economic secretary, perished in the Rangoon bombing. In many ways I have been trying to implement aspects of his vision. I am also indebted to Dr. Kim Key-won who was instrumental in sending me to meet Dr. Kim (Jae-ik) in early June 1978. At that time Dr. Kim Key-won was the director of research at the newly formed Korea Institute of International Economics, whose successor is the Korea International Economic Policy Institute (KIEP). Dr. Kim Key-won later became Korea's ambassador to the United States. After a distinguished career as a technocratic, he remains a senior advisor to Goldman Sachs and a source of continued inspiration.

My debt is also unpaid to Kim Mahn-je, at that time president of Korea Development Institute (KDI), who felt I was a tax on his budget at EPB; and successive presidents of KDI who shouldered the burden of my salary in those far-off days.

In 1999, I returned to KDI as a visiting professor. By then the KDI had through brand extension formed a graduate school of policy and management. I am profoundly grateful to my many students at the KDI School of Policy and Management (the "KDI School"). KDI's MBA and MPP classes comprises mature students from some of Korea's largest companies and government organizations as well as international students, all of whom have helped, through discussion and project presentations, in developing my ideas. Without their assistance, this book would not have been written. In particular I wish to thank Sergei Kondaroy for allowing me to draw on his research for his Master's thesis, prepared under my guidance at the KDI School.

Many employees of Korea Associates Business Consultancy Ltd. (KABC) helped form important ideas during our collaboration in creating the *Chaebol Report* between 1996 and 2003. They are Jeon Jin-hwan, Kim In-soon, Choi Mi-sun, Kim Suk-hee, Kim Su-mi, Kang Se-jin and Yi Song-mi.

I would also like to single out Ron Dore for kindling my interest in the development of the Far East; James Abegglen for his assistance in my understanding of Sony; and Dr. Frank-Jurgen Richter of HORASIS, formerly of the World Economic Forum, for involving me in his "future of capitalism" project, of which partial results were published in 2006. I am equally indebted to all those who encouraged or inspired me and are not mentioned in this book.

There are many others who, in the delightful Korean phrase, "I only met in a book." The chief of these is Ichak Adizes, whose seminal work on corporate life cycles continues to be an inspiration to me and my students.

Note on the Romanization of Korean names

Korean is written in a phonetic script called *hangul*, developed in the fourteenth century. Prior to this, the educated classes wrote in Chinese, but pronounced in a Korean way.

The romanization of Korean names is a problem for both Koreans and foreigners. Should certain sounds be transcribed as "p" or "b", "t" or "d", "k" or "g" and so on, with vowels acquiring an extra "e"? The academic world has used the McCune Reischauer system for many decades. For example, in this system, the name of the founder of Samsung Electronics is written "Yi P'yong-chol." This has some important but arcane rules that has led to a simplified system adopted by nearly all Koreans. Thus his name is written in this book as Lee Byung-chul. For the past 10 years, the Ministry of Education has tried to impose a system which leads foreigners to mispronounce the resulting words and in this system chairman Lee Byung-chul becomes Lee Byeong-chol. This also changes Pyongyang into Pyeongyang and other variants.

In a book written for the business and general reader I have used the *Korean Times* version of romanization, no doubt to be condemned by strict academics and the Ministry of Education.

Introduction: The Problem of Sustained Business Success

I want to lead Samsung Electronics to become one of the best companies in the world.

Yun Jong-yong,
CEO and Vice Chairman, 1999

Samsung Electronics from the outside

Samsung Electronics is the Korean company that has it all. It has a brilliant growth pattern, superb branding success, some of the highest profits in the world until 2009, and until 2008, a CEO who took Jack Welch as his model and produced a very special company through the theory of "a state of perpetual crisis."

In setting out to write a management book on Samsung Electronics, I considered where my comparative advantage lay. The initiators—Sohn Song Mok, the would-be publisher, and Park Haeng-gun of the Korean Publishers' Association—wanted a book which was forward-looking, and which compared Samsung with Sony. They also had in mind a "business school study approach" rather than a book based on intimate interviews.

Initial contacts with Samsung Electronics did not encourage the idea that in-depth original research with the company's blessing would be welcomed. When I first began the book in 2004, many of Samsung's internal papers reflecting on the reasons for the company's success and its future were treated as closely guarded secrets. This therefore was not the right time to write a company history. An authorized study would inevitably require observation of Samsung sensitivities.

The comparative approach seemed more fruitful, since it could incorporate both wider debate and insights which a study of

Samsung by itself would not generate. In particular it allowed me to explore aspects of change management, which has been a primary teaching focus at the KDI School.

The perspective of this book is that of an experienced commentator on Korea and global business presenting neither a narrative nor an adulatory and uncritical account of Samsung's rise, but a considered analysis of the secrets of success that both business students and CEOs will want to read and consider applying to their own companies. Nor is this book an insider's "tell all" of Samsung. Samsung Electronics is a closely guarded fortress from which information is not supposed to escape. But it is a fortress whose walls are watched closely, and some perspective of the inner issues in Samsung can be gained from those observers. The sources for this book are therefore diverse. Not a day goes by without some discussion of Samsung in the Korean press or global media. For the details, I have used official Samsung sources, official government sources and a range of significant interviews and reports about Samsung made over time by international and local journalists. The Korean press has also proven to be an invaluable source on the Samsung Group, although it has in the past been reputed to have printed stories which were sometimes not factual.

Distant observation of Samsung allowed for a more reflective approach while respecting sensitivities. My long sojourn of 30 years in Korea was useful in helping me form a view of Samsung. As a professor of strategy and management at the KDI School, I taught a range of subjects. They include international marketing, the rise of the digital economy and change management among Korean businessmen in the 35–45 age group, who have been thoughtful observers of the Korean and Asian business scene. As a business consultant, I advised foreign companies who had invested in Northeast Asia, and who interacted with Samsung Electronics and Sony on a day-to-day basis.

Between 1996 and 2003, KABC Ltd. also published an annual *Chaebol Report*. Started when there was a limited sense of danger to the *chaebol* system, this report tracked in detail the evolution of the crisis that shipwrecked so many other large Korean groups and shifted Korea's economy and society onto a new track.

The moment the last updated insight is inserted, the book begins to be outdated. But Samsung Electronics continues to evolve. The fortuitous delay in publication allowed me to insert a final chapter on both the management and strategic crisis of 2008, and Samsung's initial performance during the global economic crisis. Further updates can be found on www.kabcsamsung.com.

The secrets of success

The business shelves of bookstores groan with books which promise business success. But the strongest theme of academic criticism reviewing this literature should be that, in business, success does not last. The Fortune 500 list contains huge companies that will, if the past is any guide, disappear through mergers, bankruptcies or break-ups 30 years later.[1] Half of the companies chosen by Tom Peters and Robert Waterman in 1980 as having exhibited excellence had fallen from that pedestal by 1990.[2] Ecstatic praise for IBM in the 1980s waned as IBM teetered on crisis after crisis in the early 1990s. Brief but ecstatic praise for Enron as the supermodel for the new economy from seasoned business futurologist Gary Hamel was followed by super bankruptcy and fraud within two years of the publication of Hamel's work.[3] While Jack Welch broadcasts his version of successful management formulae, the fact is that 20 years after he became chairman, the process of reform still needed work. Far from providing an elixir of eternal corporate life, Jack Welch had proved that in a big corporation an eternal struggle against the forces of bureaucracy and opponents of change, rather than just good strategy, is essential.

With so many of the best brains on the planet, both in business and academia, plus all the consulting expertise that money can buy, being available to big corporations, why do only some companies experience dramatic success? And why do many fail? Even more important, how is success sustained, and devolution from success to failure prevented? Is it possible that, as Collins and Porras suggested in 1997, companies can be built to last?[4] Or does all business success hang by a thread? Included in Collins and Porras' selection of companies built in this manner, and supported by lavish praise for its creativity by the authors, was Sony, on the threshold of a decade of troubles.

Two giant electronics companies entered the twenty-first century side by side. Sony, formed in 1946, was the brainchild of its legendary president, Akio Morita.[5] Samsung Electronics followed 23 years later, driven by a team of people under the ultimate leadership of the chairman of the Samsung Group first, Lee Byung-chul, the founder of Samsung, and, after his death in 1987, his son, Lee Kun-hee. In 2000, Samsung Electronics had sales of US$28 billion, and Sony Corporation sales of US$70 billion. As far as electronics companies in components and appliances went, these two companies were near the top of the league, and only Matsushita and Philips had larger turnovers.

The two giants, one Korean and one Japanese, were competitors in many core areas, especially in dynamic access random memory (DRAMs), appliances and cell phones. Samsung was growing at about 25 percent per annum, and Sony, after a series of defeats in the previous 20 years, was growing at only about 5 percent per annum. Through the Betamax disaster of the later 1980s—where a reputedly superior product lost out to an allegedly inferior one which became industry standard—and through the loss of core production-skill leadership—for example, in DRAMs—Sony faced a Samsung surge on the rise of mobile phones and DRAMs, and new technology such as liquid crystal displays (LCDs).

Although our study is primarily focused on the rise of Samsung Electronics, its immediate past and its near and long-term future, inevitably we must look at Samsung's competitors both in Korea and throughout the world and at the distinctive issues facing a Korean corporation compared with a corporation domiciled in Japan or elsewhere in the world. It is natural to compare it most closely with Sony, since this is the company Samsung benchmarked and targeted itself against in the early twenty-first century. But if Samsung is like the old Sony of 10 or 20 years ago, the Sony of the early twenty-first century and the Samsung of the same period are very different. Understanding these differences could help explain why Samsung may continue to grow, and why Sony may continue to flounder, despite a heralded expected turnaround in 2006–07. By late 2008 Sony had made little progress, despite its reforms.

The theme presented is an external assessment of Samsung Electronics' achievements in relation to the PR goal, set in 2002, to build the company (then with a turnover only half that of Sony) into an innovative company that would not only overtake Sony, but would outshine it in nearly every field, notably in brand value followed by a growth in sales. Samsung's audacious bid was framed by Eric Kim, the Korean-American who was then head of marketing, where the goal was posed as "achieving the same brand recognition" as Sony.

What has been discovered is a remarkable team which CEO Yun Jong-yong had assembled to create an enterprise which now stands a chance of becoming the world's largest electronics company—a dream Samsung has harbored since the 1980s.

This is also a case study about the evolution of Korea's leading enterprise, about how a sterling company handled its corporate life cycle, and how it built and maintained its lead. What is evident is that Samsung Electronics harnessed a talented team that helped it progress from being a sub-contractor to a manufacturer to a leading creator of many electronic items. This talented team also helped Samsung Electronics grasp opportunities to accomplish what had been a dream in the 1980s. Samsung Electronics took substantial risks in its pre-emptive investment to achieve its goals. It kept its winning team refreshed by constant vigilance and talent renewal.

Later in the book we will find that Samsung employees put leadership ahead of the excellent personnel development courses and structures which Samsung Electronics (SEC) evolved in the 2000s. The same quality can be seen in the relentless work ethic of the company's Suwon campus. That leadership came primarily from Yun Jong-yong, who was to be nominated by *Fortune* as Asia's leading businessman in 2000 and was one of the 12 most powerful business leaders outside of the US in 2003.[6] But in the Korean context, this could not only come from Yun, because above him was chairman Lee Kun-hee. Samsung Electronics Corporation is not as independent an entity as Sony. The Samsung Group, as Korea's largest *chaebol*, is a conglomerate stretching through a bewildering range of businesses. The relationship between the chairman of the group and the CEO of Samsung Electronics must be introduced first. The full interrelationship between Samsung Electronics and the Samsung Group will be outlined later.

If Lee and Yun had not seen eye to eye, Yun would not have been appointed as CEO of Samsung Electronics in 1996, and would not have been given the freedom accorded to him by the chairman. Lee Kun-hee is special among the *chaebol* leaders. He is the third son of the founding chairman, Lee Byung-chul, who was himself a commanding figure in the Confucian mould. But Kun-hee was very different from his father. He believed that the chairman could not be the tireless captain of the ship, but should, rather, be a visionary going ahead of his captains.[7] This is consistent with what Bill Gates has done later in life, withdrawing from the everyday life of

Microsoft to spend time thinking about the future.[8] As chairman, Kun-hee made it a daily ritual in the 1990s to watch NKN news in the morning. He then summoned his captains to lunch to discuss what the news meant for Samsung, and what Samsung should do about the news. This was still a Confucian lunch, in which no one dared to eat except the chairman, so the captains rushed to eat before the meeting in the basement of Samsung building.[9] No Wall Street baron could quite match this combination of business and tradition.

The Samsung Group prides itself on being the partial creator of modern Korea. But we have to recognize that Samsung Electronics was both a shaper and a product of Korea. Samsung Electronics helped highlight Korean strengths in business, and in recent years has had the wealth and foresight to buy its way round many shortcomings of the Korean model through outsourcing beyond Korea. The Korean consumer's desire for new things supported Samsung's drive into consumer products in the early twenty-first century. Samsung could not escape the changes overtaking Korean society.

Korea has also evolved with Samsung Electronics. The so-called IMF crisis of 1997 (the Korean term for the Asian crisis) was an important wake-up call and stimulus for Korean management at every level. Eric Kim, after he quit as chief marketing officer in 2004, said:

> I think it was the financial crisis that literally put Samsung at the edge of dying, that forced them to rethink everything. Yes, initially there was a major resistance, a major barrier, but on the other hand because of the Asian financial crisis, there was also the view that they had no other choice. There was nothing else they could do but this.[10]

For CEO Yun, it was more; it was the coming of the crisis that allowed him to tentatively challenge everything about his company. Yun recognized the crisis as a time for change. Reputedly a long-term fan of Jack Welch's writings, he had no qualms about downsizing the workforce when the crisis hit, a very un-Korean thing to do in a company which was in better financial state than most Korean enterprises at that time. Nor did he hesitate about selling off divisions which seemed to him to be sub-standard or out of place in the Samsung Electronics that he envisaged.

The Korea of 2009 is very different from that of 1997. The pre-global crisis world of 2007–08 offered different opportunities from that of 10 years before. Korea in 2007–08 was also much less like the Korea seen in 1987 or 1977 during Samsung Electronics' infancy or adolescence. The whole of Korea Inc. learned the lesson of 1997 well. We shall see later that even before the current crisis Samsung Electronics faced new tensions as its role in Korea changed. This is where we will introduce the concept of the "Korean voice": the voice of those who did not fully absorb the lesson of the 1997; and the "global voice": the voice of those who absorbed and adjusted to the lessons of 1997. In the arguments, dialogues and disagreements on strategy which divided Samsung Electronics at the end of the first decade of the twenty-first century lies the division between those who want to challenge everything, and those who feel that the company has got where it is by being true to its origins. Both sides were to be shaken by a succession of crises in the period after 2007: a slowdown in the drivers of business growth in 2007; the political issues which led to the resignation of the chairman in 2008; the triumph of the Korean voice, which led to Yun's resignation a month later; and the onset of the global economic crisis which hit sales from October 2008. In the changes between 1997 and 2008 lies part of the essence of the life-cycle model of corporate change which, this book argues, is at the heart of the search for the corporate elixir of life.

The corporate life cycle and product cycles

Academic discussion of business success has largely taken one of three directions. In one direction lies product portfolio choice and strategic direction—these give the company competitive advantage and financial success. Advocates of the strategic causes of success have generally argued for pursuing a narrowing range of core business, but with no guidance on what to do if the core business becomes a dying business. Much of the work in this direction is derived from the codification of Michael Porter and other theorists, and the work of the big strategy consultants.

The second direction looks at change management in preventing the company from shifting from extreme success to severe problems. The direction of change management is largely case-history driven—this relates to the treatment of problems, or the symptoms of change, rather than the prevention of problems. In essence much of corporate restructuring and reform have been aimed at preventing the need for change management at its root. Despite this preference to avoid change there is also a debate on whether companies can be built to change, in the way that Collins and Porras argued that they could be built to last. Porras was to write an introduction to Lawler and Worley's *Built to Change*, which reminded readers that "over the last decade about half of the Built to Last companies have not been able to sustain a high performance level."[11] Does Samsung Electronics have the qualities which Lawler and Worley believe should exist in Built to Change companies? Or does it have something more, or something less? We will review this in the final chapter.

The third direction in academic discussion, which can in itself become the whole story in business success literature, is to concentrate on great CEOs as corporate saviors in the tradition of Jack Welch and Louis Gerstner. The story of Samsung Electronics also includes the concept of a great leader or perhaps more accurately, as it always is, a great management team.

Leaving the question of technology choice, organizational structure, leadership and even product portfolio on one side, a plausible argument for the failure of businesses over time is that like products, and like people, companies also have a life cycle. A great company should be able to rejuvenate itself and prolong business success. This is what Samsung Electronics was able to do in 1997–98 to prepare itself for a decade of outstanding success in which leadership and product portfolio and strategy all played their part. This rejuvenation, whether in General Electric or in Samsung Electronics, is not something that by itself lasts forever. Yun's solution was to try to create a culture of "continuous crisis." In 2007, chairman Lee accentuated the call to respond to crisis and initiated changes which had been only partly implemented when he left the company. While a sense of crisis may help keep the company young, it does not heal fundamental flaws, nor rejuvenate the employees of the company.

Why do companies have a life cycle? Like living creatures, companies are born into an environment which shapes them and moulds their formative years. Both the successes and failures of the early years shape the rules by which the senior managers run the company. Michael Dell's bad experience with the cost of holding out-of-date inventory in the early 1980s bred the Dell model of zero inventory. But those managers who learned the first corporate lessons also age. Men in their thirties in 1969, when the company was founded, had reached their sixties by the time of the financial crisis of 1997. Products that were fresh in the 1970s were, in the world of electronics, rapidly outdated many times over by the 1990s. The giants of the first generation of the digital IT industry—Gates, Dell, Jobs, and Khosla and McNealy—all crossed the 60-threshold about the same time.

The ossification of a company comes from many sources. More specifically, it comes from those who try to impose rules on how the company operates and then preserve those rules after the circumstances have changed. Jack Welch and others have identified this as the corporate bureaucracy. These are the senior managers who create and police the rules by which they think the company should operate, whatever the chairman or vice chairman says.

One of the most readily understandable models of the corporate life cycle was evolved in the 1980s by Ichak Adizes, who pioneered many of the aspects of analysis of the internal life of the corporation. Figure 1 below sets out his framework of a company's life cycle.

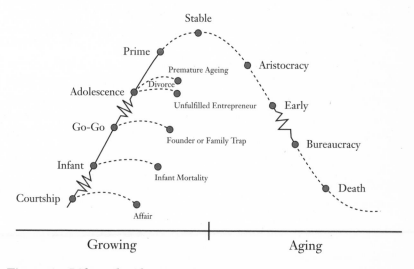

Figure 1   Life cycle of companies
Source: Adizes[12]

It is important to remember that the life cycle measures the total life cycle of the organization. This includes its ability to change, and this is best measured first by sales growth, and later by sales growth and profitability.

In this model of how companies grow and age, Adizes posits that successful companies go through a pre-adolescent "go-go" phase, if they survive infancy. They later go through an adolescent phase in which growth is rapid and then reach a plateau in which growth is no longer exponential but limited. A company with a substantial market share will face limits to its growth proportionate to the growth of the market. The company therefore is mature. If it is well managed and flexible, it is in its prime. It is easy to slip from the prime phase into the stable phase, where it is maintaining its position but is neither growing nor declining. From here, it is easy to slip into the declining ages of the life cycle—the "aristocracy" and "bureaucracy" phases. Companies fall into these phases partly because of their previous success. They then fail to change or trim costs on non-essentials or tend to put their resources into the wrong "next new thing." Adizes argues that the main issues are not about market share or portfolio choice, but about the balance between flexibility and control within the organization. This is where the development of too much control limits flexibility, or where too much flexibility in a large organization leads to a decline in efficiency. His model is based on a curve which looks something like Figure 2.

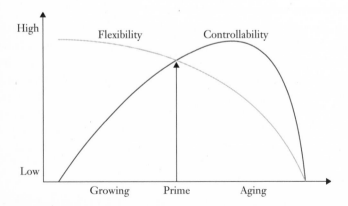

Figure 2　Flexibility and control in corporate life cycles

Source: Adizes p.3 (Figure 1)

Adizes debunks the notion that size and time are the causes of growth and aging, or that large companies with long traditions are old, and small companies with no tradition are young. He says: "I have diagnosed 100-year-young and 10-year-old corporations … Young means the organization can change relatively easily … Old means … the organization is inflexible; it has little propensity to change."[13]

Adizes wrote his seminal work in the 1980s, dealing primarily with large and small American corporations. His analysis of "adolescence" is a good description of the new electronics companies of the 1980s and early 1990s. He also treats aging as a natural phenomenon. When a company reaches the "stable" stage, it cannot be simply rejuvenated and left alone, as Jack Welch discovered. "Change is like gardening," Adizes says. "If you work at it, the weeds are taken out and the flowers will bloom. If you do not maintain the garden, the weeds will overtake the flowers."[14]

This approach does not explicitly take into account the sociology of human organizations. Deep in the DNA of a human organization are the cells that cause aging. In the human body these represent a complex process in which cells reproduce and renew more slowly. In the company, the equivalent is "bureaucratic cells." Like fat cells, which are necessary, bureaucracy exists in all organizations. But like cancer cells, the bureaucracy in organizations could grow endlessly. The result: the body moves from healthy fat among the tissues to obesity. In the company, the life cycle typically passes from fitness to an aristocratic phase, and then through stages of bureaucracy.

This analogy can be extended to plot the growth of companies by plotting sales over time. Adizes' thinking is that the aim of all companies is to attain or reach their "prime." He suggests four success factors which are necessary in various combinations throughout the sequence of life cycles relating to the quality of decisions made collectively by the organization. These are described as combinations of the collective organizational management skills: P (Performing), A (Administering), E (Entrepreneuring) and I (Integrating).[15]

P: Performing is fulfilling the purpose of the organization which, in most instances, involves satisfying the needs of the constituencies (I would have written "customers" or "markets") for which the organization exists.

A: Administering refers to the ways by which to systematize, make routine, and program the resources and activities of the organization so that "the right things are done at the right time and with the right intensity."

E: Entrepreneuring refers to proactively—not reactively—providing for change.

I: Integrating is developing a culture of interdependency and affinity, "so as to nurture the unique corporate 'religion' . . . by changing an organization's consciousness from mechanistic to organic."

Obviously, a different combination of skill sets is required for each phase of the life cycle if an organization is to reach or return to the prime or stable phase. As Adizes so brilliantly (and patiently) explains, problems occur when an organization has a combination that may be appropriate for one stage of the life cycle but inappropriate (if not fatal) for that in which it now resides. Therefore, the prime or the stable phase is achieved when the functions of P, A, E, and I are in proper balance. All organizations should maximize Performing and Administering. Those organizations which have a greater need for Entrepreneuring than Integrating will be found in the prime stage on the curve; others which have a greater need for I than E will be found in the stable point. "Any time one of the PAEI roles is missing, a mismanagement style of leadership will repetitively occur."[16]

Because the ideal combination, the ideal balance, will always be a "moving target" under constant "attack" by internal as well as external forces, each organization must constantly be aware of what that ideal combination should be. Change is the only constant. This is a constant which Koreans understand well, and which will be analyzed in detail in later chapters. This explanation may work retrospectively in an analytical situation, but does not give much guidance to the CEO who wants to know whether his company has the right combination for its stage of development. Both Welch and Gerstner knew that companies at a certain level had too much Administering and proceeded to "nuke" the bureaucracy.

Unlike many other business areas, the electronics industry during the 1960s had the additional risk of coping with fast-moving technology. Risk is about opportunity as well as danger, yet the majority of literature on risk management is about danger rather than opportunity. Hyundai set out to build its business in industries (ships and automobiles) in which price was more important than new technology. Samsung itself had built huge companies based on sugar and seasonings, and textiles; and LG on chemicals for household and industrial consumption. In 1969, Samsung Electronics embarked on a journey to compete in an industry in which change would be relentless; and in which using yesterday's technology for too long would lead to tomorrow's failure.

There is an argument that the endless succession of new technologies suited the Korean character, with its restlessness and desire for quick change. By contrast, Sony, although not always the most Japanese of companies, was slowed by Japanese caution. Sony produced a bewildering range of technologies but hesitated to adopt them, particularly after the Betamax disaster. Mere restlessness is not enough where technology is concerned. Technology must be created, and the winning technology selected. In the history of choosing the wrong technology, the name of Sony is forever linked to Betamax, an allegedly superior video technology, which was forced off the road by VHS, an allegedly inferior technology which became the industry standard.[17]

Similarly, the Windows and Office systems also swept away superior software which could not compete with the desire of the market for an industry standard rather than for excellence. Samsung had to choose—and has to continue to choose—the correct technology and business areas through which to succeed. In this, Samsung's often-stated aversion to consumer products—compared with Sony's positive embrace of consumer products and its willingness to leave components to others—is an important ingredient, and part of Samsung's success story.

Whenever things seemed to go wrong, Samsung tended to be much more concerned about the product cycle than about the corporate life cycle. This was not surprising given Samsung Electronics' reliance on DRAMs, and its experience in dealing with this that led it to leadership position. It is part of the argument of this book that it is for precisely this reason that many companies fail. For those practicing change management, the concept of a corporate life cycle is not necessarily the core theory on which much practical advice is based. Yet once it is incorporated into company analysis, it becomes an obvious and major explanatory factor in deciding why a company needs to change and how it came to this point. It was at the life cycle age of 40 that Sony's vitality began to run out. Many of Samsung's competitors are older than 40. This is despite Adizes' belief that the chronological age of a company is not important and that life after 40 for a corporation is no different than before. But 40 years is an obvious danger point. Within Samsung or Sony or any other company, anyone who started work when the company began will be over 60 years of age, and those who joined in its early years, not much younger. A company can age because its management ages. But it can be rejuvenated by a younger management.

Hence, the "outsider CEO" theory of corporate change and recovery, much loved by Wall Street investors, is that a new broom sweeps clean. However, a new broom does not always manage to sweep clean. Where it does, it sweeps out all the "old think" managers. A CEO from outside the company, like Gerstner, owes nothing to the past, and generally will feel free to choose new executives who are dedicated to the new program. But for an oriental, family-managed company, it is not easy to bring in a CEO from outside. And what if the "old think program" is in the DNA of most, if not all, Koreans and Japanese, and not just a few old guys? This was the crisis Sony experienced in 2005, when the best man for the job seemed to be a *gaijin* rather than a Japanese, because all Japanese who shared the same cultural DNA were unsuitable for the job.

In the electronics industry, technological and market change is probably faster than most. It might be thought that, by 2000, the chances of a new electronics company emerging to challenge existing companies (except in China or a fast-growing domestic market) were probably limited. A study of how Samsung Electronics grew shows that a new company could arise based on a sizeable local market and the creation of economies of scale in components (which Hamel and Prahalad term "core-products" or "products which go into finished products").[18] While a group of wary competitors circle, waiting for signs of weakness and scrambling to get to the next "big thing" first, a new generation of companies can arise, producing yesterday's technology and building up core competencies and a large market share of a virtual market.

Did Sony find itself in this trap when it hit 50? Sony teemed with innovative departments ready to produce new products in 1997, yet its path into the twenty-first century was fraught with difficulty. Sony showed all the signs of aging in both structure and organization and in product choice. It believed that its future lay in its brand's strength to sell new products. The PlayStation was to be the new Walkman. Yet in 2007, PlayStation III came a year late and was outsold by Microsoft's Xbox 360 and Nintendo's Wii. The failure highlights the electronics manufacturer's dilemma—end-user products not containing proprietary components have a limited profit potential. We shall refer to this as the "multi-competitor dilemma."

This is not a definitive market truth. There are other models that seem to work. Dell makes no components but continues to drive its market share upwards based on a quite different business model. Michael Dell's model has been to work with the company's suppliers to produce the latest computers and never to be stuck with old components (a decision based on a painful experience in its early days). As Thomas Friedman has observed, Dell represents the perfection of the global supply partnership model.[19] Samsung supplies the memory card, mother board, LCD screen, battery and power adaptor for Friedman's Dell computer, but Dell had alternative suppliers in Asia for all except the memory card.[20]

This book sets out to analyze Samsung Electronics from the perspective of the struggle for leadership in the electronics industry, and the universal struggle to keep a company free of bureaucracy. In 2005, George Gilder, an American technology analyst and author of the *Gilder Technology Report*, was quoted as saying: "Samsung is now the anti-Sony;" but by 2009 it might be seen as a member of the same family.[21]

Samsung Electronics is the largest company in Korea and has been since the 1980s. In one sense, it is unique. In another sense, it is merely the largest of the successful Korean corporations. Samsung also faces risks. Gilder likened Samsung to "the old Sony," having "much of the spirit of Sony 10 years ago."[22] How will Samsung avoid a crisis in the next few years as it faces new competition? Will those who wrote disparagingly of Sony in 2005 also express the same sentiments about Samsung in 2015? Is Samsung built to last?

George Gilder attributed Sony's decline to its layers of bureaucracy. His view underlines the core issue for Samsung. Samsung is driven by its "spirit," its "non-MBA term" for how it does things. To understand the "spirit" of Samsung in managerial terms, we have to first understand its tools for change management. To keep a company "young at heart" is a continuous battle. Yun fought this every day with his slogan of the company being in "perpetual crisis." In 2007 he was joined by his chairman, who also sounded out this "cry of crisis." As the final chapters of this book show, this sense of crisis was not misplaced. Although Yun's concept of creating a sense of "perpetual crisis" helped Samsung Electronics stay on its toes, it may have institutionalized crisis, rather than prepared the company for the moment when it reached the limits of the model which had driven it for 10 years. These are the issues which this book will explore.

Endnotes

1   Collins, James C. and Porras, Jerry I. 1997, *Built to Last: Successful Habits of Visionary Companies*, New York: HarperBusiness.
2   Ibid.
3   Hamel, Gary 2002, *Leading the Revolution: How to Thrive in Turbulent Times by Making Innovation a Way of Life*; see also Hamel, Gary and Prahalad, C. K. 1994, *Competing for the Future*, Cambridge, MA: Harvard Business School Press.
4   Collins and Porras, op. cit.
5   Sea-jin Chang's *Sony versus Samsung* (Wiley, 2008), appeared after the text was finished, but before the final chapter was written. A good account of the ongoing problems at Sony was given by Sion Barry "Welshman's Tough Task: Restructure Sony"; http://www.walesonline.co.uk/business-in-wales/business-news/2009/01/22/welshman-s-tough-task-restructure-sony-91466–22749758/; accessed May 10, 2009.
6   "The Man Who Shook Up Samsung," by Louis Kraar, *Fortune*, January 24, 2000; "Foreign Powers," by Clay Chandler, Janet Guyon, Cait Murphy, and Richard Tomlinson, *Fortune*, August 11, 2003.
7   Interviews with the elder Lee, founder of Samsung, suggest that Kun-hee learned part of his management style from his father; see Chapter 2.
8   "In Secret Hideaway, Bill Gates Ponders Microsoft's Future," by Robert A. Guth, *Wall Street Journal*, March 28, 2005.
9   Private communication with former Samsung executive.
10 www.principalvoices.com/beijing.html, May 16, 2005; accessed April 4, 2007.
11 Jerry Porras in Lawler, Edward E., III and Worley, Chris 2006, *Built to Change: How to Achieve Sustained Organizational Effectiveness*, San Francisco, CA: Jossey-Bass: V–XII.
12 Adizes, Ichak 1988, *Corporate Lifecycles*, Paramus, NJ: Prentice Hall: 79.
13 Ibid.: 2.
14 Ibid.: 276.
15 Ibid.: 115–39.
16 Ibid.: 2 and 276.
17 The Betamax story has been told many times. A good up-to-date version can be found at: http://en.wikipedia.org/wiki/Videotape_format_war, accessed May 10, 2009; see also "In Sony's Stumble, the Ghost of Betamax," by Ken Belson, *New York Times*, February 26, 2006.
18 Hamel and Prahalad, op. cit.: 215–9.
19 Friedman, Thomas L. 2005, *The World is Flat: A Brief History of the Twenty-First Century*, New York: Farrar, Straus & Giraux: 517–8.
20 Ibid.
21 *New York Times* article: http://www.nytimes.com/2005/03/10/business/worldbusiness/10rivals.html?oref=login
22 Ibid. Also quoted in "Samsung Is Now What Sony Once Was" by James Brooke/Saul Hansell, *Seoul Times*, March 9, 2005.

1

The Life Cycle of Samsung Electronics

The life of a man is short, but that of a corporation must never be.

Lee Byung-chul[1]

Courtship and infancy

What did Lee Byung-chul, founder and chairman of the Samsung Group, think he was founding in January 1969? Globally, the electrical industry was at the end of its first electronic transformation, from valves to diodes and transistors. The American and European electrical industry was under siege by the Japanese industry—Sony, Matsushita, Toshiba and Sanyo. The Italians were taking the European whitegoods market by storm. In Korea, American and Japanese companies—including Motorola, Signetics, Fairchild Semiconductor, Control Data, Victor, and Canon—were in the process of setting up ventures to take advantage of cheap labor costs and moderate-quality labor.

In all probability, Lee mainly had his eye on his local competitor Goldstar Electronics (now LG Electronics). Founded in 1959, Goldstar was sweeping the local appliance market, as Korea's high tariffs and cumbersome non-tariff barriers limited the supply of imported products to the domestic market. Goldstar's founders, the Koos, had linked up with the founders of Lucky (at that time involved in clothing and chemicals), the Huhs, to form a new rival to Samsung called Lucky Goldstar. This would form a *chaebol* which could seek to challenge the Samsung Group in every field. And Lee was not happy: unlike Lucky Goldstar, the Samsung Group was not then the favorite of Korea's military rulers, led by President Park Chung-hee.

When Park had come into power eight years earlier, Lee, the richest man in Korea, had spent six months in exile in Japan, negotiating the terms of his return, which included the surrender of his ownership of most of the Korean banks, and the creation of a new chemical fertilizer plant as a penance. A scandal involving Lee's eldest son over the sale of saccharine related to this new plant led to the confiscation of the plant and the political unacceptability of his first son as the future heir of the Samsung Group.

South Korea in the late 1960s was still one of the poorest countries in the world. It had been 18 years since the end of the Korean War, one that had left the agricultural South divided from the industrial North. During the war, more explosives had been used on the Korean peninsula than in the entire Second World War. While most of these explosives had fallen on North Korea, rebuilding South Korea had been a slow task in a country riddled with corruption and without a vision for the future. However, this changed on May 16, 1961 when a group of young military officers seized power, and put planned economic growth first. Only one thing had gone right in the first five-year plan period (1961–66)—exports grew. When the harvest was good (40 percent of GDP hung on the success of agriculture), Korea's economy, which is buoyed by exports, grew.

Between Lee, the rich patrician from Daegu in the South-east, and Park, the peasant's son from nearby, there was no love lost. A supplementary account of this rivalry is given in the next chapter. For now it is enough to note that Lee was determined to make Samsung excel in every field of endeavor. In 1968 the government passed a law for the promotion of the electronics industry and this unlocked the door to a license for Samsung.

Chairman Lee was already the richest man in Korea under the old regime, but his surviving enterprises also prospered in the new era. He began to think about changing the name for his group of companies. Until the mid-1960s, he had called most of them "First" or "Best"—the word *cheil* in Korean means much the same. But now he launched new companies reviving the name of Samsung—Three Stars—which he had used in the 1930s and 1940s. Many people thought this new name reflected a conscious desire by Lee to compete with Three Diamonds, the literal translation of "Mitsubishi."

Consumer electronics was a natural field to enter. Rural electrification had become a major part of Korean planning from 1968 as the supply of electricity began to match demand. Every Korean household wanted a TV set, an electric fan and a refrigerator. The Japanese were finding that labor costs were rising as the Japanese miracle pushed its economy to new heights. South Korea was a country that most Japanese businessmen felt they knew well from their colonial presence up to 1945. It was a country in which all those now over the age of 35 had been forced to learn Japanese. After the unpopular treaty which President Park signed with the Japanese in 1965, forcing the Japanese to pay reparations for wartime and colonial damage, the Japanese were allowed to officially invest in Korea.[2]

Consequently, in the courtship there was no shortage of suitors. Japanese companies were eager to utilize Korea's low-cost, but disciplined, labor. Because of historic animosity stemming from the colonial period, they preferred to create joint ventures. It was suddenly easy to get Japanese technology, components, and partners, not just for Lee, but for almost any Korean company. The Samsung group was armed with joint-venture and technology partners from Japan, including Sanyo and NEC. For Lee, who had studied at Waseda University in the 1930s and whose wife was Japanese, Japan was a second home, and his entire corporate structure was built on the concept of Japanese excellence as interpreted by Koreans. For the richest man in Korea and one comfortable in dealing with the Japanese, it was easy to find whatever technology Samsung needed. In 1969, alongside Samsung Electronics, Lee also founded Sanyo-Samsung Electronics to manufacture black-and-white TVs.[3]

The Japanese were the biggest investors in Korea in the late 1960s and early 1970s. But much of this promised investment—including a Toyota car plant—never arrived. In 1974, oil prices doubled and the Japanese pulled back much of their investment, especially from Korea, where they encountered continuing hostility. Korean industrialists hesitated as a mistaken government policy on private lending in 1972 almost brought business to a halt, and then two years later when OPEC brought the world economy to a halt.

Samsung Electronics, which started off manufacturing home appliances such as television sets and refrigerators in January 1969, entered the microprocessor manufacturing business (as it was then called) by taking over Korea Semiconductor in 1974. At the time, there were doubts as to the wisdom of this quantum leap, from being an assembler of consumer electronics to a producer of basic components. In 2005, Lee Kun-hee, chairman of Samsung since 1987, explained how the management of Samsung Electronics, citing the company's lack of technology in the new field, had tried to dissuade his father and himself from initiating the microchip business in 1974. Lee said that he and his father decided to move into the semiconductor business as they were already convinced that, as the nation has virtually no natural resources, the high-tech industry was the only means of survival for the Korean economy. As Lee said in 2004, "Preemptive investment is critical to success in the chip industry since missing the timing for an investment will generate a huge loss."[4]

Thirty years earlier this was far from obvious to most Koreans. Rich as the Lee family and the Samsung empire were, committing money to a new business meant diverting a lot of resources that the company could use to add profitability to existing businesses.

Worse, Korea Semiconductor, which had a plant in Puchon in the Kyonggi province, was on the brink of bankruptcy only two months after its foundation. With the economy faltering, and the Japanese, expecting the worst, canceling nearly all their planned investment in South Korea, Samsung's managers saw this new investment as too risky. There were serious doubts about how South Korea, always short of foreign exchange, would survive in a world of high oil prices. Naturally, those around the Lees warned against jumping into a new industry that they knew little about.

Chairman Lee had already created a culture in which he listened to his senior managers. So father and son, rather than go directly against the ideas of their executives, funded the takeover of Korea Semiconductor privately, and only merged it with Samsung Electronics in 1979. Consumer electronics was seen as the leading business. Semiconductors were seen as items which would fit into these appliances, a source of import substitution more than of profit.

Given that the leading semiconductor companies had begun their businesses in the 1950s, just a few years after the first semiconductor transistor was invented in 1947, Samsung made a relatively late start. In 1976, Samsung Electronics succeeded in manufacturing the semiconductor transistor, and also installed mass production facilities of 3-inch silicon wafers in its Puchon plant.

At the consumer end of the industry, the Korean government deliberately blocked the entry of Japanese-finished consumer electronics. It was possible to smuggle in Japanese goods, but it was not possible to import them legally. The Korean government was determined to make an external competition-free environment for its electronics industry. Samsung did not stop at TVs and semiconductors but proceeded to create a total of six different electronics companies.

The government's thinking—governed by the simple idea that exports were good and the domestic market was secondary—was that consumption was waste.[5] For this reason, color TV sets could not be sold in Korea, and all domestic broadcasting was in black-and-white, although the American Forces Korea Network (AFKN) broadcast in color and those who had smuggled in TV sets could watch these English broadcasts in color.

In 1977, a young Ira Magaziner (later to be industrial adviser to President Clinton) stopped by the Samsung Electronics center at Suwon, while working for the British government as a consultant looking at color TV technology. As he was to put it later: "A few years before, Korean black-and-white televisions had begun arriving in England. At first, British TV producers hadn't been concerned. The Koreans gained only a small market share, and besides, this was exactly what developing countries were expected to do: compete in 20-year-old products."[6] Fifteen years later there would not be a UK-owned TV manufacturer.

Magaziner was not very impressed by Samsung Electronics:

> The company's electronic division, in Suwon, an hour's drive from Seoul, wasn't much. The factory floors were bare concrete, and people were hand-wheeling parts to and from the production line. I moved on to Samsung's research lab, which reminded me of a dilapidated high-school science classroom. But the work going on there intrigued me. They'd gathered color televisions from every major company in the world—RCA, GE, Hitachi—and were using them to design a model of their own.[7]

The chief engineer told Magaziner that rather than buy parts from overseas, Samsung was going to make everything itself.

Magaziner did not believe the company because he thought it could not find the engineers who could accomplish this.

In 1982 he returned, working for GE's microwave division and aiming to source cheap microwave ovens. At that time only the Japanese and American firms could make microwave ovens, but the Koreans were close behind. First he was struck by the color television line. "This was different—as automated as any TV plant I'd seen in America," he said.[8] He was also surprised to find that the company was making its own tubes for the TVs, right down to the glass in a joint venture with Corning. But he was most impressed with the change in the R&D lab which had gone from a school science room to a large modern operation: "Everything Samsung had said it would do in 1977, it had done."[9] Samsung was also ready to offer a way to allow GE to make money out of microwaves by producing them at a price that GE could not refuse.[10]

Go-Go Growth (1983–95)

By the 1980s when Samsung's six electronics companies were merged into two, Samsung Electronics and Samsung Semiconductors, electronics made up 42.1 percent of the group's industrial workforce, and about 10 percent of the total workers in the Korean electronics industry. Goldstar was still ahead, employing 14 percent.[11]

Problems with the Korean government continued. Samsung had to fight off an order to move the company's semiconductor operations from Suwon (where it had moved from Buchon) to Kumi, where the government planned to have all Korea's semiconductor plants located alongside the state-funded Korea Institute of Electronics Industry (KIET). Only Samsung was strong enough to resist this order. Its answer was to merge both companies.[12]

Why did Samsung Electronics Corporation (SEC) continue to invest money in components? The answer to this strategy lay at the heart of what it meant to be Korean in the 1970s and early 1980s. Despite escaping from Japanese colonization in 1945, Korean industry remained heavily dependent on Japanese know-how and even more on Japanese components. Samsung Electronics strategists could see that they were basically assemblers. As they disassembled the world's best TV sets, they saw the same components in many of them. Unless they could penetrate into the component business,

Korean industry would forever be dependent on the Japanese, who were now dominating the electronics industry. Did Samsung managers realize that they would be building up a core competence which would eventually allow them to out-compete the Japanese?

The Samsung Group began to make rapid strides in the semiconductor business with the "Tokyo Declaration" by chairman Lee in February 1983 where he announced that Samsung was making full inroads into the semiconductor industry. Ten months later, Samsung Electronics announced that the company had placed Korea in the third spot in developing the high-speed memory chip, behind only the US and Japan. Samsung lagged behind the US and Japan in developing the 64K DRAM by four and a half years. This meant that the Japanese and Americans enjoyed high prices; but when Samsung entered the market, the price for DRAMs fell dramatically and fell further as others followed.

Samsung engineers worked hard to narrow the technology gap with their top-tier competitors. In 1984, one year after the Tokyo Declaration, the company had narrowed the gap in its 256K DRAM development to three years. Samsung developed the 1Mb DRAM in 1986, the 4Mb DRAM in 1988 and the 16Mb DRAM in 1989, shortening the lead time on each occasion. In 1992, it gained the technological initiative in the global memory-semiconductor market by developing the world's first 64Mb DRAM.

During the 1980s, Korea was also undergoing historic changes. In 1980, a second military revolution had taken place which brought Chun Doo-whan to the presidency. In 1986, the democratic movement prepared for the overthrow of the military dictatorship. This did not take the dramatic form of violence. Chun Doo-whan did not step down from power as Synghman Rhee had done in 1960 in the face of massive demonstrations, nor did the KCIA chief assassinate him as Park Chung-hee had been assassinated in 1979. In the face of the determined will of the Korean people, Roh Tae-woo, Chun's designated successor, made a June 1987 declaration that free presidential elections would be held. Chun allowed these elections to take place in 1987 and Roh, a co-conspirator of the December 1979 military coup that rushed to fill the power vacuum after Park's assassination, was elected, as two opposition leaders fought one another and split the vote. But Roh allowed the democratic forces to continue their protests, allowing unions to form in all major industries and beyond. He presided over an era of prosperity in which Korean wages rose 250 percent and inflation only 50 percent, doubling every Korean consumer's income.

Also in 1987, Korea acceded to the requests of the US government to open key markets, allowing the import of cigarettes, cars and other consumer items, and to allow foreign investment in the life insurance market. This liberalization did not extend to Japanese products, which gave Korea's electronics industry a further 10 years of protection.

These changes did not upset the growth pattern of Samsung Electronics. The strong cohesive culture of the company prevented the formation of unions, but Samsung Electronics continued its high wage policy. The company continued to produce both consumer products for which there was a surge in demand from 1986 onwards, and showed increasing competence, especially in TVs and, above all, in DRAMs.

Adolescence: Rejuvenating Samsung Electronics— The Yun era, phase 1 (1996–2000)

With the 64Mb chip in 1992, Samsung Electronics had entered the border zone between go-go and adolescence. It was time to change and restructure. Samsung had achieved a core goal to take leadership in DRAMS, but what should its new goals be? DRAM chips supplied 50 percent of the company's profits in 1995, and provided 35 percent of the total sales of the Samsung parent company. In 1995 Samsung was now at the leading end of the product price cycle. This meant that it was ahead of the global supply curve and enjoyed initial high profits. But when the rest of the manufacturers caught up, Samsung's profits would fall, and this would happen in early 1996, when a global oversupply of microchips caused prices to fall drastically. Since the early 1990s, Samsung has led the global market in DRAM semiconductors, the memory chips that are vital to almost every digital product we use. During the 1990s price slump, as competitors like Hitachi and NEC were backing away from the chip business Samsung dived further in, introducing two new lines.

In 1996, sales of Samsung Electronics fell for the first time, by 2.1 percent from 16.2 trillion *won* (about US$20 billion) to 15.87 trillion *won*. Facing considerable pain in this cyclical movement, Samsung executives began to look again at its then-inefficient consumer electronics division, which had been neglected in favor of manufacturing microchips. Samsung had market leadership in television sets and the company began to aggressively market these abroad. But before Samsung could develop an effective strategy to cope with both the promotion of TVs and the problem of the DRAM price slump, the whole of Korea was engulfed in a financial crisis of unparalleled proportions.

The Samsung Group was lucky that in December 1996 chairman Lee had appointed Yun Jong-yong as CEO of Samsung Electronics. Forty-nine-year-old Yun, a long-serving engineer and a great admirer of Jack Welch and the corporate restructuring movement he led, was eager to apply many of the same ideas to Samsung Electronics. This marks him as a very unusual man within the Korean corporate universe of the 1990s. While most CEOs at the time were very able men, they lacked a sense of global vision or regard for Western companies. None of them had had experience of restructuring their companies or of ever downsizing. Rather, they were all growth specialists who had experienced double-digit sales growth almost every year since the early 1980s, and whose only financial skill was in borrowing new money to pay back old money.

If Samsung Electronics was to experience more than organic growth that was heavily dependent on product cycles, it would have to do something different, or change gear. Without this, there was every possibility that the company would develop signs of falling into the aristocracy cycle where Korean-style complacency was developing. This form of complacency was a more dynamic form of the disease than that seen in Western management, but complacency nonetheless. Samsung Electronics was by then already the largest company on the Korean stock market. It was one of the most prestigious in the Samsung stable, and was overstaffed with highly competent Samsung men who did not have to try too hard to be successful.

By the time Yun took the helm in December 1996, Samsung Electronics was primarily known for manufacturing microchips. Its consumer electronics products were regarded internationally as cheaper and lower-quality imitations of leading brands such as Sony and Mitsubishi. In Korea, other brands such as LG Electronics and Daewoo Electronics were experiencing surges in consumer confidence that were chipping away Samsung's market share.

At this time, the Samsung group was intently focused on its new auto company, which was preparing to make its first sales. Samsung Electronics was a major investor in the auto company, holding 50 percent. The Korean economy appeared to be defying gravity, continuing to grow at 8 percent per annum and growing visibly richer. Yun, as president of Samsung Electronics, was expected to preside over this successful company in which decision-making was decentralized, and in which each executive had wide discretion in making his own decisions.

Yun had other ideas. Although an engineer by training, he had evolved a set of management principles modeled along what Welch did at GE. He could see strong parallels between Welch's descriptions of GE in 1980 and Samsung Electronics (and most other Korean companies) in 1996. In 1988, Yun had completed a senior executive course at the Massachusetts Institute of Technology's Sloan School, where Jack Welch's achievements were being praised. In 1996, Robert Slater's 1993 book on Welch's work at GE was popularizing Welch's achievements.[13]

Yun brought to his job a lingering regret that he had studied engineering and not philosophy. "I just think I was very curious about everything ever since I was young, and curiosity just leads you to natural science," he told Eric Minton of Industrial Management in 1999.[14] Although Yun was more interested in studying philosophy, he had entered Seoul National University to pursue a degree in electrical engineering (a field often called "electronics"). "Korea was a poor country then, so I knew that if I majored in philosophy I would not have a job."[15]

Yun was born on January 21, 1944 in Yongchun, part of the Southeastern province of Kyungsangpukdo. He joined the Samsung Group in 1966 after graduating from Seoul National University's School of Engineering. Three years later he moved to the newly founded Samsung Electronics Company, where he worked on televisions. In 1977, he was promoted to head the Tokyo branch, which was concerned largely with relationships with the Japanese electronics companies in selling components and obtaining sub-contracts, and in sourcing and buying the Japanese components that went into every Samsung product at the time. Samsung-branded products were not on sale in Japan, and Japanese products were not legally available in Korea.

An equally important function for those in Tokyo was to keep track of the next generation of Japanese products. The Tokyo office was also a good place to meet the chairman. Lee Byung-chul spent several months each year in Japan., and the Tokyo office was responsible for keeping in touch with the chairman's day-to-day needs and orders. In Tokyo, Yun was able to establish relationships with both the first chairman and the future chairman.

This was a good base from which to start a string of high-level appointments within Samsung Electronics. In 1988, Yun was promoted to vice president. In March 1990, he rose to the position of vice president and representative director of the Consumer Electronics Business Group. He was appointed the Consumer group's president two years later. Outside of Samsung Electronics, he was establishing his reputation as a leader in South Korea's electronics industry. In November 1990, he received the Korean government's bronze medal for his contribution to the electronics industry, followed by a gold medal in May 1992. In that same year, he was named the most successful manager of the year by the Korea Management Association.

During Yun's time at the consumer products division, Samsung Electronics was investing heavily in research and development. "Producing high-value products with the next generation consumer electronics and improving product images among consumers are our main goals," Yun told the *Christian Science Monitor*.[16] Yun temporarily left Samsung Electronics in December 1992, to become president and CEO of Samsung Electro-Mechanics. He then headed Samsung's Display Devices division for two years from 1993, and managed its Japan headquarters in late 1995 before being called back to Samsung Electronics by the chairman.[17]

Samsung's chairman, Lee Kun-hee, who felt Yun had done well in consumer electronics, charged the new CEO of Samsung Electronics with the specific task of accelerating the company's growth and diversifying its portfolio at a time when the chip industry was in cyclical decline. Yun wrote in 2005 that in 1996 and 1997:

> . . . the market plummeted for major product lines, including semiconductors, IT devices, audio/video products and home appliances. Retail prices for mainstay items continued to fall . . . The record profits achieved

by our semiconductor division in 1995 distorted the
perception of the entire company's financial standing.
The revenue structure and product portfolio worsened,
jeopardizing the very survival of the company.[18]

This problem was far from apparent to most Samsung
Electronics executives. On appointment, Yun initially thought
that the world's memory-chip industry would recover from the
previous year's decline. He also increased funding for research and
development of consumer electronics. Still adhering to a mentality
of viewing greater market share as an ultimate goal—a common
perception in East Asian corporate philosophy, as opposed to
an emphasis on profits in the West—Yun spoke of plans to hire
more workers.[19]

In 1997, Yun's ideas and rapidly developing skills were
essential. Initially, he thought of embarking on expansion, so he
concentrated on new areas of growth. As part of this process, in
January 1998 he introduced the Global Product Manager (GPM)
system which would make the GPM, rather than the centralized
decision-making process, responsible for product management. Yun
was already emphasizing that marketing, rather than manufacturing, was part of the way forward.[20] But within a few months it had
become obvious that Korea was caught in its worst economic and
financial crisis since independence.

On December 3, 1997, South Korea's Minister of Finance
and Economy, Kang Kyong-shik, signed an accord with the IMF
which inaugurated what the Koreans called "the IMF era," or as it
is commonly called in English "the IMF crisis." The crisis had in
fact started 11 months earlier, in January 1997, with the collapse of
Hanbo, a mid-ranking *chaebol*—the Korean word for the curious
kind of conglomerate which the Korean system had generated. By
December, despite the best efforts of the government, 14 of the top
30 business groups in Korea had fallen into bankruptcy. With them,
they had taken most of the domestic banks and, almost as a by-product,
the confidence of foreign banking institutions and investors. Many
more groups teetered on the brink of bankruptcy, protected only by
government restrictions on debt repayments, which in turn forced all
banks into a state of near bankruptcy.

Korea had ring-fenced its financial system with the intention of
pushing consumer savings into industrial investment. Because Korea

had a continuous current account deficit, these banks had also borrowed abroad. While the government could keep the *chaebol* on life support by preventing domestic banks from recalling their loans, there was no restriction on foreigners trying to collect their debts. As a result, by late November Korea was on the verge of default on its extensive foreign debt. The foreign debt problem, rather than the corporate crisis, required the attention of the IMF. Korea, unlike Japan or Taiwan, had had an endemic current account deficit throughout its 36-year growth marathon and owed the world's banks enough, it was believed, to threaten the world financial system. Korea had exhausted its foreign exchange reserves by November 1997, and was within hours of default on foreign short-term borrowing. This required drastic action by both the government and the private sector.

The term "IMF crisis," used by Koreans to describe the brief period of about six months from December 3 that the government lost decision-making power,[21] does not mean that South Korea believed that the IMF was having a crisis or caused the crisis. A better description of this whole crisis was that it was a *chaebol* crisis, rather than a financial crisis. The sequential collapse was induced by the over-ambitious investment plans of the 30 top business groups within an inadequate macroeconomic environment. The *chaebol* managed to survive as business groups under legislation which was expressly designed to prevent them from existing! We will examine in detail how unique the *chaebol* was as a Korean institution in the next chapter.

What contributed to the excessive foreign borrowings by Korean companies? Control of foreign exchange and a fixed exchange rate plus high domestic interest rates had made it attractive for both corporations and banks to borrow heavily abroad, both on a long- and short-term basis. Foreign banks had been happy to supply funds as, in most cases, Korean banks acted as intermediaries because the Korean financial market was still closed. These borrowings were thought of as sovereign debts by both sides.

These short- and long-term loans pulled down more and more companies during 1997. Korea's impractical bankruptcy provision in the Commercial Code exacerbated the problem—even Korean blue-chips came under pressure. The chairman of LG summed up the issue accurately by saying that no company in the world could survive the sudden withdrawal of all its credit. More accurately, no company in the world with a debt ratio of over 100 could survive such action by the banks. Almost no Korean company had a debt ratio that low. The Samsung Group's debt-to-equity ratio in 1997 was 356 and Samsung Electronics' was 300. The resulting impact of this high debt ratio was the rapid erosion of profits through having to make high interest repayments. In 1996 Samsung Electronics had a very respectable operating profit of 1.44 trillion *won* (about US$1.8 billion) but after deducting interest charges, the net profit was only 160 billion *won*, or US$202 million. The Samsung Group had planned to invest between US$12 billion and US$15 billion during 1998–2000, but had earnings of just US$160 million in 1996.

Because Samsung, LG, and SK survived without a dramatically visible crisis like those happening to Daewoo or Hyundai, the assumption was that these *chaebol* were in good shape at the end of 1997. This was not at all the case. The Samsung Group had huge debts of about US$4 billion, most of it borrowed from Samsung Electronics, and servicing this debt eroded net profits. Furthermore, the Samsung Group's profits were sunk into Samsung Motor Company, which had no revenue. In 1997, Samsung Electronics Corporation had sales of 18 trillion *won* (US$22 billion), a marked improvement on 1996. Its net pre-tax income was US$108 million. But this net profit masked the fact that many product lines of Samsung Electronics Corporation, notably the consumer products division, were unprofitable. Samsung Electronics was kept in the black by one product line, DRAMs. A net profit of US$108 million was woefully inadequate to keep the steady reinvestment in new DRAM production facilities going. Samsung Electronics needed to borrow more money every year to keep up with its competitors. Its local competitors, LG Semiconductor and Hyundai Electronics, needed to borrow about the same amount with much lower incomes.

The entire corporate expansion of Korea had been built on debt. The less well-managed local competitors, LG Semiconductors and Hyundai Electronics, were bankrupt by the end of 1997 based on their debt-servicing needs. More bad news was to come. The IMF was convinced—based on its Latin American experience—that capital flight was a high danger and that interest rates should be raised to 20 percent to encourage capital to remain in Korea. In fact, this was a complete misunderstanding of the mechanism needed to prevent a currency flight on the Korean *won*. But it took a year to convince the IMF that this measure was unnecessary.[22] During that year, every company in Korea struggled with the surge in the cost of local debt servicing. Joseph Stiglitz, then chief economist at the World Bank, later wrote that this mistake made the 1998 recession much worse than it needed to be.[23] Many small Korean companies and many large companies perished unnecessarily as a result of this mistake.

Against this backdrop of financial chaos in Korea, Yun's work on restructuring Samsung began. It was not until the second half of 1998 that Yun could get a consensus for a "resolute restructuring program." In his words, "A policy called 'Concentration on Selective Resources' was adopted, and all units or functions not considered strategically important were sold, discontinued or spun off."[24] In one year Yun cut the company's debt by US$13 billion; reduced investment; and pared its 84,000-man payroll by 30 percent without labor unrest. He was also ruthless in selling or closing down parts of the operation which did not make money. In 1998, it was rumored that this could include the entire consumer products division.

This moment gave Yun his chance to practice the lessons derived from Jack Welch. Under the Concentration on Selective Resources program, Yun looked at the whole company from the perspective of its resource base. He and his team concluded that the company, far from needing new employees, only needed two-thirds of the existing managers and workforce. He adopted a management reform program called "3P Innovation" which focused on Products, Processes and Personnel.[25]

Yun streamlined the company and made costly operations more efficient. He laid off more than one-quarter of the workforce, but managed to mollify the labor management council because both factory workers and managers were involved. He pulled the plug on 52 products and removed 45 companies from the Samsung Electronics stable. "The restructuring was painful but necessary," he told Ravi Velloor of *The Straits Times* (Singapore). "It is this bitter pill that we were prepared to swallow that has helped put Korea on the road to recovery."[26]

A horrendous external distraction that emerged at this time may have saved Samsung Electronics. The Korean government is prone to meddle in business affairs. While some meddling may be highly productive, other meddling imposes huge burdens on business. Somewhere in the decision-making machinery, President Kim Dae-jung had been sold on the idea of swaps or "big deals" between the *chaebol* on a gigantic scale which would involve taking two or more loss-making companies and merging them into one entity.

The government proposed that Daewoo Motors would take over Samsung Motors, and Samsung Electronics would take over Daewoo Electronics, Korea's number three consumer electronics company. Samsung might have landed the better deal, since Daewoo Electronics was, on paper, a successful company, and Samsung Motors was a dead dog. But for those around Yun, who were considering closing down the consumer products division, it was far from attractive to be handed a purely consumer products company, with massive overseas investment and unclear debts. Both groups spent a lot of energy resisting the deal and Samsung was ultimately saved by the collapse of Daewoo Group in 1999. Because of the collapse of both the deals and of Daewoo, Samsung in turn had to put its motor company into liquidation. This meant writing off more than US$2 billion of Samsung Electronics' assets.

Under the same "big deal" policy, LG Semiconductor and Hyundai Electronics were forced to merge, to create Hynix. (Technically Hyundai "acquired" LG Semiconductor, including the debt which in the end helped create the collapse of the old Hyundai group in 2000. After 2000 Hyundai split into several groups.) Samsung attempted to stand above the other groups in crisis, resisting all orders from the government to restructure. It is claimed— and this is probably true—that in 1998 the newly-elected South Korean president, Kim Dae-jung, threatened to cut off Samsung's bank credit if the company could not reduce its debt, which stood at about three times its equity.

The one saving grace in the 1997 crisis was the devaluation of the *won*, which fell from about 800 *won* to the US dollar to 2,000 *won* in the last six weeks of the year. In the short term, this created further liquidity problems for any Korean company which had debts in US dollars, but it created a super-competitive economy when it came to exports. The *won* had been overvalued in the mid-1990s as Koreans had paid themselves handsome salaries without regard for profitability—part of the cause of the crisis. The *won* rebounded to about 1,250 to the US dollar by the end of 1998, but did not cross the 1,000 frontier until 2005. This meant that Samsung and other exporters made money, and could grow rapidly to repay domestic debt and refinance FX debt. Korean pay rates could remain at their current levels in Korean *won*, but become highly competitive in international terms during this period.

In 1997, Samsung Electronics had sales of 18 trillion *won* (US$22.5 billion). In 1998, its sales were 20.8 trillion *won* (US$16 billion). Although the sales growth constituted a 15 percent rise in *won* terms, the weakness of the Korean currency meant a drop in dollar income of 71 percent over 1997 figures.

During 1998, each dollar in exports brought in more *won*. The company's financial position was helped by DRAMS exports and a reduced reliance on consumer sales in Korea. Samsung Electronics had more than US$259 million in earnings during 1998, almost tripling the results of the previous year. By implementing his changes, Yun paid off the company's US$4.7 billion debt, and Samsung's share price on the Korean stock exchange more than doubled from December 1997 to April 1999. DRAM chip prices rose again, as Yun had predicted they would, providing another source for the immense increase in Samsung's profits. "Half the credit goes to our restructuring and the other half to the booming demand in DRAMs and LCDs," Yun told Ravi Velloor.[27]

During this period, Samsung's attention was drawn towards the rest of the world, especially the US where the "new economy" and the Y2K issue was creating a boom for everything connected to IT. Samsung Electronics' TVs, mobile phones and the flat screens first produced in 1995, all found ready markets. The voice of Samsung Electronics America grew within the organization, perhaps reminding some managers of the way Sony had moved to the US in the 1960s. As part of an effort to make Samsung a multinational corporation and to decrease bureaucracy, Yun had already set up regional headquarters in the US, Europe, and Asia as part of the group's strategy of diversification. While these changes were intended to gradually ease the temporary slump of the microchip industry, the Asian financial crisis derailed any plans to expand Samsung Electronics over the next several years.

In June 1999, the Korea Management Association named Yun the most successful CEO in Korea. At the end of that year, as a mark of the chairman's favor, Yun was promoted from president to vice chairman of Samsung Electronics—second only in the entire Samsung hierarchy to chairman Lee Kun-hee—exciting the envy of his colleagues both within Samsung Electronics and the Samsung Group as a whole.

Prime: From DRAMS to world leadership—The Yun era, phase 2 (2000–07)

In Adizes' model of the corporate life cycle, prime is the optimum point in the life cycle curve. This is where the organization achieves a balance of self-control and flexibility. He describes the characteristics of "prime" organizations as:

- Functional systems and organizational structure
- Institutionalized vision and creativity
- Results orientation; the organization satisfies customer needs
- The organization makes plans and then follows up on those plans
- The organization can afford growth in both sales and profitability.[28]

Nothing describes Samsung Electronics more aptly. The scale of the financial revolution which Yun and his team wrought between 1997 and 2000 can be measured by Samsung's sales, which grew from 20.8 trillion *won* (US$16 billion) to 32 trillion *won* (US$28 billion). Much more impressive was the fact that net profit rose from 123.5 billion *won* (US$94.6 million) to 6 trillion *won* (US$4.8 billion), giving CEO Yun considerable leverage to grow the company and to prepare for more aggressive goals without borrowing.

Yun had rescued the company from financial crisis by implementing a new corporate philosophy within its ranks and by enhancing its research and development wing. Tackling the inefficiencies of the old Samsung philosophy, Yun introduced cash-flow principles to Samsung Electronics and emphasized profits over market share. One of his innovations was ensuring that consumer products were not made for foreign sale before they were ordered. Workers were offered an opportunity to study modern techniques in marketing and productivity through a school set up within Samsung Electronics, and large bonuses were given for outstanding performances.

Yun, who repeatedly described himself as "the chaos-maker," said he "tried to encourage a sense of crisis to drive change. We instilled in management a sense that we could go bankrupt any day."[29] In 1998, this could literally have been true and this gave Yun the confidence both to put the reform drive into Samsung Electronics and to continue it as a philosophy. The downfall of Sony during the period when Samsung was playing catch-up only confirms the efficacy of the "continual crisis" philosophy.

Yun's astute reading of how digital convergence would impact consumer electronics also kept Samsung at the forefront of development. In the early 1990s, he had been the head of consumer electronics. He continued to observe the switch from analog to digital format in the future of every consumer device made by Samsung. He saw amazing opportunities in the globe's enthusiasm for the digital age, and the birth of digital convergence. The technological innovations that Samsung was working on had placed the company ahead of the pack in the digital revolution. "With the digital age, we can catch up with our competitors . . . We were 30 to 40 years behind in the analog age, but in the digital age, the playing field has been leveled."[30]

Moving away from Samsung Electronics' previous dependency on the DRAM market, Yun also focused on building new and high-quality consumer electronics. Early into the recovery process, he pinpointed the mobile phone market as an especially lucrative one. Samsung Electronics supplied athletes, staff, and others at the 1998 Winter Olympic Games in Nagano, Japan, and at the 2000 Summer Olympic Games in Sydney, Australia, with 25,000 pieces of wireless communications equipment. The South Korean population alone provided a large demand for mobile phones, but Samsung's exposure at the Olympic Games provided a boost to the international reputation of its consumer electronics. In 1999 Samsung struck a deal with the cell-phone service provider Sprint PCS, through which Sprint would market Samsung-built phones in the US. Other Samsung products developed at the time included internet music players and flat-panel LCDs.[31] Yun expressed the company's desire "to become a world-class company in the digital era, and in particular we want to become the best in terms of digital convergence and core components."[32]

Following the restructuring, Yun touted the virtues of "digital convergence," in which many electronic functions, using the same microchips, are combined into one product. Digital convergence is used in such products as mobile phones that double as game-playing, internet-enabled computers. This required the development of a new microchip set, and Samsung, because of its premier place in microchip production, was in an ideal position to lead the development of such technology. The results were such products as color-screen mobile phones, smaller notebook computers, and enhanced camcorders. As Yun explained it:

> The IT industry is heading towards convergence. TVs, camcorders, mobile phones, PCs and other digital devices are being connected together through networks. We make all of these products and we make the chips needed to operate them. We are better placed than any other company in the world to enjoy the benefits of digital convergence.[33]

This, of course, was after the "tech-wreck" in the US which pushed most US hi-tech companies on the defensive. Samsung continued to pursue the digital era because, for it, the mobile phone was the first wave of digital convergence. By 2001 Samsung Electronics had a truly diverse line of products. Twenty percent of Samsung Electronics' revenue came from semiconductors, compared with 35 percent from digital media (including PCs) and 25 percent from telecommunications. By March 2002, Samsung Electronics was also the world's largest supplier of flat-panel monitors and DRAM chips, and the third-largest supplier of mobile handsets.[34]

In October 2002, the company reached a deal with the International Olympic Committee to be the "Official Wireless Communications Equipment Partner" for the 2006 and 2008 Olympic Games. That same year, Samsung also introduced an internet-enabled refrigerator and the world's smallest portable DVD player. Profits, which were US$2.7 billion in 1999, rose to US$5.7 billion in 2002.

Yun had high ambitions for Samsung Electronics. "I want to lead Samsung Electronics to become one of the best companies in the world," he explained. "When this goal is achieved, I want to visit historical and cultural sites around the world to pursue my study of philosophy."[35] Yun's achievements were honored when he received *Fortune Magazine*'s "Asia's Businessman of the Year" award in January 2000 and CNBC's Asia Business Leader Award in November 2002.

We have to consider what would have happened to Samsung Electronics if Yun had not become CEO. As Andrew Ward observed in 2003:

> In 1996, Mr. Yun was not the obvious choice of leader for a company in urgent need of painful restructuring. As a Samsung veteran who had risen through the

company's ranks, he might have been expected to protect the status quo. Instead, Mr. Yun turned out to
be an aggressive reformer. A third of Samsung's workforce was shed, lossmaking businesses were sold, costs
were trimmed and the company's rigid management
structure was shaken up.[36]

Samsung Electronics would certainly have restructured but
would have concentrated on production rather than marketing
and branding. Downsizing would have been limited and product
areas that were unviable would have been kept in-house. An ardent
campaigner against complacency, Yun set in motion processes to
break down habitual tendencies and bureaucracy within Samsung
Electronics. In a 1999 address to all employees he said: "Timing and
speed will determine (the) life and death of a company in the digital
era. Thus we must take the initiative in eliminating the 'Five Ills'
of complacency, habitual practices, formality, authoritarianism and
egoism; and equip ourselves with sound management fundamentals
represented by speed, simplicity and self-regulation."[37]

Yun described the Five Ills as factors that cause major but
unseen damage to the organization, including delayed decisions,
poor inter-departmental co-operation and communications, unnecessary meetings, and massive paperwork.[38] In order to ensure that
managers were able to access the company at all times, Yun dis-
tributed notebook computers and mobile phones to his staff. To
combat bureaucracy and reduce costs, he set up a memo system on
his computer that enabled employees to contact him directly with
their complaints or ideas.

Although the Samsung Electronics team were divided over
the appeal of consumer products, they felt even more threatened
by dependency on DRAMs. Yun, particularly, wanted to reduce
Samsung's reliance on commodity semiconductors, whose profits
varied wildly depending on the ups and downs of the product cycle.
In 2000, operating income for semiconductors was US$4.8 billion
or 82 percent of Samsung Electronic's income base and 38 percent
of total sales. In 2001 chip prices would slump again, and Samsung's
semiconductor profits would fall with them.

But where would equally profitable lines come from? Yun had
pruned the company of most of its loss-makers, and yet 62 percent of
sales was only making 18 percent of the operating revenue. With the

coming renewed slump in DRAM prices at the end of 2000, where was Yun to make up for lost profit?

Supercharged prime: Catching up with Sony

One of Samsung Electronics' main challenges at the end of 2000 was trying to figure out how to finance the next round of investment for the next generation of commodity chips. Was there a way to make consumer products more profitable?

One man in the marketing division believed that stronger branding was the way to go. This man was Eric Kim, a Korean American, who persuaded Yun to spend money in the US market in 2001 to promote consumer products in America. He argued that this would raise the brand image of consumer products and allow new products to command a price premium. A reporter captured Kim's early days:

> Although Yun speaks through a translator in a formal reception room at the Seoul headquarters, he seems to relish the battle for the consumer market as much as 46-year-old Kim, a native son he enticed back in 1999 from a Dun & Bradstreet software unit. The casual Kim meets visitors in his airy office. As an outsider in a tradition-bound *chaebol*, or conglomerate, he can strike some elders as audacious. So be it. Samsung has just rolled out a $470 million global advertising and display campaign to establish itself as the "digit-all" company.[39]

So Kim got the go-ahead to market a strong brand for products focused on digital technology. "Through market research, we've found that people are tired of techno-snobbery. They want leading-edge technology at a good price," Kim said.[40] In 2002 Eric Kim, now newly-appointed global marketing director for Samsung Electronics, announced the company's goal of reaching the level of Sony's brand equity by 2005. This challenge to Sony, and indirectly to all other electronics companies, caught the imagination of the world's business writers. Coming from a company which in 1998 had considered abandoning consumer electronics as part of its portfolio, the challenge represented a major shift in policy driven by the vision of the digital era in which Samsung could sit at the center. Many within the company did not believe that this was possible, or that marketing should take this role. Nor did they like the American turn that the company was taking.[41] Eric Kim and CEO Yun saw eye to eye on this goal and they had a ready listener in the chairman of the Samsung Group, Lee Kun-hee. (Indeed, this was something that might have met with the approval of Sony's Akio Morita, who had expressed the view that "Management of an industrial company must be giving targets to the engineers constantly; that may be the most important job management has in dealing with its engineers.") The goal to beat Sony, whose products were at this stage selling at a premium, had been Yun's ambition since he took charge of Samsung Electronics in 1996. The task was not to find a new product area to drive the expansion of the company, but to seek the integration of everything Samsung did to achieve premium status.

The market's reaction to Samsung Electronics' audacious ambition was mixed. While some thought it laughable, others felt Samsung Electronics had the makings of overtaking the industry giant. Sony's CEO, Nobuyuki Idei, certainly wasn't laughing. To him, Samsung was already on the verge of overtaking Sony. After all, Samsung was already the second-most recognizable consumer electronics brand in the world, according to New York-based consultancy, Interbrand. Another observer, Graeme Bateman, head of research in Seoul for Japanese investment bank Nomura Securities, was of the opinion that Samsung was no longer making poor equivalents of Sony products but making products consumers wanted.[42]

Those who listened carefully realized that Samsung was doing more than just advertising—it was changing its entire brand positioning and making entrepreneurial marketing the driving force.

For a company which up until the 1990s was concentrated on producing electrical goods for other manufacturers, Samsung Electronics had a huge undertaking. It was now seeking not only to raise the awareness for its brand but to break away from being associated with discount stores such as Wal-Mart and Target in the US. To create the demand for its products, the company relied on targeted channels—high-volume electronic-goods chains and prominent independent distributors—to boost sales and volume. It formed strategic alliances with Best Buy, Sears, and J&R Music & Computer World. Samsung Electronics certainly had the vote of one of its resellers. "This company is very oriented toward the future," said Michael London, executive vice president at Best Buy, the biggest US electronics seller, adding: "Their products are now high-value and sophisticated."[43]

The first two years of this campaign were impressive. By 2003 Samsung Electronics had sales of US$36 billion and pre-tax net income of US$4.98 billion (see Figure 1.1). Moreover, the extra US$8 billion in sales compared with 2002 was based on much more profitable sales. In 2004, the company crossed the US$50 billion mark in sales, adding US$14 billion and doubling net income based on mobile phones, flash memory and LCD screens. By then, it had a market capitalization double that of Sony. Samsung had gone from crisis to triumph. During the same period Sony had encountered nothing but trouble.

Between 2002 and 2004 Samsung Electronics doubled its sales. And it began to run close to Sony on a number of measures. In 2005 it achieved its goal of having a higher brand value than Sony, reaching number 20 on Interbrand's top 100, with a value of US$14.9 billion. Sony was number 28, with a brand value of US$10.7 billion. But this was not quite the achievement it appeared, since while Samsung's brand value had risen 186 percent, Sony was the fastest-falling company of 2005, with only two-thirds of the brand equity it had had in 2000.[44]

When Eric Kim set his sights on overtaking Sony, he did not realize that the Japanese company was in such trouble. The fact that Sony's brand value was falling fast was only a warning of the magnitude of Sony's troubles. In March 2005, Sony did the

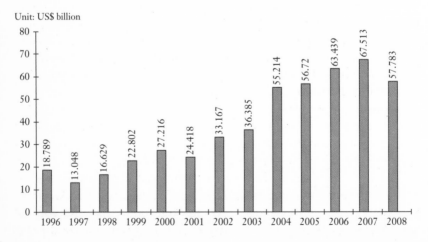

Unit: US$ billion

Figure 1.1   **Samsung sales growth**

unthinkable—it appointed an American, Howard Stringer, to head its entire operation. No Japanese consumer products company had voluntarily turned to an American for leadership. But Sony is no ordinary Japanese company. It is one of the flagships of Japan Inc. In adopting this shift, Sony was admitting to the necessity to reshape the company to cope with the rising competition. The media was quick to identify Samsung Electronics as the key competitor.

By contrast, Samsung had pursued a lean corporate structure since 1997. Increasingly, it delegated authority to front-line managers around the world and assigned almost a quarter of its far-flung staff of 88,000 to research and development. In 2005, Samsung Electronics saw ultimate success. Interbrand showed Samsung had conclusively beaten Sony in brand valuation. However, Samsung was faced with inherent weakness, as we shall see later. The Korean way of accounting created some problems for Samsung Electronics against international competitors. At the same time, by the end of 2005, Eric Kim had left Samsung for Intel, and the brilliant entrepreneurial marketing campaign was about to unravel.

In 2005, Samsung Electronics was South Korea's largest company in sales revenue terms, as it had been for many years. It was now also Korea's most profitable company and was one of just nine companies in the world with a net profit of over US$10 billion. Samsung Electronics continuously represented about 27 percent of the capitalization of the Korea Stock Exchange. By this time, 69 percent of its shares were owned by foreigners. It was still controlled by the Samsung Group, which cumulatively owned 20 percent of its shares, as explained in the following chapter. Its nearest Korean rivals, in terms of size, were Hyundai Motors and LG Electronics, each about half the size or lower in turnover terms, and far below in profit terms. Samsung Electronics' major products were now DRAMs, LCDs, handphones, and consumer appliances. In 2005, the company ranked thirty-ninth in Fortune's Global 500 companies.

The problems of stable going on aristocracy (2006–present)

Prime is the last phase of youth, and is followed by the first phase of aging, which is the "stable" cycle, later followed by "aristocracy." This hardening of the arteries is usually accompanied by a growth in the power of the bureaucracy versus the other aspects of management. Sony was layered in bureaucracy in 2005. When Jack Welch became chairman of GE, one of his main aims was to "nuke the bureaucracy" earning him his early 1980s sobriquet "Neutron Jack." GE, as a conglomerate, was already decentralized and Welch's contribution, by simplifying the bureaucracy and management structure, was to increase control while emphasizing flexibility and entrepreneurialism which he had experienced in the plastics division.

Although Samsung Electronics was focused on being lean, it had yet to learn the true lesson of decentralization. One aspect of organization which the conventional life-cycle model does not consider is the impact of decentralization and empowerment, especially in a centralized Asian context. "Aristocracy" perfectly describes this situation where a divisional structure based on products, as adopted by Sony in 1995 and Samsung in 2005, creates a set of semi-autonomous business satraps[45] contending for resources and power.

Decentralization became a way of handling diversity and allowing flexibility in many organizations, normally under a divisional structure, as seen during the later 1980s and 1990s. Samsung Electronics, in particular, did not embrace such a structure until the early twenty-first century.

When CEO Yun wrote about Samsung Electronics' change agenda, he put great emphasis on the "processes" part for change. It is important to remember that the life-cycle concept measures the total DNA of the organization, which includes its ability to change, and this is best measured by sales growth and profitability. In 1996, on the basis of the Yun reforms, a rejuvenated Samsung Electronics managed to avert settling into stable complacency by soaring into a new life, and a line of rapid growth. By the beginning of 2006, however, the company had lost its marketing entrepreneurialism shine, and was showing signs of aging.

The product cycle exhibits the same sort of dynamics as a company's life cycle. In 2006, 80 percent of Samsung's revenues were coming from semiconductors, principally DRAMs, and NAND flash memory (used for storage devices), LCD screens and mobile phones, and in each sector new challenges were emerging.

At this juncture of its growth, Samsung Electronics was far from its 1992 days. Its DRAMs normally commanded higher prices and fatter margins because the bulk of its memory revenues come from specialty products, including graphics chips for game consoles and high-density memory modules for heavy-duty servers. "We move up to higher-value chips if other companies catch up," Hwang Chang-gyu, president of Samsung's memory-chip unit, told *BusinessWeek* in 2006.[46] Its fastest growth came from flash memory, which can hold data even when electric power is turned off. Samsung, in 2005, wasn't able to keep up with the voracious demand for flash-memory chips that go into cell phones, MP3 music players, digital cameras, camcorders, and other handheld devices.

In 2004, Samsung controlled 55 percent of the US$2 billion market for NAND flash memory, used mainly in removable cards that store data, music, and image files. With a sprouting portable digital-products field, the NAND flash-memory market globally hit US$7 billion by 2005, and continued to grow.

Samsung Electronics was also somewhat shielded by the commoditization of the DRAM and LCD-panel markets as a result of the strong demand for LCD screens from growth in the notebook PC market, the increasing replacement of cathode-ray-tube computer monitors as well as consumer preferences for flat-screen TVs. In the second quarter of 2004, Samsung's LCD sales totaled US$948 million, up 42 percent from the first quarter, to account for 11 percent of its US$8.6 billion in second-quarter sales.[47]

Samsung Electronics was also riding high in the mobile phone market. It had proved that a Korean company is capable of building a brand through a top-down marketing strategy. By focusing only on mid- to high-end phones, it sold 25 million units in the first half of 2004, grabbing about a 10-percent share of the market, to be the world's number three in mobile phones, after Nokia and Motorola. It introduced well over 100 models globally in 2004, including those that allow users to download and view up to 40 minutes of video and watch live TV. "We're confident we'll get stronger," Chu Woo-sik, Samsung's vice president, declared in 2006.[48] In 2007, Samsung continued to climb, to reach the number two spot in the mobile phones market; but Nokia also increased its lead.

But in 2006, when chairman Lee and vice chairman Yun surveyed their product portfolio, they saw that growth was hitting the ceiling. Without entrepreneurial marketing, Samsung's brand value was rising slower than that of other companies. After more than 12 years of energetic growth, the energy was waning. Companies in the aristocracy phase tend to still be cash rich, but characteristically try to raise profits by raising revenues, not by cutting costs.[49]

Faced with this, Lee called for a new vigor to be injected, not only in Samsung Electronics but the whole Samsung Group. The new slogan was: "creative management." As usual, Yun championed active cost-cutting, prepared to reorganize and rejuvenate Samsung Electronics.

For Samsung, this was *the* moment to return to the state of "continual crisis." Change, however, was going to deal Lee and Yun a series of blows. If one talks of a "continual crisis," as one might talk of the continual ebbing and flowing of the tides, what should a company do when a real tsunami hits it? In 2007 growth slowed down and profits fell as semiconductor prices sagged, which offered a chance for Yun's critics to raise their voices. Then a political scandal affecting the Samsung Group was to force the resignation of chairman Lee in April 2008. The unleashing of an underlying tension between "the Korean voice"—forces within the company—and "the international voice," at a moment when the product portfolio was no longer yielding growth, resulted in Yun also resigning a month later. Finally, the onset of the global financial crisis in 2008 required all the skills that Yun had honed, but demanded them of a new team. As the following chapters will show, a company at the prime stage in its life cycle will cope with the problem very differently from a company at the aristocratic point.

Endnotes

1 *Time*, July 19, 1976.
2 "Papers to Help End Debate on South Korea-Japan Normalization Talks—Analysts;" Summary of a Yonhap News report on the release of documents relating to the 1965 treaty in 2005 posted August 25, 2005, Red Orbit http://www.redorbit.com/news/business/220909/papers_to_help_end_debate_on_south_koreajapan_normalization_talks/; accessed July 26, 2009.
3 This account follows Tony Michell's From a Developing to a Newly Industrialized Country: The Republic of Korea, *1961–82*, ILO Employment and Industrialization No. 6, Geneva, 1988:139–50; and the longer working paper which preceded it.
4 "Samsung to Invest W25 Tril. in Chip Production Lines Until 2010," by Kim Sung-jin, *Korea Times*, December 6, 2004.
5 In 1980 I took part in a fierce dinner party debate between Kim Jae-ik, the director of the Economic Planning Bureau, Bela Belassa of the World Bank and others about whether the domestic market should be subordinated to the export market in an export-led economy.
6 Magaziner, Ira and Patinkin, Mark 1990, *The Silent War*, New York: Vintage Books: 22.

7   Ibid.: 23–4.
8   Ibid.: 30–1.
9   Ibid.
10   Ibid.: 33.
11   Michell, op. cit.: 146 and footnote 39.
12   Ibid.: 144.
13   Slater, Robert 1993, *The New GE: How Jack Welch Revived an American Institution*, New York: McGrawHill.
14   *Industrial Management*, July 1, 1999: 10.
15   Quoted in *Current Biography International Yearbook*, H. W. Wilson Company (2003), at: http://www.hwwilson.com/Print/cbintl2003_yun_biography.htm; accessed July 8, 2007.
16   *Christian Science Monitor*, October 15, 1992.
17   Wilson, op. cit; accessed July 8, 2007.
18   Yun Jong-yong 2005, "Samsung Electronics" in *Global Future*, Arnoud de Meyer *et al* 2005, Singapore: John Wiley & Sons (Asia): 57–8.
19   Wilson, op. cit. http://www.hwwilson.com/Print/cbintl2003_yun_biography. htm; accessed July 8, 2007.
20   Yun, op. cit.: 60–1.
21   KABC Ltd., *The Chaebol Report* 1999, Vol. 1: 23–30.
22   Stiglitz, Joseph E. 2002, *Globalization and Its Discontents*, New York: Allen Lane: 105–10.
23   Ibid.: 89–128.
24   Yun, op. cit.: 55.
25   Ibid.: 56.
26   Interview, *The Straits Times*, Singapore, October 4, 1999; cited in Wilson, op. cit. http://www.hwwilson.com/Print/cbintl2003_yun_biography.htm; accessed July 8, 2007.
27   Ibid.
28   Adizes, Ichak 1988, *Corporate Lifecycles*, Paramus, NJ: Prentice Hall: 56.
29   "South Korea Company: Reign of the 'Chaos-Maker,'" Andrew Ward, *Financial Times*, March 13, 2003.
30   "Look Out, Sony (Samsung Aims to Be Leading Electronics Brand)," by Heidi Brown, *Forbes*, June 11, 2001.
31   Wilson, op. cit.
32   Minton, Eric, "A Philosophy of Change," *Industrial Management*, July 1, 1999; profile on Yun Jong-yung, CEO of Samsung Electronics Co. Minton won the Magazine Association of Georgia GAMMA Silver Award for Best Feature Writing or Reporting—Business to Business, 2000, for this profile.
33   Ward, op. cit.
34   Andrew Stevens for CNN International's E-Biz Asia, May 12, 2001.
35   Minton, op. cit.
36   Ward, op. cit.
37   Yun, op. cit: 61
38   Ibid.
39   *Wall Street Journal Asia*, July 28, 2005.
40   Ibid.

41 This theme is taken up in later chapters of the book, where opposition to the approach of Yun is described as driven by "the Korean voice." Eric Kim came closest to talking about it in his *Harvard Business Review* video interview with John Quelch (see http://harvardbusinessonline.hbsp.harvard.edu/relay.jhtml).

42 Quoted in "Samsung Moves Upmarket," by Frank Gibney, Jr., *Time*, March 25, 2002.

43 Ibid.

44 *BusinessWeek*, Interbrand Report, 2006.

45 Semi-autonomous provincial governor of the Persian Empire. *Wikipedia* describes the satrap's role this way: "Whenever central authority in the empire weakened, the satrap often enjoyed practical independence, especially as it became customary to appoint him also as general-in-chief of the army district, contrary to the original rule. 'When his office became hereditary, the threat to the central authority could not be ignored' (Olmstead). Rebellions of satraps became frequent from the middle of the fifth century. The great usurper Darius I struggled with widespread rebellions in the satrapies, and under Artaxerxes II occasionally the greater part of Asia Minor and Syria was in open rebellion."

46 "Samsung: A Rosy Future for Memory Chips," by Moon Ihlwan, *BusinessWeek*, September 25, 2006.

47 Ibid.

48 Ibid.

49 Adizes, op. cit.

2

Samsung Electronics and the Samsung Group: The Burden of the Korean System

My greatest pleasure comes in meeting the challenge of making money.

Lee Byung-chul[1]

The *chaebol*: Frankenstein monsters created by legacy government regulation

All Koreans are taught that history has subjected Korea to a series of invasions. Korea had lost its independence between 1905 and 1910 and, during the Second World War, was a colony of Japan. The failure to create a plan to set Korea free in the various conferences of the Second World War (at Cairo, Tehran, and Potsdam) was one of the significant diplomatic bungles of the twentieth century, and led directly to the Korean War and to the division which resulted. North Korea was occupied by the Russians, who fairly quickly handed over to a Korean administration. South Korea fell under the rule of the American military government in Japan.

In 1945, General MacArthur's team, bent on democratizing Japan, instigated a program known as *zaibatsu* dissolution. The *zaibatsu*, family-owned conglomerates controlled by a holding company,

which had dominated Japanese industry, were to be beheaded—
holding companies were prohibited and family shares confiscated.
The aim was to create a democratic Japan in which power was not
concentrated. Under the military government, when legislation was
passed in Japan, the same regulations were passed in Korea, as a
former Japanese colony, as ordinances. The first Korean National
Assembly made all these ordinances into laws. Holding companies
were illegal in Korea until the early years of this century, and
difficult to create, even after gradual deregulation.

The Samsung Group is a conglomerate or *chaebol* (meaning
"big money"). It is important to understand that all these *chaebol*—
Samsung, Hyundai, LG, SK, and others—which have become
household names around the world, do not (or did not until after
2005) exist in the legal, consolidated sense that General Electric
or the Sony group of companies exist. Only since 2007 have some
of the large Korean groups struggled with the new legislation to
create holding companies. Samsung is not yet one of them. Since
all of these were family firms, how was the family to control the
group? As the founders of the Korean business groups built their
businesses, they could not consolidate holdings in a single business
group, but held their companies through individual shareholdings
or corporate cross shareholdings. As late as 2007 the concept that
it is more rational to have a proper holding-company structure was
just being debated seriously, with the LG and SK groups taking the
lead. Further, as a "modernizing" trend, in the 1970s the Korean
government forced each *chaebol* to make each major company in
the group a listed company. This meant that each *chaebol* was partly
owned by the founder or his family, by private and institutional
investors, and by other companies in the group. Each conglomerate
had to create a structure of cross-holdings which became a shareholder's nightmare.

Legally, there could be no holding company, and shareholding, as in the case of Samsung Electronics, is circular. This is
the burden of the Korean system. The circular nature of shareholding is illustrated in this succinct, but potentially confusing,
Datamonitor summary.

> Samsung Electronics' largest shareholders are Samsung
> Life and Samsung Corporation. Samsung Corpora-
> tion's largest shareholders are Samsung SDI and

Samsung Life. Samsung SDI's major shareholder is Samsung Electronics. Therefore, [due to the nature of such circular shareholding,] if you control Samsung Life you control the whole Samsung group. Samsung Life's major shareholder is Everland, and Everland's major shareholder is Lee Jae-yong, an executive of the company and the son of group chairman Lee Kun-hee.[2]

Lee Jae-yong became Everland's biggest shareholder when he acquired 630,000 shares in 1996. Everland issued convertible bonds that Lee then acquired and switched over to shares. Lee's three daughters also acquired 630,000 shares between them in this manner. This transaction was to become the cause of multiple investigations over the coming 13 years.

This irrational structure imposed by Korean law placed extra burdens on the rich, large companies in all groups. Samsung Electronics was required to hold shares not only in its own related subsidiaries, but also non-connected companies in the Samsung family. In the case of Samsung Electronics, it had to hold shares in Samsung Motors (until 2000), Samsung Card (until 2007), and Samsung Capital.

In the 1997 financial crisis, the IMF was persuaded that the *chaebol* were responsible for the crisis (rather than the contorted financial structure imposed on them by law) and efforts should be made to destroy the groups and break them up into separate companies divorced from the founding families' control. Ironically, the government allowed each group (which did not legally exist) to create a restructuring office which would implement the reforms the government was directing. The truth is that the entire system was responsible, and if the *chaebol* were monsters, they were nonetheless rational attempts of businessmen to grow their businesses within the rules created by Korea Inc. Much government effort went into this regulation to little effect; what was required were legal holding companies.

The objection to the holding structure came from policymakers who realized this conundrum: the owners of the big *chaebol* would be too rich when resources could be concentrated in the holding company.

Outside the business world, the Korean public tends to have a hostile attitude towards the *chaebol*, ranging from mildly negative to extremely hostile. This tends to be reflected in the press and government policy. The Samsung Group itself is far from immune from this feeling, as is reflected in the final section of this chapter.

Lee Byung-chul and the Samsung Group

Chairman Lee was born in February 1910 to wealthy landowners. In the 1930s, he was sent to Waseda University, the leading private university of the day in Japan, and the preferred Japanese university for Koreans. University in Japan in the 1930s, like universities in Northeast Asia until recently, was not so much a place to study (unless you were a poor student who needed a scholarship, which required perfect grades) as a place to establish lifelong friendships. Lee did not finish his degree. But he did build a circle of friends and began to formulate the dream of a business group which would lead Korea into the future. This dream inspired the inception of the Samsung Group. Lee began to build his future empire trading in Masan in 1935. As a young businessman in Masan he showed something of his technique to outclass the competition. Noting that his competitors all used slow ox-carts for distribution, he bought a motor truck—and soon left the competition in his dust, "howling blue murder."[3]

Samsung itself is said to have originated with the rice-trading operation which Lee founded in 1938 in Daegu. Samsung Corporation later became the flagship company of the group. In the 1940s and 1950s, Lee called some of his companies, which were based around trading, textiles and food, "Samsung;" and most he called *cheil* (meaning "the first" or "best").

When Korea became independent in 1945, Lee began to expand his business empire, founding Samsung Trading Company (soon to become Samsung Corporation) in 1948, and the powerful food company Cheil Jedang in 1953, the same year that Samsung Corporation opened its first overseas branch in Japan. His businesses extended during the 1950s through banking, insurance, real estate, trading and manufacturing and processing.

By the late 1950s, Lee was already the richest man in Korea, and this following a decade of war in which Korea's rural landed wealth was destroyed. Lee was one of a new generation who learned how to profit from the wartime and post-war situation and used his growing empire to acquire bank and insurance companies, as well as an increasing range of industrial entities. The majority of these were acquired rather than created. At the time, Lee's philosophy for establishing a new business was to "pounce on it when the market is at rock bottom."[4] During the 1950s he made a great deal of money out of exporting tungsten, one of South Korea's few minerals which could earn foreign exchange.

The student revolution of April 1960 swept away the old corrupt regime of Syngman Lee, which was followed by 13 months of troubled democracy and, later, a military coup led by General Park Chung-hee. Above all, Park was determined to stamp out corruption, and this put him in conflict with Korea's richest man. Lee's six-month exile in Japan ended with his agreement to surrender his ownership of Korean banks and to establish a new chemical fertilizer plant. A subsequent scandal involving his eldest son led to the confiscation of the plant and began a difficult period in the life of Lee's group of companies in which his competitors had better access to the government than he did.

For nearly 15 years, Lee's companies were to suffer from being at the back of the queue for licenses and favors, including the preferential bank loans needed to build new industrial plants. In this era, the government strictly controlled the businesses which companies could enter by limiting licenses, except wherein areas which were declared open (as the electronics industry was in 1968).

The one route to growth that did not depend on government favor was to buy companies in trouble. Lee's life insurance company, the largest in Korea, and his Cheil Foods and Samsung Corporation, the trading company, were all cash-generating machines.

Lee also prepared for future conflict with the government. In 1965 he founded a newspaper and in 1967 told a *Time* reporter that this was his favorite business—the Joong-Ang Mass Communications Center, headquartered in a nine-story Seoul office building where he worked, surrounded by teak-paneled walls and a collection of oriental pottery. Joong-Ang includes a television station, South Korea's most popular radio station, and the *Joong-Ang Ilbo*, a daily newspaper with a circulation of 325,000.[5] "Mass communications," he said, "are the best way to prevent bad politics." But, as *Time* noted, "They also happen to be a pretty good channel through which South Korea's biggest businessman can talk back to his various critics."[6]

In the late 1960s, the Samsung Group (Lee had decided to name all his new companies "Samsung"—"three stars"—rather than Cheil)

found itself handicapped in the next stage of Korean industrialization. In 1971, encouraged by the success of POSCO, the state-
owned integrated iron and steel company, President Park started
on a "Heavy and Chemical Industry Plan" which would in 10 years
build the future of Korea's industrial might. Much criticized by
neoclassical economists as departing from Korea's competitive
advantage in cheap labor, this plan handed out government finance
to favored *chaebol* which promised to build the next generation of
Korean industry. Samsung was still at the back of the line at this
stage. Huge state-planned projects in shipbuilding, oil refineries
and petrochemical plants and machinery sectors went to rivals such
as Hyundai, LG, SK, Hanwha, and other groups. Lee was forced
to watch as the upstart Hyundai, founded by the son of a poor
peasant family with no education, built an industrial empire to rival
his own. In the 1970s Hyundai Motors and the new Daewoo Motors
became increasingly successful.

To get into heavy and chemical industries, Samsung had to
wait until smaller companies got into trouble and then buy them
to build Samsung Heavy Industries, as it did when it bought the
shipyard of Daesung Heavy Industry in Koje in the 1970s. (It wasn't
until the liberalization of industrial licensing in the late 1980s that
Samsung was allowed to build its own petrochemical complex.)
The one license no one could deny Samsung, however, was the
new General Trading License issued to seven trading companies in
1975 which gave each of them a new freedom in financing exports.[7]
Because of this unique access to export and import finance, Samsung
Corporation was able to further enhance its leadership.

At the end of the 1950s, Lee was the richest man in Korea.
Within the next 20 years, he created a formidable business machine.
His fellow businessmen referred to him as the man with the golden
touch. They also viewed him with fear. Lee did not suffer critics or
competitors gladly.[8] A *Time* journalist who interviewed him in 1967
described his approach: "Lee's approach to business is a combination of Oriental grace and karate chops; the combination has made
enemies for him ever since he left college in Japan 33 years ago and
went into business as a rice miller."[9] Nine years later, *Time* described
him thus:

> Outwardly, "B.C." is mild-mannered and looks a bit
> professorial behind gold-rimmed spectacles. He clearly

enjoys wealth. His home is a palatial retreat 25 miles South of Seoul, set amid 1,200 acres of landscaped gardens and lawns where peacocks strut. Lee also has a world famous collection of ancient Korean pottery— the ultimate sign of luxury—and a fine disdain for the Korean chore of entertaining visiting businessmen. His greatest pleasure, he says, comes in meeting "the challenge" of making money.[10]

By the later part of 1970s, Lee had made his peace with the government only to find a new regime in power in 1980 which tore away his broadcasting network, TBC, and left him bitter for several years. Increasingly, Lee's ambition was to rival Hyundai in making cars. In the early 1980s, he signed an agreement with Lee Iacocca of Chrysler, expecting that the inclusion of a foreign investor would allow him a license to make cars to compete with Hyundai Motor Company. Instead, Hyundai was granted a license to enter the electronics industry in 1983, concentrating on chips and components rather than consumer appliances. Hyundai's entry into Samsung's semiconductor turf was no doubt one of the causes of Lee's so-called Tokyo Declaration of February 1983 in which he proclaimed that Samsung would become the world leader in semiconductors. Despite Hyundai's entry into electronics, Samsung had to wait until 1993 before it was granted an auto license. It came too late for Lee, who had passed away in November 1987. It was his son and succeeding chairman Lee Kun-hee who was finally allowed to create Samsung Motors.

Under the Korean system preventing the formation of holding companies and circular shareholding structure, whichever subsidiary had the resources to create a new investment was chosen to invest in a new group venture. The subsidiary with the most resources to borrow overseas and domestically at that time was Samsung Electronics. So Samsung Electronics became the largest shareholder in Samsung Motors. The first cars were just rolling off the production line in Busan as the first rumbles of the IMF crisis of 1997 were beginning to shake the weaker conglomerates.

At Lee's death in 1987, key parts of the Samsung Group were inherited by his daughters and relatives. Cheil Jedang became a separate group in its own right, as did Shinsaegae, Chongju Paper (which became Hansol Group), and Joon-gang Ilbo (which became Byucksan Group). The Shilla Hotel went to another daughter.

These independent groups thereafter followed their own fortunes, collaborating where appropriate. The Samsung Group passed to Lee Kun-hee.

How would his son continue his legacy? The heavy-handed government controls created by Park were gradually dismantled in the late 1980s and early 1990s. This meant that Samsung could enter any industry, but so could its competitors. It particularly irked Samsung that Hyundai was persistently classed as bigger than Samsung by the Korea Fair Trade Commission, the government agency charged with monitoring the *chaebol*.[11]

The coming of age of Lee Kun-hee

Lee Byung-chul had spent a lot of time deciding which son should be his successor. Lee was successful because he demanded efficiency over tradition. As early as the mid-1960s, he shocked family-conscious Koreans by abruptly firing two of his three sons who were Samsung managers. "They were not fit to hold executive positions," he explained to a journalist 10 years later.[12] One of his sons dropped out of business and the other started what was, until its bankruptcy in 1997, the highly successful Saehan Media Group. With Kun-hee, Lee had worked carefully to produce a successor who would continue his work. For six years after his father's death, the new chairman worked to establish himself with the senior Koreans who had been his father's colleagues, finally proving himself by obtaining the license for Samsung Motors in 1993. The founding of Samsung Motors may almost be regarded as an act of filial piety on the part of Lee Kun-hee. He persuaded himself that electronics were becoming increasingly important in the automobile industry, and that while Samsung had no competence in the auto industry, the prowess in electronics would make Samsung Motors a future leader in the industry.

From this point on, Lee began to stamp his own mark on the whole group. Chu Woo-shik, head of investor relations in 2007, recalled that in 1993 there began a period of soul-searching when Lee announced that Samsung executives must "change everything except your wife and kids."[13] This became known as the "Frankfurt Manifesto," where Lee set out an agenda to make Samsung special, to challenge everything, and to work towards a new standard of design. It was intended to be compared with the Tokyo Declaration of 1983. To set the Samsung Group apart, Lee declared that unlike other working companies, Samsung would work from 7am to 4pm (the normal working hours in Korea being 9am to 6pm). To enforce the change, Lee would dial internal numbers at random and if someone answered the phone he would say: "This is the Chairman, why are you still at work?"[14]

Lee found that it was not easy to change the quality of Samsung's products or to get employees to change their work culture. He pushed the HR training programs in Yongin to change their course offering. He also resorted to dramatic gestures, including the incineration of cell phones at the factory in 1996 (see below). He also replaced the head of Samsung Electronics with Yun Jong-yong and sent Samsung's top managers to the US to learn from Jack Welch and GE's long-term reform efforts.

Lee continued his father's style of not attempting to micro-manage everything within the group, unlike the leaders of some other *chaebol*. In 1999, he described his role in this way:

> Before the financial crisis, I was half a step behind the front lines. I left [some] of the decisions to individual CEOs, but I didn't want to stay too far back. Recently, I moved one step further behind [the front lines]. I am most interested in how the twenty-first century will unfold and what we need to do to prepare. These are the strategic issues on my mind. This is where I am spending most of my time rather than getting involved in day-to-day management.[15]

The Samsung Group and the IMF crisis

Samsung's real challenge was to come during the IMF crisis in 1997. Although the government was determined to break up the *chaebol*, it recognized that in dealing with the groups it needed to encourage a central organization in each group which would undertake the restructuring. The Office of Restructuring gave the chairman of each group the power he had sometimes lacked in the past.

It took several years for people outside Samsung to realize the strength of Samsung's planning. When the Asian financial crisis broke out in 1997, many conglomerates crumbled, but Samsung, under Lee's firm leadership, used the situation to cut off unnecessary parts of the business to focus on its core activities—electronics and finance. In the process, 14 group affiliates were sold, and about 50,000 employees (about 60 percent of whom came from Samsung Electronics) had to leave group companies.

If surviving the IMF era was a contest, the Samsung Group was the winner. The Samsung Group office had predicted an increase in sales of only 5.8 percent at the outset of 2000. In fact sales grew by 19.8 percent, the increase coming chiefly from Samsung Corporation and Samsung Electronics, although many smaller Samsung subsidiaries increased their sales by about the same percentage. The Samsung Group also increased the number of its subsidiaries, particularly in the area of the new economy. With unconsolidated net profit of over 8 trillion *won* (US$8 billion), the group was four times as profitable as its nearest rival (LG) in absolute terms.[16] Only two groups (POSCO and Daelim) recorded a net profit to sales ratio higher than Samsung's 6.4 percent. But this did not occur without pain.

Part of the pain came from the government and part from the financial situation of its subsidiaries. The government ordered all *chaebol* to nominate three core areas of business and to shed all non-core areas as well as to drastically reduce the number of subsidiaries they owned. Samsung refused to identify its last one or two core business sectors, but shed 231 non-mission critical layers or under-performing units in the period 1999–2001. The group also reduced the number of major subsidiary companies from 65 to 34, as shown in Table 2.1. But by 2001, the total was back to 51.

Table 2.1   Samsung's main businesses following restructuring

1998		Post-Restructuring
Electronics		Electronics
Finance		Finance
Services		Services
Machinery	→	Trading
Chemicals		**34**
Automobiles		
Shipbuilding		
Distribution		
Clothing		
Real Estate Development		
65		

Source: KABC, *The Chaebol Report*, 2000, Volume 1.

In 1998, Samsung was participating in 10 areas of business. After restructuring, it was essentially participating in four: trading, finance, electronics, and services, with options on two more. However, the creation of 24 new-economy companies essentially created a new business area.

Considering the size of the group and its efficiency in terms of turnover to assets, and the relative profitability of some of its subsidiaries, notably Samsung Electronics, the group should have been in a position to expand in any direction it chose. In 1999, Lee said the IMF era imposed tough external limits on the group, the state of the local economy, and internal trade agreements: "Our challenge is to work within these limits with the givens of a new economic order, and continue Samsung's progress towards becoming one of the world's most powerful brands."[17]

The critical issue was what to do with the "black hole" companies—the companies that were hopeless loss-makers. Samsung had three major black-hole companies at the start of 1999, as shown in Table 2.2.

In 1998, Samsung Watch—a consistent loss-maker—was merged with Samsung Precision and became a major machine-making company, a move described by business consultancy KABC as "a good benchmark of its future management capacity."[18]

For Samsung Motors there seemed no hope but liquidation. This would mean writing off 4 trillion *won* (US$4 billion) of investment borrowed from Korean and foreign banks by Samsung Electronics and Samsung Life. Samsung was saved by Renault, which had picked up Nissan during the crisis of the late 1990s, and was now ready to absorb the Samsung Motors plant, which had been engineered by Nissan engineers working with Koreans. Samsung ended up owning 20 percent of a foreign-owned

Table 2.2 Samsung's black-hole companies (losses in 1997 year)

Samsung Motors	–667 billion *won* (–US$667 million)	(in receivership)
Samsung Commercial Vehicle	–72.4 billion *won* (–US$72.4 million)	(liquidated)
Samsung Watch	–6.8 billion *won* (–US$6.8 million)	(merged)

Source: KABC, *The Chaebol Report*, 1998, Volume 1.

company—Samsung–Renault Motors—with Samsung Life and Electronics still owing the creditors about 2.7 trillion *won* (US$2.7 billion). The earlier decision to hold on to Samsung Commercial Vehicles may have been with the intent of merging the company with Samsung Heavy or of trying to sell to a group like MAN or Volvo or Renault. In practice, the company was unsellable and was later liquidated.

In 2000, although Samsung Commercial Vehicles was off Samsung Electronics' books and Samsung Motors was about to be acquired, the group still had other big loss-makers, although not quite in the "black hole" category. The group had managed to stem losses at Samsung Techwin (the new name for the merger of Samsung Watch and Samsung Precision) and Samsung Electro Mechanics, but Samsung General Chemicals continued to lose money, while Samsung Heavy—the ship builder—re-emerged as a major loss-maker, despite the disposal of the Construction Equipment division to Volvo in 1998.

During 2000, the Samsung group had 13 major companies (up from 11 in 1998) with a turnover ranging between 40.6 trillion *won* (US$40.6 billion) and 13 trillion *won* (US$13 billion). Three made a loss in 1999; two made a loss in 2000.

From 2001, with the rapid growth of Samsung Electronics and the general recovery of the Korean economy, the Samsung group resumed leadership of the *chaebol*, the more so because its nearest rival, Hyundai, had been forced to split into several groups (the most notable being Hyundai Motors Group) under different sons after the death of its founder in 2000.[19]

The Millennium Plan: Samsung's entry into the twenty-first century

Lee Kyun-hee's interest in how the twenty-first century will unfold has found expression in what has become known as the Samsung Millennium Strategy. Samsung's long-term goal in 2000 was to complete a move to a holding-company structure (still illegal in Korea at the time), with about 20 subsidiaries and 100 affiliates worldwide.

At that time Samsung had three subsidiaries with more than 20 trillion *won* (US$20 billion) in turnover: Samsung Corporation (40 trillion *won*), Samsung Electronics (34 trillion *won*) and Samsung Life Insurance (20 trillion *won*). All were large companies. Two other electronics companies built this total further. Three subsidiaries were close to the 5 trillion *won* category: Samsung Heavy Industries; Samsung Display Devices; and Samsung Fire and Marine Insurance, whose growth in 2000 was dramatic. The only other major companies after Samsung Electro-Mechanics and Samsung Chemicals would have been Samsung Fire and Marine Insurance (see Appendix).

In early 2000 the group announced that it would set up six divisional companies within Samsung Corporation (which was to become the mother company).

The six, which may be compared to single business units, were to be:

- Internet shopping mall
- New e-business sector
- Chemicals
- Information and communications
- Machinery equipment
- Construction.

It should be noted that Samsung Electronics was not part of this strategy, and the relationship between Samsung Corporation and Samsung Electronics was to be left unclear. Within this strategy Samsung's "World's Best" strategy was to raise the portfolio of No. 1 products in the world from 12 to 30 within three years and to 50 within five years. Samsung's Millennium Strategy was to find new business opportunities in existing flagship enterprises and in new businesses which were unrelated but within Samsung's core capabilities, such as internet and digital businesses. On top of this ambition, Samsung still had to demonstrate how to handle its other loss-making companies, which had appeared in 2000.

Under this scenario, the expectation was for the Samsung group to further merge its business units during succeeding years. This seemed to have been resisted, partly by Samsung Electronics, which had its own interests in the new economy.

The 2000 strategy would seem to have restricted Samsung Electronics to products, and to put software—including Samsung's growing software and systems company SDS and its many spin-offs—with Samsung Corporation.

At the time, Samsung was suffering from the loss of staff to start-ups, and the Unitel group—Samsung's successful internet family—was spun-off to be listed on KOSDAQ to be able to offer staff stock options. As performance after 2000 shows, the result of this stand-off (for want of a better phrase) between Samsung Corporation and Samsung Electronics was to spawn many new subsidiaries. At the same time, Samsung had introduced both economic value added (EVA) and EVA-linked bonuses throughout the group. From the ownership point of view, Samsung subsidiaries had issued shares sequentially to consolidate family and large company ownership. This process was to be completed to permit the listing of Samsung Life during 2000. (However, as at 2009, Samsung Life was still not listed because of regulatory concerns.)

The role of the chairman since 2000 had not been central to the day-to-day management of the company, and some thought that Samsung, like SK, could survive the loss of its chairman (there were continuing fears about Lee's health at this stage) without losing its headway. But Lee Kun-hee drove the Samsung Group in a very different way from other chairmen and had a longer-term vision than any other Korean chairman.

In this Millennium Plan, the major growth company was to be Samsung Electronics, followed closely by Samsung Corporation (see Table 2.3). These were very aggressive targets, particularly for Samsung Electronics, at a time when industry forecasts for Samsung Electronics in 2005 were 45 trillion *won* (US$45 billion) at most. The new forecast assumed that Samsung could keep its leadership in DRAMs, mobile phones, and LCD displays. Many market watchers thought that this must envisage acquisitions and start-ups as well.

To grow the whole group, Samsung Life Insurance needed to expand overseas to sustain group growth momentum (see Table 2.4). This was something Samsung Life had failed to do in the past. It remains a wild card for the future. It was Samsung Fire and Marine which established a branch in China first.

So in the Millennium Plan either Samsung Corporation or Samsung Electronics, or both, could have been used as the vanguard for Samsung's future expansion. If one were looking for a model where Samsung Corporation and its diverse potential holdings might be in 2005, one might have looked again at Japan's Itochu. In 1997, total turnover of Samsung Corporation was 29.7 trillion *won* (US$29.7 billion) at pre-November 1997 exchange rates while Itochu's turnover was around US$160 billion in 1996. Samsung Corporation achieved 34 percent growth in turnover rate in the first

Table 2.3 Basic management plan targets (trillion *won*) for 2005 under the Millennium Plan

Samsung Electronics	70	8.4	Home, mobile, personal multimedia, core electronic parts
Samsung SDI	15	1.9	Mobile display, second-generation battery
Samsung Electro-Mechanics	10	1	Internet parts, filters, precision electronic parts
Samsung Techwin	2.5	0.25	Semiconductor equipment, parts and fiber-optic systems
Samsung Corp.	50	0.63	Internet business, venture investment
Samsung Fine Chemicals	1	0	New medicines for cancer, AIDS, electronic materials

Source: KABC, *The Chaebol Report* 2002, Volume 1.

Table 2.4 Samsung's future: Turnover projections

Samsung Corporation	40	70
Samsung Electronics	34	70
Samsung Life Insurance	20	40
Samsung Heavy Industries	4	6
Samsung Display Devices	5	8
Samsung Fire and Marine Insurance	3	6
Samsung Electro-Mechanics	3	6
Other Companies	11.1	34.2
Total	**120.1**	**240.2**

Source: Korea Associates Business Consultancy and EABC Forecasts 2001.

half of 1998 compared to the same period in 1997. This was considerably higher than the 23 percent growth seen in 1997, 25 percent in 1996, and the 15 percent seen in 2000.

The Millennium Plan did not outline Samsung's financial-sector plans. The group did not make it clear whether it envisaged two Samsungs: one in manufacturing and one in finance and possibly each represented by a holding company, or whether the two would be more closely integrated in the future—something which the government strongly discouraged. Until 2007, the government strategy favored a divorce between financial holding companies and manufacturing companies, and this would certainly be applied rigidly on a group as big as Samsung. For Lee and Yun, who looked to GE as a model, such a separation was not attractive and it was better to be silent on financial provisions.

The manufacturing services and digital group within the Samsung stable would have a turnover of about 140 to 150 trillion won (US$140–150 billion) while the financial group would have a turnover of a minimum of 50 to 70 trillion *won* (US$50–70 billion), grouped around Samsung Life; Samsung Fire and Marine; Samsung Card; Samsung Capital; Samsung Securities; and whatever financial companies Samsung chose to favor. In 1998, Samsung Life had increased its turnover from 14 trillion *won* (US$14 billion) to nearly 19.3 trillion *won* (US$19.3 billion), and 20 trillion *won* (US$20 billion) in 1999. Samsung Life had flatlined by 2000.

The one thing the Millennium Plan required was more investment and, as a result, Samsung's debt equity ratio rose from 146 percent in 2000 to 266 percent in 2001, although the company had planned to reduce the ratio to 124 percent by 2002. The spike in debt ratio reflected more realistic accounting, and also the financial burden of expansion. Samsung's short-term debt rose 18.7 percent in 2000 from 12.4 trillion *won* (US$12.4 billion) to 14.7 trillion *won* (US$14.7 billion). Total bank debt was 18.1 trillion *won* (US$18 billion), up 5.62 percent.

Essentially, the chairman had prepared his group for expansion in the twenty-first century and he could potentially steer his fleet of companies in any direction. One fear among investors was that Samsung Electronics' profits could be siphoned off to bolster the fortunes of, say, Samsung Card. While this might not be illegal, it certainly would not please investors in the electronics unit. "In terms of business, this is a top-notch company," said Jang Ha-sung, Korea's leading advocate for transparency and scourge of the *chaebol*; "But in terms of corporate governance, it is still in the nineteenth century."[20]

Samsung's structure and management

Samsung, again the largest of the *chaebol*, was arguably the best group from a managerial-competency standpoint and from the point of view of group financial management, and had managed to hold together its group structure in a synergistic way. However, this structure suffered internal threats—brought on by the Korean system of cross-holdings and the need for the chairman to pass on his inheritance—as well as external threats caused by systemic risks among Korean financial institutions which could have an impact on Samsung's financial companies.

Lee Kun-hee was under close government scrutiny on two counts. The persistent issue was the transfer from 1996 onwards of blocks of shares in various Samsung companies—mainly using the unlisted leisure company Everland as the vehicle—to his son Jae-yong at untraded prices. The second was the final resolution of Samsung's obligations to Samsung Motors' debt. The latter erupted in 2006 as the valuation data for the collateral pledged by Lee Kun-hee to the creditors showed a gap of about 1.4 trillion *won* (US$1.4 billion). This gap was to be plugged by Samsung companies, and not by Lee. This had various *chaebol* ill-wishers and minority shareholders crying foul. Lee was also under health pressures. He had serious treatment for cancer at the end of the 1990s and in 2000 was believed to be in limited remission. He made a remarkable recovery subsequently.

Samsung Electronics surges forward and Samsung Corporation falters, 2000–06

The Millennium Plan envisaged that Samsung Corporation would continue to grow, and rival its fast-growing cousin Samsung Electronics, bolstered by its "new economy" dimension which would revolutionize its trading function. Between Samsung Corporation and Samsung Electronics there was a long-running smoldering rivalry. Samsung Corporation, being the oldest company, saw itself as the true heart of Samsung. When Yun was promoted to vice chairman of Samsung Electronics in 1999, while the head of Samsung Corporation remained merely president of his company, feathers were further ruffled. But when Samsung Corporation was handed the key to the new economy, Samsung Electronics was deemed to be equally upset. Samsung Electronics was telling the world that it would be the leader of the digital age, but its cousin was given the keys to the content door.

In August 2001, *BusinessWeek* ran an enthusiastic article about Samsung Corporation's success in e-business. The article featured the company's successful online seafood exchange, FishRound.com, in which Samsung Corporation had a 70 percent shareholding. The company's president, Roh Sang-hong, told the magazine that FishRound had already attracted 271 of the largest fish wholesalers and retailers in the Asia Pacific region and had traded US$94 million worth of frozen fish. He expected trade volume to hit US$250 million by the end of 2001 and FishRound to be profitable by March 2002.[21]

According to the magazine, Samsung had been on a quest to grow its online business. Since April 2000, it had launched four other e-marketplaces to trade steel, chemicals, textiles, and medical supplies—all products it also traded offline. This online business was expected to help Samsung reduce the tedious physical process of matching buy or sell orders by turning to computerized online matching. By the end of 2001, Samsung expected its five e-marketplaces to handle US$2.8 billion in trades, surging to US$7 billion the following year.[22] At least half of these trades were to come from new customers, helping generate an estimated US$45 million in fees for the sites that year. By mid-2002, Samsung expected all the sites to be profitable. "Samsung has a clear idea of where B2B fits in its future," John Lee, an associate at McKinsey & Co.'s Seoul office, was quoted as saying.[23]

The aggressive e-market development added up to what Samsung's Lim Young-hak, vice president of the corporate planning team, termed a 10-year war to become the world's most wired trading company. "We want to be among those setting business standards in the twenty-first century," he said, as he outlined expectations that cost savings and new cash generators would push Samsung Corporation's profits up 160 percent, to US$150 million, by 2003.[24]

The e-dream didn't last. The world was not ready for the online trading venture that Samsung Corporation had envisaged. While Samsung Electronics went from strength to strength, Samsung Corporation was restructured from a company with 34 trillion *won* (US$34 billion) in turnover in 2001 and 36.9 trillion *won* (US$37 billion) in 2002 to about 9 trillion *won* (US$9 billion) in succeeding years. The reason was that, up until 2003, Samsung Corporation had been responsible for much of Samsung Electronics' exports, operating like a Japanese trading company on wafer-thin margins. In 2001, 63 percent of Samsung Corporation's sales were electronics. From 2003, Samsung Electronics handled its own exports, leaving Samsung Corporation to continue the non-electronics business and to absorb Samsung Engineering and Construction.

Net profits were hardly affected and Samsung Corporation was able to close down some unprofitable operations which the company had maintained for the electronics company. The founding company had been irrevocably overtaken by Samsung Electronics. From 2003, the Corporation became increasingly well known for its construction dimension, taking on major development work in Dubai and elsewhere.

Other Samsung companies continued their mixed fortune. Samsung Electronics was forced to absorb Samsung Card and bail it out during the 2002–03 credit-card crisis. Samsung Techwin went from strength to strength, reaching almost 3 trillion *won* (US$3 billion) in 2006 with 158 million *won* in net profit. Samsung Petrochemicals became a joint venture with Total of France in 2003. The other members of the electronics family continued to grow. Samsung Digital Systems became one of Korea's largest software providers, and SDI and Samsung Electro Mechanics continued to develop investing overseas but reaching sales of only about 3 trillion *won* (US$3 billion) in 2006, no more than in 2000. Samsung Display Devices, renamed Samsung SDI Ltd., achieved sales of more than 6 trillion *won* (US$6 million) in 2006, despite the problems of the cathode ray tube (CRT) industry globally as it was replaced by digital technology.

Above all, the monolithic Samsung Life company dominated Korea's life insurance market with a share that has varied between 50 and 60 percent. The government hesitates about allowing this privately held company to go public because this would instantly reinforce the Lee family's wealth and the family's shareholdings in major companies like Samsung Electronics. Given the public hostility towards the owners of the *chaebol*, this is something no government to date has been willing to permit. Chairman Lee Byung-chul's achievements were that two of his shrewd bets have paid off: the first being creating a life insurance company in the 1950s in a nation which had nothing to save; and the second, creating a semiconductor colossus in the 1970s when the country had no infrastructure to support it.

Prognosis, inheritance, and Samsung's public image

In 2007 chairman Lee Kyun-hee announced the need for a further period of total restructuring of the Samsung Group. The issues involved are discussed in later chapters, but as the *Chosun Ilbo* expressed it: "Last year, Samsung [Group] posted 141 trillion *won* (US$150 billion) in sales and a net profit of 10.7 trillion *won* (US$11.4 billion). Samsung's sales account for almost 20 percent of Korea's GDP: it is Korea's flagship business conglomerate. We should be worried when a conglomerate like Samsung feels an urgent need to restructure."[25]

In looking at Samsung Electronics from the outside, it is easy to forget that it is part of a larger group. While it has a considerable degree of independence, Samsung Electronics is firmly attached to the Samsung Group's fortunes. Although foreign shareholdings represented 51 percent of Samsung Electronics in mid-2006, Samsung Life Insurance owned 7.3 percent, Samsung Corporation owned 4 percent, and other Samsung companies and members of the Lee family added another 5 percent. Since Samsung Life and Samsung Corporation were either owned by the Lee family, or by other Samsung companies (including Samsung Electronics subsidiaries; the theme park company Everland; or by the unlisted virtual holding companies of the Samsung Group), the ultimate management voice lies with the chairman of Samsung—Lee Kun-hee and his successor.

The relationship between the chairman and the CEO of Samsung Electronics has already been discussed and its benign nature in shaping the progressiveness of this company emphasized. There is another issue which attracts the attention of the Korean public and the authorities, and this is the question of inheritance. From the onset of his health problems in the later 1990s, Lee Kun-hee began the process of transferring his wealth to his son, Lee Jae-yong, who is already the major shareholder of Everland. In May 2007, two directors of Everland were convicted (though not imprisoned) of assisting in a shell game (which all the *chaebol* play) to allow shares to pass from one family member to another from as long ago as 1996. The executives were found guilty of breach of trust for selling Everland shares to Lee Jae-yong and others at well below the market price, resulting in 8.9 billion *won* (US$8.9 million) in losses to the company.

The Korean public takes an austere view of this game and, in the people's view, it damaged the claims of the Republic of Samsung to represent the Republic of Korea. The *Chosun Ilbo* billed this as another rebuke for Samsung.[26] It has to be remembered that though the event took place more than a decade ago, this was the key moment in which Lee Jae-yong was able to convert the bonds into shares and become the largest single shareholder in Everland, with 25.1 percent. Through his majority stake in Everland, Jae-yong was able to exercise control of Samsung Life Insurance and Samsung Electronics through cross-shareholding, eventually becoming the controlling stakeholder in the Samsung Group.

In its ruling, the High Court said: "The decision by Everland's board to issue the CBs [Convertible Bonds] took place without a quorum and is therefore void, while the issuance of the CBs and allotting them to Lee Jae-yong and others constitutes a breach of trust."[27] In its ruling, the court also added: "Their behavior breached trust since it went beyond the boundaries of conventional fundraising and affected the ownership structure by hoarding CBs with a third party."[28]

In the view of the *Chosun Ilbo*, because the board's decision was void, the act of issuing the bonds was also void and Jae-yong's controlling stake in Everland could also be interpreted as being void. The court, however, did not draw that conclusion, saying that in order to protect the sanctity of deals "there can be instances where completed issuances can be viewed as being valid according to corporate law."[29] But it added that since this incident was not a conventional transaction and involved the transfer of management control to a third person, "it cannot be concluded that the issuance itself is entirely valid."[30] The court left open the possibility that the CB deal could be voided.

In the newspaper's view, the Supreme Court's ruling would have wide implications for not only the leadership succession but also for the Samsung Group's entire ownership structure. It reckoned Korea's image was dealt a blow by the ethical and legal dispute under which management control at the Samsung Group had been transferred. "Samsung must take a good long look at itself to see why this happened," the paper said.[31]

Other media voices also took up this issue, continuing the level of criticism against the *chaebol* in general. *The Korea Times* reminded its readers that a recent survey by the Korea Development Institute had revealed that the majority of Koreans felt negative about Samsung and other *chaebol*, and that the *chaebol* themselves were responsible for this feeling. Respondents to the survey cited immoral management, accounting fraud, illegal stock transactions among family members, and tax avoidance.[32] This is an issue which is likely to dog Lee Jae-yong as he moves towards succeeding his father. The younger Lee was heavily criticized when he was moved into the corporate planning department of Samsung Electronics in 2001. In 2007, at age 40, he was named chief customer officer, a title held in a few US companies such as United Airlines and Sears. This effectively made him vice president of the company. His succession would move him out of Samsung Electronics into the chairman's office, where he would have to face the ongoing matter of the convertible bonds issue.

Samsung Electronics was eager to convince its shareholders that shareholder value was central to the company's policy decision, whatever the games at the top. In its annual report for that year, the vice chairman stressed that in 2006 Samsung Electronics had spent approximately 40 percent of its net profits on enhancing share-holder value by paying dividends of 5,500 *won* per share and had repurchased shares worth 2 trillion *won* (US$2 billion).[33] Samsung Electronics has emerged clearly as the brightest of the three stars that make up Samsung's name. At the end of 2008, it accounted for about half of the turnover of the Samsung Group and about 70–80 percent of the group's profit. The political issues described in this chapter represent some of the special characteristics of the Korean government and popular attitudes towards the wealthy and their *chaebol*. The fact is that the Samsung Group is still prevented by government regulation from having a transparent group structure, and this may continue for a long time. Samsung Electronics has operated successfully in this environment, despite the fraternal rivalry between the senior Samsung companies.

Events were to get significantly worse after the 2007 High Court decision, with allegations of widespread bribery by the Samsung Group being spread by a would-be whistleblower who had once headed Samsung's legal affairs department. Kim Yong-chul, who worked as an attorney at Samsung from 1997 to 2004, claimed he took part in creating over 7 trillion *won* (US$7.5 billion) in slush funds for Samsung. Kim described the conglomerate and the Lee family as a "force mixed with injustice."[34] The affair broke on the eve of the 2007 presidential elections, and an independent prosecutor was only appointed to investigate the allegations in January 2008, when President Roh had little more than a month left in office, and when his successor, the business-minded Lee Myung-bak, was already deeply involved in the transition planning for his new government. As a result, the prosecutor was forced to cut short his investigation and conclude only that Lee Kyun-hee had been guilty of tax evasion.[35] Lee surrendered all corporate positions in April 2008, and his son was given responsibility of overseas subsidiaries. Had Frankenstein reined in the monster? The implications for Samsung Electronics can only be considered in the context of other internal issues, which are described in the succeeding chapters.

Endnotes

1 "Korea's US$500 Million Man," *Time*, July 19, 1976.
2 "Samsung Electronics Co., Ltd. SWOT Analysis and Company Profile," Datamonitor, June 12, 2007; accessed September 30, 2007.
3 *Time* 1976, op. cit.
4 Ibid.
5 "South Korea: B. C. Lee's World," *Time*, April 28, 1967.
6 Ibid.
7 Michell, Tony 1988, "From a Developing to a Newly Industrialized Country: The Republic of Korea, 1961–82," ILO Employment and Industrialization No. 6, Geneva: 95–9, and the longer working paper which preceded it.
8 *Time* 1976, op. cit.
9 *Time* 1967, op. cit.
10 *Time* 1976, op. cit.
11 KABC, *The Chaebol Report* 1996,Volume 1.
12 *Time* 1976, op. cit.
13 See http://210.118.57.197/AboutSAMSUNG/SAMSUNGGROUP/Chairman/InthePress/Press2002.htm; accessed May 17, 2009.
14 Private communication.
15 "The Hard Road Ahead: Interview with Lee Kun-hee,"*Asiaweek*, November 12, 1999.
16 KABC, *The Chaebol Report* 2000, Volume 1.
17 *Asiaweek*, op. cit.
18 KABC, *The Chaebol Report* 1998, Volume 1.
19 KABC, *The Chaebol Report* 2001, Volume 1.
20 Interview in *New York Times*, May 20, 2006.
21 "E Biz or Bust, Samsung Bets Big on On-line Trading," by Ken Belson and Moon Ihlwan, *BusinessWeek International Edition*, August 6, 2001.
22 Ibid.
23 Ibid.
24 Ibid.
25 Editorial, *Digital Chosun*, July 30, 2007.
26 "Another Rap over the Knuckles for Samsung,"*Digital Chosun*, May 30, 2007.
27 Ibid.
28 Ibid.
29 Ibid.
30 Ibid.
31 Ibid.
32 Editorial, *Korea Times*, June 7, 2007.
33 Samsung Electronics Annual Report 2006.
34 "Prosecutors Launch Probe into Samsung Bribery Scandal," *Korea Times*, January 10, 2008; "Samsung's Lee Family Accused Of Corrupt Dealings," by Shu-Ching Jean Chen, Faces in the News, *Forbes*, November 13, 2007.
35 "Samsung's Chairman Steps Down,"englishnews@chosun.com, April 29, 2008.

3

Samsung and Sony Compared: The Tale of Two Life Cycles

Samsung is the new anti-Sony.

George Gilder

Prologue

Eric Kim articulated Samsung Electronics' ambitious goal of lifting its brand equity level to match that of Sony when he was appointed the company's global marketing director in 2002. This throwing down of the gauntlet was a brash assertion by Samsung Electronics, challenging Sony as well as other Korean companies. The move was also brash given that in 1998 Samsung Electronics had considered abandoning consumer electronics as part of its portfolio. Internally, this move was not without its detractors, but Eric Kim and CEO Yun saw eye to eye on this goal. They also had the backing of the chairman of the Samsung Group, Lee Kun-hee, having convinced him that this was an attainable target for the company. In fact, it had been CEO Yun's ambition to overtake Sony since he took charge of the company in 1996.

In the early years, between 2002 and 2004, Samsung Electronics doubled its sales. It also began to run close to Sony on several fronts.

In 2005, Samsung achieved its goal of having a higher brand value than Sony, reaching number 20 on Interbrand's top 100, with a value of US$14.9 billion. In the same year, Sony was positioned at number 28, and was valued at US$10.7 billion. However, Samsung had not yet reached Sony's brand value of US$16.41 billion, achieved in 2000.[1] As Samsung's brand value rose, Sony had become the fastest falling company of 2005 and seemed unable to stem the decline, even going as far as to appoint a Westerner, Howard Stringer, as the CEO in March of that year. During the period 2005–09, Stringer struggled with the process of bringing change management to a company which had reached a point in its life cycle where change was extremely difficult for the organization. In the corporate fiscal year that ended March 2009 (like nearly all Japanese companies, Sony follows the government year of April–March, which makes direct chronological comparison with Western companies difficult), Sony experienced its first net loss for 14 years of US$1 billion.[2] A further round of factory closures and job losses was announced, with the CFO stating that "as far as the restructuring measures go, it's not that we're doing anything that different. We are just going another step."[3]

The life cycle of Sony

Courtship and infancy

Sony Corporation was founded in May 1946 as Tokyo Tsushin Kogyo (Tokyo Telecommunications Engineering Corporation). The company's founding prospectus highlighted the philosophy of Sony's incorporation as: ". . . the establishment of an ideal factory, free, dynamic, and pleasant, where technical personnel of sincere motivation can exercise their technological skills to the highest level."[4] In 1958 the company changed its name to SONY (from "Sonus," meaning "sound") because the original Japanese name was impossible for non-Japanese to pronounce or remember. The company was led by two remarkable men Masaru Ibuka and Akio Morita, who acted as co-chairmen. The two men had met during their military service and founded the company. Morita persuaded his family to invest in the company. Ibuka, who was then 38, was to look after production, and Morita, then 25, came to be the marketing genius.

Go-Go

From the word go, Sony was always determined to be different. It started producing magnetic tapes, before moving to transistor radios in 1957. While other Japanese companies were producing exports on sub-contracts, Sony opened its showroom in Fifth Avenue in New York in 1962, followed by the Ginza in 1966 and Paris in 1971—all built round the concept that without a unique brand image revolving around unique products, Sony could not become a leader in the electronics industry. The goal in the 1960s and 1970s was to have consumers associate the name "SONY" with unique, high-quality products.[5] Morita decided that in order to succeed he should run the company from overseas and Sony opened its office in the US (Sony Corporation of America) in 1960, listed ADRs (American depositor receipts) on the New York Stock Exchange as early as 1961 and was co-listed on the NYSE by 1970.

Sony moved some of its manufacturing abroad in 1959, to Hong Kong, and to Shannon in the Irish Republic. It opened its first US plant in San Diego in 1972. Alongside this development, an American became president of Sony Corporation of America in 1966, and by 1972 both the president and vice president were Americans. Management was rapidly localized alongside production and R&D during the 1970s and 1980s.

While Sony was becoming a true multinational on one level, it remained Japanese on another. In this respect it reflected what Professor Hirotaka Takeuchi describes as the "two Japans." On the one hand, there was a competitive, global and world-class Japan; on the other, was a Japan that was inward-looking, uncompetitive (or anti-competitive) and mediocre.[6] For Morita, although he pushed the company outwards, the most important mission for a Japanese manager was to develop a healthy relationship with his employees, "to create a family-like feeling within the corporation, a feeling that employees and managers share the same fate. We will try to create conditions where persons could come together in a spirit of teamwork, and exercise to their heart's desire their technological capacity."[7] He felt that there were three kinds of creativity: "in technology, in product planning, and in marketing."[8] The technology would be Japanese.

Sony reached a peak in international recognition with the introduction of the Walkman in 1979. The device was created by audio-division engineer Nobutoshi Kihara for Morita, who wanted to be able to listen to opera during his frequent flights across the Pacific. Morita is said to have hated the name "Walkman" (it was originally branded "Soundabout" overseas) and asked for it to be changed, but gave up after being told that a Japanese promotion campaign had already begun using the name and would be too expensive to change. The Walkman introduced a change in listening habits, allowing people to carry their own choice of music or other audio material with them. It was the forerunner of all mobile devices.

Adolescence and Prime

Sony made many consumer appliances, but it was the Walkman which made Sony a global brand. The sales revenue continued to climb and it seemed that Sony could do no wrong. Its leaders had been right about the transistor radio, the Walkman, and the CD-player format and business model. But when it introduced the video player in 1976, the company departed from its previous model and went instead for a high-price product, aiming at 100 percent ownership of the market, either by sale of its own products or through licensing. JVC also took up the video-player challenge but using a different format (the VHS rather than the Betamax format used by Sony) and destroyed both Sony's market and its confidence in marketing and product innovation.

It should be remembered that when Sony started producing video-players, it owned 100 percent of the category. The defeat of the Betamax format by VHS became a classic technology marketing case study, creating the phrase "to Betamax," wherein a proprietary technology format held by a single company is overwhelmed by a format allowing multiple, competing, licensed manufacturers who can offer a lower-cost product. Apple's lead in desktop computers being overcome by the IBM PC is another example. Sony's confidence in its ability to dictate the industry standard backfired when JVC made the tactical decision to engage in the open sharing of its VHS technology. By adopting this route, JVC sacrificed substantial potential earnings but that decision ultimately won the standards war. During the late 1970s and early 1980s, manufacturers were divided: on the Betamax side were Sony, Toshiba, Sanyo, NEC, Aiwa, and Pioneer. On the VHS side were JVC, Matsushita (Panasonic), Hitachi, Mitsubishi, Sharp, and Akai. The clinching point (as with the Windows system) was not superior quality but consumer usability. Betamax produced tape which recorded for one hour, while VHS offered three hours of recording time. The simple utility of VHS operations outweighed Betamax's questionable technical superiority. By 1984, 40 companies were utilizing the VHS format, in comparison with Betamax's 12. Sony finally conceded defeat in 1988 when it too began producing VHS recorders. When Sony ceased to make Betamax recorders at the end of the 1980s, it became a more Japanese—in the sense of being more cautious—and a less visionary company.

Stable: Changing the leadership

The transition from "prime" to "stable" in a company's life cycle has no obvious boundary. Just as Sony was admitting defeat in the Betamax wars, in the late 1980s it made what might be regarded as a fundamental and strategic mistake—entering a mature business area it did not fully understand through acquisition. Sony acquired Columbia Pictures Entertainment, including Universal Studios (1989) and CBS Records (1990), and moved into what would be described a few years later as the "content business." Sony believed that because it understood the hardware of entertainment systems, it could understand and make a profit from the content business. This belief was strengthened by the successful introduction of PlayStation in December 1994, which included separate content sales. (The work on the PlayStation— initially through Nintendo—in fact, stretched back into the 1980s.) Sony's management was further lured by the "new economy" hype in which the knowledge economy was touted to be the true income earner, while hardware-makers were seen as second-rate companies.

However, Pictures and music are completely different businesses, each with its own risk profile and revenue streams. The way they were structured in the early 1990s, neither was ready for the digital age.

Sony turned 50 years old in 1996. This was preceded two years earlier by a change of CEO. Then honorary chairman Ibuka became chief advisor and Morita, who was recuperating from illness, was appointed honorary chairman in his stead. These changes meant that the two founders had distanced themselves from the direct management of the company. The new chairman, Norio Ohga, who had been president for 12 years, chose Nobuyuki Idei to fill his former position.

In what was to be his last mission as president, Ohga had just completed a restructuring of Sony under which the different divisions were made into separate companies. His plan was for the company to be led not by a single charismatic figure but by a team of executives—a chairman and CEO, a vice chairman, a president and chief operating officer, several chief officers and divisional presidents. By introducing a new system, he had hoped to encourage divisional presidents to take the initiative in their respective fields.[9]

This restructuring process was to be part of a move allowing generational change to help rejuvenate the aging company. But what it ended up doing was introducing layers of bureaucracy which slowed the company.

When Ohga announced Nobuyuki Idei as his successor in March 1994, the business community was surprised. Idei had been appointed managing director in charge of advertising, public relations, and product design just the previous year. It was time for the third creativity, marketing, to be employed. Idei can be contrasted with Eric Kim of Samsung. Ohga's selection reflected the same market-driven thinking. Idei had joined Sony 35 years earlier, wanting to work for a company that he thought would succeed in the European market. During the 1960s and 1970s, he had spent close to a decade in Europe. He then moved on to overseeing the audio, computer, and VCR business operations, even though his background was not in the engineering field. In the 1990s, as a director in charge of advertising, product design, and public relations, Idei concentrated his efforts on promoting the Sony brand image.

Between Kim and Idei there were three important differences—one was generational, one geographic, and one a matter of timing. Kim had come up through the digital world in the hi-tech era, whereas Idei had come from the old-tech era of mechanical electronic engineering. Equally important, the "new economy" ideas which were fermenting in the US in the late 1990s were not fermenting in Europe at the end of the 1980s in a pre-internet and pre-digital age.

The selection of Idei was indicative of the direction in which Ohga was trying to lead Sony, as he explained later: "Sony needs someone who is not necessarily an engineer, but appreciates technology; someone who recognizes the latest technological developments and has the foresight to see future technology trends; someone who understands the software business; and someone who has a global perspective. All these indicators led to Idei-san."[10]

Aristocracy, bureaucracy, the lost decade and corporate change

Sony at 50

In 1996, to celebrate Sony's fiftieth birthday, the new management took 20,000 employees and their families to Tokyo Disneyland. Japan rode the Asian currency crisis of the 1990s without calling in the IMF. As the world's second-richest country, with the largest foreign currency reserves and a persistent current account surplus, it had no need of the IMF. But it had an urgent need to change, which it could not face up to. After the collapse of the bubble economy at the end of the 1980s, Japan had not only entered the Asian corporate crisis in the early 1990s well ahead of other Asian countries, but had also entered what is popularly termed "the lost decade." There are those, like James Abegglen, who have argued that this is a misnomer:

> The period from 1995 to 2004 was not a "lost decade," as is often described, but one put to vigorous and effective use. Nor has it been a decade of "stagnation." It has been a decade of critical reshaping of the strategies and structures of the *kaisha* ["corporations"]. It has been a decade of vitally needed redesign, and far from being stagnant, has been a decade filled with putting in place urgently needed new programs.[11]

Although this may have been true for Japan as a whole, for Sony—Japan's best-known company—the redesign and reshaping did not go far enough, while the division of the company into different subsidiaries encouraged bureaucracy and infighting.

In the 1995 financial year (see Table 3.1), Sony had sales of US$44.75 billion and experienced a net loss of US$3.29 billion, its first loss since 1989, but also its last loss until 2009.[12] Its sales and net income during the early 1990s showed the classic financial characteristics of a company urgently in need of restructuring. Sales in yen terms were more or less static, and net income fell dramatically in 1993 and 1994 before the loss seen in 1995.

The company's annual report placed the blame for the loss on the write-off of goodwill and additional losses in the second quarter seen in the Pictures Group.

Table 3.1 Sony's sales and net income FY 1991–95

	Yen in millions						Dollars in thousands		
	1995	1996	1997	1998	1999	2000	1996	1998	2000
ASSETS									
Current assets:									
Cash and cash equivalents	¥475,555	¥459,339	¥428,518	¥423,286	¥592,210	¥626,064	$4,333,387	$3,206,712	$5,906,000
Time deposits	16,173	32,605	52,518	107,139	24,304	6,138	307,594	811,659	58,000,000
Marketable securities	66,617	28,420	120,094	169,209	117,857	107,499	268,113	1,281,887	1,014,000
Notes and accounts receivable, trade	675,111	923,566	1,066,314	1,230,799	1,135,598	1,156,065	8,712,887	9,324,235	10,906,000
Allowance for doubtful accounts and sales returns	(48,185)	68,763	(93,732)	(114,911)	(122,015)	(100,596)	(648,708)	870,538	(949,000)

In April 1994, Sony abolished its product groups in the electronics business and introduced the new corporate structure with eight independent companies. This move was to allow the eight individual companies to create their own management goals, and have their own financial statements—a strategy intended to accelerate decision-making. In practice, this backfired because it simply created more levels of bureaucracy. In 1995, Sony completed its first-year launch of PlayStation, a product thus far hidden away under "others" in the corporate accounts.

Sony expected its operating environment to grow increasingly challenging as a result of the uncertain direction of the Japanese economy, the high value of the yen, and fierce price competition. It promised to introduce ever-more-appealing products, new dimensions of product integration, and R&D; and more streamlining of the company. But most of these promises could not be met.

Ohga and Idei outlined three core strategic challenges for Sony:

- In its principal area of electronics: to further strengthen Sony's leading position in audio visual while developing its IT business.
- In its entertainment business: to foster a deeper understanding among company management and employees of the entertainment industry so that Sony can secure a firm foothold.
- To integrate the electronics and entertainment businesses to create totally new business opportunities, to evolve into a truly global total entertainment company.[13]

Bearing these things in mind, it is easy to see why Sony was so excited by the PlayStation, which during the 1990s and early 2000s was to restore some of the luster lost by the Sony brand. The PlayStation was based on Sony's own proprietary processor and, above all, the product linked the electronics and entertainment strands of the business. But a US$5-billion business was wagging the tail of a US$70-billion business, and Sony faced death by what may be termed the "multiple competitors dilemma."

Sony at 60

By March 2003, almost 10 years after the restructuring and with the same management team, Sony had increased its sales by 64 percent, from US$44 billion to US$72 billion, and had a net

profit of US$1.38 billion. Part of this was simply due to the posi-
tive impact of changes in the exchange rate. In yen terms, the net
income of ¥144 billion was only 23 percent higher than the
¥120 billion of 1992. In dollar terms, it was the difference
between US$923 million (¥130 = US$1) and US$1.38 billion
(¥104 = US$1)—that is, 50 percent higher. During the same period,
Samsung's sales increased by 300 percent. It was Sony's last good year.
What followed was what is known in Japan as the "Sony Shock."[14]

In 2003, Sony announced a big earnings shortfall and sliding
sales in its mainstay electronics division. According to Allen Wan,
the Asian bureau chief of CBS's MarketWatch program, Sony's
problems could be attributed to a dearth of exciting new products,
and a lack of focus arising from its diverging interests ranging from
music, to movies, to chips. Wan said some market watchers saw
Sony's problems as self-generated.[15]

In 2004, Sony announced that in its first quarter (April–June)
operating profits had plummeted 90 percent from the previous year.
Investors in Tokyo and New York hammered the stock down by
15 percent in the following two trading sessions. Reporters flooded
the company with queries about what had gone wrong. Analysts
openly questioned Sony's commitment to develop an all-internet,
all-the-time strategy in preparation for the day when its mainstay
consumer electronics and video game machines no longer dominated
the company's earnings.[16]

Sony officials did their best to deflect all this alarmist specu-
lation about the future of one of Japan Inc.'s flagship companies,
pointing out that information technology and electronics manufacturers worldwide were in the grip of a precipitous and unavoidable
slowdown in corporate and consumer spending. As an illustration
of the lack of panic, Sony's chairman, president and chief financial
officer were reportedly going ahead with the summer vacations they
had planned.[17]

To many, Sony's abrupt slide was a troubling indicator that its
problems went deeper than a temporary drought in demand. The
company had launched uncertain and unprofitable initiatives such as
an effort to sell music online, and it had spent heavily on the development of a web-surfing game machine to succeed the PlayStation.
Restructuring charges at consumer-electronics subsidiary Aiwa also
contributed to losses. According to Yukihiko Shimada, consumer-
electronics analyst for Credit Lyonnais, the consumer-spending

boom of 1999 and 2000 hid Sony's "structural problems," which were more than cyclical. Shimada's assessment was: "The company has overextended itself . . . In other words, Aibo the robot dog isn't ready to roll over and play dead, but it isn't altogether frisky, either."[18] While senior management told themselves that the cycle would recover, in fact the problems inside Sony were not ones which an upturn in the market could solve. Further, if the management had looked across the East Sea at Samsung in Korea, they would have found a company in the same business area that was growing rapidly despite the alleged problem in the business cycle.

It was not just Sony, however, that was suffering from the rising competition from Korea: all corners of Japan's hi-tech industry were being affected by the slowdown. Matsushita Electric Industrial, the maker of Panasonic products, reported its first quarterly loss since its stock was listed in 1949. Another Japanese electronics giant, Fujitsu, said it would take a one-time $2.4 billion restructuring charge to pay for a reduction in capacity, and Fujitsu's chief rival, NEC, said it would lay off 4,000 people by 2005 because of the slump.

Other analysts accepted the Japanese industry's explanation about a downturn in the global market. "Sony is a global company linked to the global economy," said Masahiro Ono, consumer-electronics analyst with UBS Warburg in Tokyo. "When world demand for consumer electronics slows, it shouldn't surprise us that Sony reports bad financial results."[19] But as we saw earlier, Samsung's growth in the same period gave no such indication of a global slowdown in demand.

Analysts were still obsessing about the tail, noting that the PlayStation division was now making a loss and was facing an onslaught from XBox. "Sony used its muscle against Nintendo and Sega when it launched the PlayStation, and took a big market share. Now, Microsoft is going to try to do to Sony what Sony did to others," wrote one analyst.[20] No one pointed to the fact that Samsung was continuing to go from strength to strength, because it remained linked to the portfolio of core components as well as appliances.

Aging companies often look to acquisitions to save them. In the content business, Sony toyed with purchasing MGM. Commentators were impressed:

> If Sony buys MGM it would create a movie business
> big enough to rival America's entertainment giant,

Time Warner. That would be something of a triumph; in 1994 Sony was the laughing stock of Hollywood after writing off $2.7 billion of reckless spending at its movie division. With its film business now earning solid profits, it has made a preliminary bid of $5 billion for MGM, jointly with two private equity firms, Texas Pacific Group and Providence Equity Partners, who would put up a lot of the money.[21]

The on-again/off-again merger was finally consummated in 2005, after being formally announced in April 2004. Content wise and in terms of films that could be made into video games this was an interesting move in association with Comcast, the US cable network giant in partnership with private equity firms. In terms of saving the core business it was a continuing distraction.

Sony's management therefore decided it was time for a change and brought in the head of its US division, who had managed something of a turnaround in the US despite Samsung's competition in June 2005. Howard Stringer was both an outsider and outside the technological circle and had been a CBS journalist who had risen to serve as the president of CBS (1988–95), and who had joined Sony as the head of Sony Corporation of America in 1997 after two years of running a TV and media company.

Stringer was not the obvious choice. Many thought that Ken Kutaragi, the father of PlayStation, was the logical choice. Kutaragi's latest creation, the handheld PlayStation Portable, had just been released and was selling well. (An estimated three million units were sold within three months of release in Japan and the US.) But instead of ascending in the dramatic management reshuffle that put Howard Stringer in the chief executive's chair, Kutaragi was demoted and lost his seat on Sony's board, though he still ran Sony Computer Entertainment, Inc., the company's game subsidiary.

As one commentator noted:

It appears the 54-year-old Kutaragi's outspoken nature, in a corporate culture that's oiled by consensus, may be to blame. Independent and shockingly frank by Japanese standards, Kutaragi hasn't held back from criticizing company decisions.

In January, he told the Foreign Correspondents' Club in Tokyo that fellow executives had been overly restrictive in controlling Sony content in a world where consumers of digital movies and music want hassle-free access. Asked what he would do if he were running Sony, Kutaragi said the company must revive its original innovative spirit, when it boasted engineering finesse with the transistor radio, Walkman and Trinitron TV.[22]

During the first quarter of 2005, at age 59, Sony saw wider losses at its electronics and music affiliates. Analysts said that the results underscored how tough it would be for the new top-management team to turn the company around. However, such comments simply showed how little financial analysts knew about the problems of engineering a fundamental turnaround; which in the case of giants like IBM, took three years.[23] In Stringer's second quarter of office, the group suffered a further loss, with its consumer-products market share being chipped away. This made Sony's projection of a net profit of ¥160 billion (US$1.49 billion) for FY2005 almost unattainable. Again Sony blamed the market and analysts agreed that Sony's problems were not all of its own making and that it was operating in a weak market for electronic goods while prices were tumbling. When a company is in the bureaucracy phase of its life cycle it is normal to blame external circumstances for internal failure. Such problems were not affecting Samsung Electronics. In consumer electronics, Sony no longer offered unique "must-have" products. Even in Japan its share of digital still cameras dropped from 20 percent to 10 percent, and in portable audio Sony did not catch up with Apple's lead in MP3s, even in its home market. To earn revenue, Sony sold its flat-screen TVs below competitors' prices.

A leading digital analyst in Japan, Hiroshi Takada of J.P. Morgan, believed that "having already undertaken a wide ranging restructuring, Sony had little scope for more cost-cutting. If they are serious about recovery, they will have to pull out of [loss-making] businesses."[24] Cutting costs is one thing, but portfolio restructuring, along the lines adopted by Samsung a decade earlier, was another. Sony's global sales for the financial year ending March 2005 had slipped to US$67 billion.

Nevertheless, under Stringer some radical changes began to take place. Much of the turnaround came from some painful rethinking of the way Sony did business. By 2006 the company expected to trim US$2.8 billion in annual costs from the electronics division, in large part through layoffs and early retirements that would reduce the company's overall payroll by 13 percent, or 20,000 workers. Having closed 17 of its 70 factories between 1999 and 2003, Sony closed an additional four. At the same time, the company planned to pare its offerings in about 15 of its 137 product categories. Sony also set about cutting the number of parts it used. In TVs, it trimmed the various chassis (basic platforms) in its sets from 30 to 15, with the aim to get down to six. "When we use common chassis, production gets much easier, so our production costs drop by 30 percent or more," said Makoto Kogure, head of the television unit.[25] All told, Sony hoped to cut its parts list to 100,000 by March 2006, from 840,000 a year earlier. There was also a proposal to stop the "sleeping with the enemy" policy which had created the Samsung-Sony JV to produce LCDs. By the end of 2005, one observer noted:

> Sony insists its electronics recovery isn't simply a cost-cutting story. Instead, the company is trying for greater vertical integration, buying the bulk of key parts for its most profitable products from divisions inside the company rather than from outsiders. This technique has been tried off and on by many companies over the years, but Sony sees it as a big new strategic advantage. The TV unit, for instance, next year will start getting its LCD panels from a Sony-Samsung joint venture. And while Sony today buys many of its TV chassis from outsiders, once it reaches the half-dozen platforms Kogure wants, most will be made in-house.[26]

In this context, for Samsung to have overtaken this company in 2005 does not seem such an achievement. Like other great companies restructuring late in their life cycle, management's expectations of reforming the company in a matter of quarters, dragged on into years. By March 2008 at the end of FY 2007–08, indicators suggested that the company was finally turning around, as Figure 3.1 shows.

Sales and operating revenue were up 6.9 percent, operating income was up 5.2 times and net income 2.9 times. But just as the company was back on track, the world economy was about to fall off it and, by 2009, Sony was back at restructuring and talking about closing a further eight plants, in the US, Mexico, Indonesia and France, and laying off another 16,000 workers.[27]

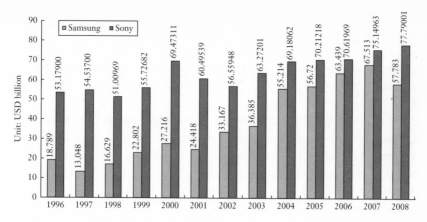

Figure 3.1   Growth of Samsung's Sales Versus Sony's 1996-2008

Source: Sony Sales—Sony Historical Data / Sony Global Website; Samsung Sales—Samsung Annual Report/FSS Korea; Japanese Yen FX—Bank of Japan; Korean Won FX—Bank of Korea

Note: Samsung's total is Korean company only (see text), while Sony is consolidated. Reduction in 2008 due to dramatic fall in value of the won.

Samsung Electronics vs. Sony

Samsung and Sony are best compared at two moments in time: during the run up to Samsung achieving its goal of overtaking Sony's brand value, and then in 2009 after Samsung had hit its "Sony moment" in 2007 and struggled to reposition itself during the global downturn.[28]

Samsung and Sony 2004–05

In 2004 to 2005, Samsung showed a much healthier financial structure than the aging Sony. Samsung's pre-tax net income was twice as high as Sony had ever achieved, and the company did not complain of a cycle of falling demand. Samsung had more accurately identified the leading sectors of profitable technology than Sony, and had grown faster. Sony seemed to be stuck in profitless growth, without dominance in any leading sector. Samsung had 88,000 employees in 2004 with average earnings per employee of US$568,200. In the same year, Sony had 151,400 employees and average earnings per employee of US$443,700. On this crude measure, Samsung demonstrated a level of productivity 28 percent higher than Sony. Nor was Samsung Electronics weighed down with the content industry, which, as we have seen in Chapter 2, had been taken by Samsung Corporation under the Samsung Millennium Plan, and that had not really produced very much.

In 2003, Samsung had passed Sony in terms of electronics sales, but adding Sony's music and media business, Sony was still the bigger company. As shown in Figure 3.2, Samsung's sales were concentrated in four major areas, where it was larger in each case, although Sony arranged its sales into seven electronics areas and four content areas.

One of the responses of the Korean government to the 1997 crisis was to increase the share of a Korean company's equities that could be held by foreign investors to 100 percent. The Korean stock

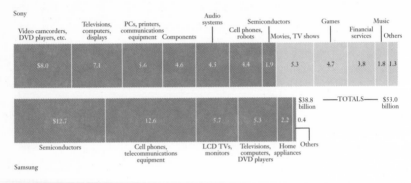

Figure 3.2   Two electronics giants: Head-to-head 2004 (nine quarters results)

Source: Business Week

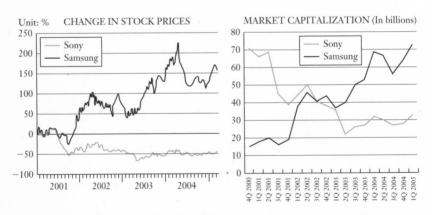

Figure 3.3   Changes in stock prices and market capitalization 2001–05

Source: BusinessWeek

market had first been tentatively opened to foreign investments with the issue of convertible bonds in the 1980s. Foreign trading on the Korean stock market was first allowed in the second half of the 1980s. Samsung Electronics was the stock of choice with 83 percent of Samsung's stocks being held by foreigners in 2004.

This pushed up the value of Samsung's shares, which had steadily risen between 2001 and 2005, while Sony's had fallen. In terms of market capitalization, in 2000 Sony had been valued at over US$70 billion and Samsung Electronics at US$20 billion. By 2002 the two companies had equal capitalization and by 2005 Samsung had a market capitalization more than double that of Sony (see Figure 3.3). Investors believed in Samsung and had lost faith in Sony.

The original Eric Kim challenge had been to overtake Sony in brand value. On the face of it by 2005, Samsung had won the challenge it had set itself in 2002, moreover it had exceeded Sony Electronics in sales, net profit, and market capitalization.

Samsung and Sony in mid-2009

In 2007, before the *won* began to tumble, the Korean company had reached 89 percent of the sales of Sony including movies and content. A further US$30 billion were added by final sales in off-shore subsidiaries making Samsung larger than Sony on a consolidated basis. (See discussion on page 195–197 and Appendix 2.)

By 2008, both companies had reclassified their sales, and Sony had spun off its music content business into a separate company. Samsung in a difficult year saw a reduced US dollar income due to the collapse of the Korean *won* from 930 to 1,450 to the US dollar, but still sold more electronics than Sony as shown in Figure 3.4 by 13 percent. As explained in Appendix 2, worldwide Samsung sold even more, but these sales are not included in this set of figures. Both companies made losses in the first quarter of 2009, but because of the different financial years, this pushed down Sony's 2008 performance and would have an impact on Samsung's in 2009. By contrast, Samsung had a resurgent second quarter, partly driven by the low value of the *won*.

Despite doubts about Samsung's portfolio in 2007 and slowing growth of sales, during 2009, Samsung continued to outsell its competitors in its established product areas.[29]

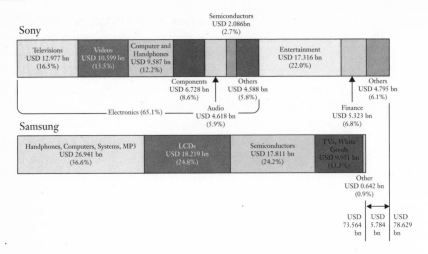

Figure 3.4   Sony's Product Range versus Samsung Product Range 2008

A tale of two life cycles

Sony and Samsung's life curves may be plotted against one another (see Figure 3.5). Adizes never suggests that comparative life cycles could be plotted, nor that these curves can be plotted in terms of sales or profits. Indeed, at each stage he suggests that different internal and external measures are appropriate for each company. Nevertheless, in making a comparative analysis of companies, the concept of drawing the life cycle of both companies on the same axes creates valuable insights.

This comparison suggests that Samsung was just entering its stable phase in 2006–07, 10 years earlier in its life than Sony. Sony had aged beyond the stable cycle and was well advanced into aristocracy and bureaucracy by 2005 when Howard Stringer took over. It was then caught up in a desperate struggle to regain a stable or, less-likely, prime mode. But for Samsung, reaching the stable phase was also entering the danger zone, most especially in electronics where "rising stars" turn into "dogs" in a very short cycle. Both companies moved from prime to aristocracy/bureaucracy at a remarkable speed.

For Adizes, this aging is related to reduced flexibility and controllability of the organization, but in practice in electronics, and probably most other areas, it relates to strategy and portfolio choice. The history of Sony illustrates some of the dilemmas of global corporations that include acquisitions in their growth strategy. Unlike Samsung, Sony has used both acquisition and decentralization

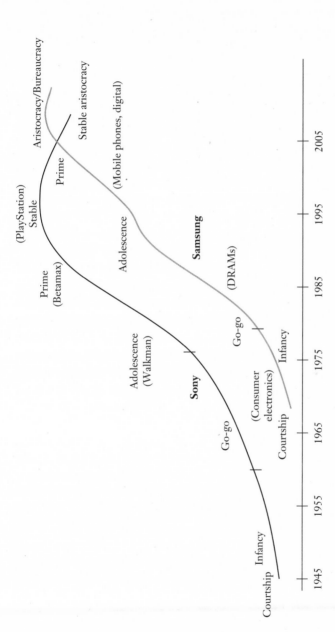

Figure 3.5 Sony and Samsung life cycles compared

as ways intended to handle the problems of organizational flexibility and control. In 1995, one of Sony's biggest problems was the question of how to handle the acquisition of Columbia Studios. Rather than increasing integration over the past 10 years, Sony has tended to pursue decentralization, without achieving positive results—in a Japanese corporate social organization, this move increased the potential for bureaucracy rather than flexibility.

The comparison between Samsung and Sony's life cycle illustrates the short time span between success and moving into organizational decline. This is not only a feature of the fast-moving electronics era or the nature of the twenty-first century. The observation that many of the "excellent" companies in the early 1980s identified by Tom Peters were in trouble by the end of the 1980s suggests that this has always been true. As CEO Yun put it on several occasions, the need for a sense of crisis in corporate life is when the company is most successful and not when it is in a crisis.

For Samsung, capturing leadership in electronics in 2004–05 was akin to having climbed to the top of a slippery pole. "The Sony moment of 2007" showed that even if Samsung had discovered the elixir of eternal business life, its rise in the early years of the new century was a combination of good strategy, good management, good portfolio choice plus good luck.[30] Could growth and success be sustained? The following pages study the actions that Samsung Electronics has undertaken to try to sustain growth and youthfulness in a difficult industry.

Endnotes

1   "The 100 Top Brands,"*BusinessWeek*, August 6, 2001; http://www.interbrand. com/images/studies/IB_SV_BW_8_6_01.pdf; accessed May 20, 2009.
2   "Sony Warns of More Losses," by Daisuke Wakabayashi and Yuzo Yamaguchi, *The Wall Street Journal Asia*, May 16–17, 2009.
3   Ibid.
4   Sony Corporation, Annual Report 1995.
5   Nobuyuki Idei in Meyer, A. 2005, *Global Future: The Next Challenge for Asian Business*, New York: John Wiley & Sons: 23.
6   Porter, Michael, Takeuchi, Hirotaka, and Sakakibara, Mariko 2000, *Can Japan Compete?*, Basingstoke: Palgrave Macmillan.
7   http://www.evancarmichael.com/Famous-Entrepreneurs/1158/Akio-Morita-Quotes.html; accessed July 10, 2009.
8   Ibid.

9   "Company History"; at: http://www.sony.net/Fun/SH/1-36/h6.html; accessed July 16, 2007.
10 Ibid.
11 *Financial Times*, July 28, 2005: 28.
12 Sony, Annual Report 1995.
13 Sony website, op. cit.
14 "Sony Unveils, Massive Restructuring Plans," by T. Uranaka, *The Japan Times*, May 29, 2003.
15 CBS MarketWatch on May 29, 2003.
16 Ibid.
17 Ibid.
18 "The Next Electronics Giant?" by Charles Cooper, *Cnet News*, November 5, 2003 at: http://news.cnet.com/The-next-electronics-giant/2008-1041_3-5102413.html
19 Ibid.
20 Ibid.
21 Ibid.
22 Ibid.
23 Ibid.
24 Ibid.
25 Ibid.
26 Ibid.
27 Wakabayashi and Yamaguchi, op. cit.
28 "Samsung's Sony Moment," by Moon Ihlwan, *BusinessWeek*, July 19, 2007, accessed July 26, 2009.
29 For further discussion, see pages 195–197. The book went to press before the 2009 consolidated results were available which were expected to emphasize this further.
30 See pages 205–212.

4

Branding Samsung Electronics

*I convinced the company we had to have a single message.
We were the new kids on the block and the block was noisy.*
Eric Kim, 2002

Samsung as an umbrella or master brand

Samsung didn't have to think about global marketing until the 1990s, although, like other Korean companies, it had been aggressively advertising its corporate name in newly emerging markets. The majority of Samsung's products sold in Western countries were either branded by other companies or were components inside other companies' products. Samsung-branded products were sold to US consumers in the 1990s, but promotion of the products was crude.[1] Whether an earlier marketing approach would have helped, or whether Samsung had now reached the point in its life cycle where a massive investment in marketing would have been justified remains a matter of judgment. This must have been an issue which vice chairman Yun reflected on time and time again as he struggled to push Samsung Electronics to new heights from 1996 onwards. To firm up his ideas, and to convince doubting colleagues, he needed an ally and he needed to demonstrate that marketing would work on multiple levels.

During the early 1990s, Samsung had developed numerous sub-brands for the American market such as Plano, Tantus, Yepp, and Wiseview. This was in contrast to its Korean and developing-market strategy of relying on its corporate name. The decision was made to focus on one brand or a "master brand." With so much media fragmentation and clutter, Samsung believed that the master-brand strategy was the only way to reach the consumer. A similar strategy was being followed by other top gainers on Interbrand's 2006 list. Asked about Samsung's move away from sub-brands to a single-brand strategy, Greg Lee, the chief marketing officer who succeeded Eric Kim, told an interviewer:

> It was a change in 1996 by our chairman, who wanted to build a brand, not just a product. There was an Asian economic crisis, and the company was in a crisis because it wasn't as efficient as it needed to be. And not having a strong brand was crippling. We also migrated to a premium-brand strategy, ditching low-end products that were selling well.
>
> . . . The story I'm trying to tell is about a big way of building a brand. It works because Samsung has one master brand as opposed to 50. We looked to the future to build the Samsung brand as iconic—one that everybody would want to have and love to have. That is what BMW has done well.[2]

In Korea, Samsung Electronics enjoys the association with the entire Samsung family of companies. Over 25 years, Samsung, as a group, steadily pursued the positioning that Samsung was the largest, most innovative and reliable of the *chaebol*, and that any product or service bought from a Samsung company would be totally reliable. Unfortunately, Samsung also had a negative image in the Korean market, with many members of the public feeling that the company was arrogant and that it "owed" Korea something. For this reason, Samsung bought LG Electronics products, because it thought that LG, being more Korea-friendly, would bring in the culture of a more friendly after-sales service.

Meanwhile, in the rest of the world, Samsung Electronics was the leading brand within the Samsung Group. The other giants of the Group—Samsung Life or Samsung Construction—had little or no presence in overseas markets, and Samsung Corporation was likely to be confused with Samsung Electronics. It was not easy for the Korean executives of Samsung to appreciate this distinction, and it took a Korean American to understand that Samsung Electronics could tap into a huge vein of new business by making its brand a household name.

Yun himself seems to have been convinced that increased marketing would bring three benefits to Samsung Electronics: it would increase the company's sales, profit margins and market capitalization.

The question was: was this the right time? Did Samsung have the qualities needed to achieve dramatic results. The only way to find out, Yun decided, was to run a test campaign in 2001. This would be aimed primarily at the US market, and if this was successful, it would go global the following year. For the 2001 campaign, Yun turned to Eric Kim.

Eric Kim entered the world of Samsung Electronics in 1999 at the age of 45. He was precisely the kind of man Yun was looking for—a late recruit from outside of the "Samsung Man" tradition. Kim was born in Seoul in 1954 and was 11 when his family moved to Los Angeles. Originally contemplating a career in the sciences, Kim majored in physics at Claremont's Harvey Mudd College. He went on to get a Master's in engineering at UCLA, before adding a Harvard MBA. After Harvard, Eric Kim worked at Lotus Development, Dun & Bradstreet, and a New York tech venture-capital firm called Spencer Trask Software Group. When he joined Samsung in 1999, he had retained enough Korean language and culture to avoid gross social blunders but had acquired enough American directness to make a difference. He was dubbed "an American who eats *kimchi*" by his Korean colleagues.[3]

At that time, Samsung Electronics was, in the words of Harvard marketing guru John Quelch, "a company dominated by hard-nosed engineers." Engineers looked on marketers as a bunch of "flower arrangers" who designed sales brochures and ran promotions on out-of-date products.[4] Likewise, marketing expenditure was an item in the budget which was either already committed to existing advertising purposes or an elastic item out of which money could be poached for other purposes.

Samsung Electronics' US campaign showed good results. Sales doubled. According to research conducted in April 2002, Samsung's 2001 global brand campaign ("Everyone's invited"— developed by FCB) helped to elevate the brand substantially. In the

US, brand awareness and preference increased to 74.1 percent from 56.4 percent over the life of the year-long campaign. During that period, consumer awareness of Samsung also increased 7.5 percentage points (from 83.7 percent to 91.2 percent). The positioning of both Samsung's first global brand campaign of 2001 and its Salt Lake City Winter Olympic Games sponsorship marketing initiatives had built the pillars on which a US$200-million global campaign would be launched in 2002.

The company's hard-nosed engineers liked the Olympic sponsorship. Koreans take sports seriously as part of their national cultural and political agenda; and of course the Olympics was viewed in Korea, while the money was spent in America. Sports promotion, itself a rapidly growing area of marketing expenditure globally, survived Eric Kim's term of office at Samsung.

Both Yun and Lee were delighted with the results of the 2001 campaign, especially with regard to visibility in the US. This success allowed Kim to persuade doubters that Samsung would be able to address and incorporate those lessons logically into its marketing initiatives. Kim was promoted to executive vice president of global marketing, and Samsung launched its new global advertising campaign designed to position the company as a leader in the digital-convergence arena.

No one in the US had paid particular attention to Kim as a marketer in his previous jobs. Although he had worked as an executive with a variety of companies—general manager at Lotus Development Corporation, CEO of Pilot Software, chief technical officer at Dun & Bradstreet, and a venture capitalist at Spencer Trask Software Group—it was Samsung Electronics that gave him the opportunity to excel. Kim rapidly demonstrated that his time at Harvard Business School had been well spent. He showed that he could apply some simple and basic marketing rules to Samsung Electronics and make a big difference.

After quickly working his way up to the top of Samsung Electronics' global marketing department, Kim realized that even without getting a larger budget he could make a real difference if he unified Samsung's fragmented advertising expenditures into a single worldwide brand campaign built around surreal, sexy and futuristic images. This was in many ways the new century's equivalent of Sony's 1980s global campaign of "those frightfully clever people from Sony" which had utilized the British comedian John Cleese and gave rise to the popular Japanese product waves of the late 1970s and early 1980s.

Under Kim's direction, the Samsung Electronics brand image was revolutionized with exciting, innovative advertising campaigns. Shrewd sponsorship deals also dramatically altered popular perceptions of the company and its products. The result was not just the doubling of Samsung's business in the US—it also caught the imagination of the business world with its goal of overtaking Sony in brand recognition. The use of the Interbrand measure for this was inspiring because it could deliver an objective assessment of value based on a rigorous methodology that could be explained to non-marketers. As John Quelch, who had taught marketing at the Harvard Business School while Kim was there, was to write a few years later with Samsung Electronics in mind:

> Many marketing managers are failing their employers. They are often creative right-brain thinkers who can dream up campaigns to drive top-line sales but they show little interest in the balance sheet impact of their promotional programs. Such marketers lack the quantitative, analytical skills necessary to drive marketing productivity; and they resist being held accountable for marketing performance, claiming that variables beyond their control, such as competitive activity, impede their ability to monitor the impact of marketing expenditures on sales results. So what must a marketing manager be able to do to succeed in a world where information rules?[5]

With Interbrand's evaluation, Samsung's marketers could show where they were in a way which would build future earnings and not just past sales. Kim had delivered to Yun the tool he needed to convince the doubters inside Samsung Electronics and to build a case for the chairman.

Although in numerous interviews Kim projected a confident image in which he made running Samsung's global marketing department seem simple, this masked the considerable battles he faced within the company. He acknowledged that had it not been for the financial crisis of 1997, he might never have been able to get Yun's backing for this venture. After he left Samsung, he said:

Samsung's history has been, as with many other Asian companies, very much in manufacturing. It started off as a contract manufacturer building for somebody else and then it grew more and more to build its own brand. But the concept of marketing really wasn't there. The basic mentality was: "Well, if I make something cheap enough people will buy it." That mindset was very strong and frankly, that mindset is quite common among a lot of the hi-tech companies and a lot of the Asian companies. If I make it cheap enough I can sell it.[6]

According to Kim, this approach was problematic in that in this diminishing-margin scenario a company could never invest in the future because it simply didn't make enough money:

So you have to get into a point where you're sufficiently differentiated and where the consumers are sufficiently willing to give you the necessary credit so that you can make enough money so that you can invest in your future. That's the sort of cycle you need to be in.[7]

"I convinced the company we had to have a single message," Kim said in 2002. "We were the new kids on the block and the block was noisy."[8]

Kim worked with New York-based Foote Cone & Belding (FCB), Samsung's global advertising agency of record, with an agenda which was to focus on how Samsung's wide array of digital products would meet the ever-changing needs of today's consumer. The advertisements, both broadcast and print, were dedicated to expanding the Samsung brand, while demonstrating the enhanced emotional benefits of the company's cutting-edge, digital-convergence products. The campaign combined communication, entertainment and information. The basic message was how Samsung's products could help to bring consumers richer and more enjoyable lives. FCB was already Samsung's US advertising agency and Kim was able to bring the global business under his aegis. This did not mean, however, that all of Samsung's US$900 million was devoted to this campaign. More than half was left for strategic market development.

Kim had planned to pull together Samsung's global spending, but he also wanted to spend more, and he was able to convince Yun that this should be the case. Samsung's investment in overall marketing activities was planned to exceed $900 million in 2002, including television and print media buys, as well as online marketing, retail promotions, collateral and point-of-purchase displays. This branding investment was an increase of more than 21 percent over 2001, and included the $200 million earmarked for this new global campaign.

Kim also wanted to make sure that he was spending his global budget wisely. To build the Samsung brand, Kim needed to invest in marketing. He recruited analysts and employed consultants to round up data from all Samsung's divisions on past marketing expenditures by product and country subsidiary, along with sales and profit results. By modeling these data, he uncovered where Samsung was overspending and under-spending. He redeployed US$100 million against higher potential product–country opportunities.[9]

In planning the 2002 drive, Kim brought with him some interesting attitudes which reflected a New York attitude to both the new economy and digital convergence—an attitude very different from what was found among Korean consumers. Kim's view was that, while many consumers thought of digital technology as an elite experience that was inaccessible to them, "Samsung prides itself on developing revolutionary technology that meets everyone's needs, whether business or personal. Our 'DigitAll' campaign depicts how exciting and accessible digital products really are, and how they've become part of our daily lives."[10] In Seoul, "DigitAll" was already part of Korean consumers' daily lives as advanced digital mobile phones were universal, based on a technology far superior to that of the US, and in Korea internet broadband access was the highest in the world. Because the Korean consumer had already adopted such a progressive attitude, it was easy for Kim to sell this program to his Korean colleagues, and many in Korea did not realize how revolutionary these Korean commonplaces would appear to the US consumer. Yun already believed that it was in digital convergence that Samsung Electronics' unique future lay.

It is important to stress that Kim did not work alone. During this period he assembled a team of talent that included Peter Weedfald, as North American consumer electronic sales, marketing, and operations senior vice president, and Jim Sanduski, who was the veteran of the team, having joined Samsung Electronics in 1995, and who presided over the visual-display product group. Sanduski also built Samsung up to the second-largest brand in digital TV during this period.

Emphasizing consumer products

The company's new campaign was to showcase a specific range of Samsung's products ("marquee products," in advertising lingo) in a wide array of digital leadership, including the convergence, mobile, and entertainment sectors. There must have been those who doubted that this program was correctly timed, given that 2001 had witnessed the technology crash following the whiplash of the dot.com bust-up. Much of the campaign was, as an anonymous blogger wrote on an electronics discussion board, "new economy hype that might have been thought more appropriate in 1999 or 2000," but was carefully repackaged. Samsung really had the products, and while the dot.com crash had left Wall Street investors and venture capitalists in gloom, Samsung was advertising the practical results of the digital age; not computers, but the tool of new living for everyone.

Products spotlighted within Samsung's advertisements included convergence communication devices, such as color LCD mobile phones and wireless handheld PCs; entertainment products, such as portable DVD players and HD-ready LCD televisions; and futuristic products, such as the company's first-ever internet refrigerator. In the advertiser's jargon, Samsung's taglines featured variants of the "DigitAll" theme, including "DigitAll Passion," "DigitAll Escape" and "DigitAll Wow." The aim was to demonstrate that consumers no longer chose products based on necessity but on want and desire—that Samsung's digital products could affect consumers' lives on an emotional level.

The campaign was launched with television spots in the US on May 16, 2002. It included broadcast and print buys in Europe, the Commonwealth of Independent States (Russia), Southeast Asia, Latin America, Africa, the Middle East and China. The campaign's "Anthem" television ad made its debut on Samsung's new 41-feet by 65-feet spectacular sign at Samsung's VIP sneak-peek lighting ceremony in Times Square. The 30-second spot featured an array of Samsung products "designed to stimulate a range of emotions, being used by consumers in a wide variety of everyday settings and geographic locations."[11]

There had to be more than merely advertising to support this campaign successfully. Promotion was only one part of the marketing mix. Products made a second element. If the positioning of Samsung was to be changed, there would have to be premium pricing, and given the nature of the distribution system for consumer electronics, a change in channels as well.

In Korea this was not necessary. Samsung had its own chain of branded stores, as did LG and Daewoo Electronics. This system of distribution had been built up over 30 years, and was only just being challenged by the rise of superstores which had begun in about 1995 in Korea. In North America, sales and marketing would need to push the higher-end retailers and downgrade the value dis-counters. Samsung was moving upmarket and it had to change its image in the West from value brand to premium brand. It helped Samsung that this premium strategy was already established in the case of mobile phones.

In most of the developed world where Samsung was seeking to expand sales, the pricing of its products and the channel would be critical. It would be hard to re-price existing products but Kim was promising the consumers of the world a constant supply of new, cool products. In a conventional fast moving consumer goods (FMCG) market, the process would take many years, but in Samsung, where the existing products could be replaced quickly, the process could take six to 18 months, provided that the distribution channels could be persuaded of the Samsung repositioning proposition.

The challenge to Sony

There were implicit long-term dangers in Samsung Electronics' global campaigns. Kim was effectively committing Samsung to developing a range of consumer products which would not be Samsung's most profitable lines, or even necessarily areas of core competence. The best way to put the company in the same league as Sony was to make the comparison deliberate and explicit, and raise Samsung's status by equating it with the company that in the public's view was the market leader.

Kim caught the imagination of the world with his PR campaign in which he announced the goal of overtaking Sony's position in brand image and brand value. While some supposed that in recent years Samsung had built a dominance in much of the developing world, and that it was in the West that it must grow, in fact Kim and his team had conducted a global exercise identifying where the markets were, how much Samsung was spending in each, and how to build the brand in each. But the hurdle was high. Out of 75 brands ranked by Interbrand, Samsung was number 43, with an estimated brand value of US$5 billion. Sony ranked 18, with a value of US$16 billion.

As Heidi Brown of *Forbes* later reported, this did not meet with full approval in Seoul:

> Eric Kim, a Korean-born American with no prior consumer-products marketing experience . . . made headlines in Japan when he told *Forbes* in 2001, in a most unhumble way, that he wanted Samsung to "beat" Sony in five years. Samsung higher-ups wrung their hands— Sony is also a customer—and reportedly reprimanded Kim for publicly baiting a customer.[12]

At the time, though, the world's business press was unwilling to suspend disbelief on this goal. Brown saw Samsung's move this way: "Now, another also-ran in the West seeks to pull a Sony. In so doing, Samsung Electronics—considered Korea's preeminent global name, although its biggest US brand presence is in lowly microwave ovens—is targeting the very path-breakers of a generation ago."[13]

This was not quite the response that Kim must have hoped for. Being described as "another also-ran in the West" was not the language that Samsung Electronics' powerful PR department was looking for.

Other commentaries were in the same vein:

> Now, the company is trying to spiff up its dowdy image in the consumer-electronics market, a task that falls to Eric Kim, its executive vice president of global marketing. The facelift seems to be working because the company's brand value has leaped up the charts,

according to brand research firm Interbrand. Still, the move has not come cheaply. Samsung has spent hundreds of millions of dollars to change its image—and the effort comes at a particularly tricky juncture.[14]

But Kim and FCB did catch the imagination and attention of the world. The 2005 results showed that Samsung was on the road to the success Kim had promised and its competitor, Sony, was in trouble partly because Samsung was stealing its market. Yun, Kim, and the Samsung team had caught the moment precisely. Three years after the launch no writer would have considered writing the skeptical commentaries seen in 2002.

Kim went further. To support his campaign he needed to get marketing involved in the next generation of consumer products. This meant he had to win the confidence of the Samsung engineers who did not think that marketing was particularly important, or that it should drive product development. Kim was determined to help make key products more appealing in global markets. He ordered a redesign of the Nexio PDA to add a bigger screen, a keyboard, and a wireless connection before its US debut. He also pushed to get Samsung products into more upscale retail outlets to improve their affinity with affluent consumers. But the real credit should go to men like Chin Dae-je, who had been head of the consumer electronics division since 2002. Working 18 hours a day, Chin spent about half his time on the road, pitching the company to retailers and analysts, and talking with Samsung representatives overseas. (Chin later became Minister of Communications in the Roh administration.)

Chin's division won several design awards, including one for its Yepp MP3 player, its digital still camera and its flat-screen TFT-LCD monitor, which also acts as a TV. Samsung ranked fourth in the US in the number of patents registered in 2002.[15] By 2003, market analysts claimed that "young consumers were ogling Samsung cell phones and flat-panel TVs the way their parents once lusted after Sony products."[16] That image change made the difference between struggling to eke out razor-thin commodity margins and enjoying fat profits as a consumer favorite.

Business analysts continued to cross-examine Kim on whether Samsung was really a consumer products company. They warned him that his moves could take Samsung into the troubled waters Sony was experiencing. One critic asked: "Look at Sony, which is known as being a consumer electronics company: Its latest earnings report said that business is doing rather poorly. Why go there? Especially when you have assets like LCDs, memory and cell phones?"[17]

Kim's reply was clear:

> Last year [2003], our revenue was about $50 billion worldwide. Our profit after taxes was close to $7 billion. In terms of profit generation, we were second only to Microsoft. That's higher than IBM and higher than any other hi-tech company. Our latest earnings report had very strong results. I agree that consumer electronics is a tough business, but we're winning.[18]

To the objection that Samsung was winning because of its ability to produce to very large economies of scale, and that DVD players were a flash boom as the new product replaced video players, Kim replied:

> DVD is an example where it was on a very-fast-declining price curve. We believe TV will become another digital center for the home. DVD prices have come down a lot, but we're leading the charge in LCD TVs, which are premium-priced. Who would have guessed a few years ago that people would pay thousands of dollars for a TV? The fact is, we invested heavily prior to that in flat-panel technologies which gave us leadership in monitors and then took that technology to TVs.[19]

Samsung believed that the LCD TV was a classic example of the new era for digital products. Kim put it this way:

> The LCDs follow Moore's Law.[20] The winners of this game will be those who can drive the cost-reduction curve rather than follow. We have the world's largest scale in terms of capacity, the world's most advanced technology, and we're one of the top brands. So we're leading this charge. Now prices will fall. This is the game. The ones who are not able to lead the price curve are the ones who end up the losers. The same

thing happened with wireless phones. Why do you think some of the best companies, like Ericsson, Sony and Panasonic, have essentially gotten out of the wireless phone business?[21]

Kim's point was also that PC growth had definitely fallen to less than 5 percent growth annually. Not surprisingly, most IT players were desperately searching for growth areas. The likes of Dell and Gateway were getting into the consumer electronics space but Samsung was an old hand at the consumer electronics game.

Kim was also unfazed by the potential threat of Dell and Gateway in the total convergence field, where consumer electronics and computing came together and where Samsung lacked presence in the US PC business. "My basic point is that CE (consumer electronics) is a different business," he said. "You can't simply extrapolate that because Dell is a powerhouse in PCs, they will automatically be one in consumer electronics. They may or may not be."[22]

Kim's analysis, reflecting that of his colleagues at Samsung, was precisely that Samsung Electronics could now be the master of each technical change because of its lead in basic component supply, which most of its competitors lacked. As mentioned in earlier chapters, it was Samsung's total portfolio which allowed it to take the lead in the consumer electronics area. The decision of some of its competitors to retreat or combine in the area of mobile phones is analyzed in the next chapter. Above all, the real driver of the cost of a modern consumer product was in the core components. It was this belated recognition which led Sony to join Samsung in an unprecedented venture to make LCDs (which we will discuss further in Chapter 10). As long as this was true and Samsung remained at the forefront of component technology, Samsung Electronics could become both a true consumer electronics company and a components manufacturer. There remained an element of "riding on the tiger's back" in this equation. To maintain its brand image, Samsung needed to continue to produce new products and new technology. Likewise, there was the question of whether consumers really had loyalty in the area of consumer electronics.

As one analyst pointed out:

On the product innovation side of this—Kim and Samsung can sell a great story marketing-wise, but it has to be backed up—I'm just wondering about consumer loyalty in this day and age. With Samsung, for example, just how much did you have to keep producing new models almost for the sake of producing new models just to keep at that cutting edge? Just how important is that now?[23]

Kim's analysis was that there were two aspects to this from a marketing standpoint: one was brand-related; the other, product-related. Brand is beyond any particular product. A company armed with a strong brand stands a better chance of success when it introduces new products than a rival which doesn't own a strong brand. The strength of the brand grows with the complexity of the market—as new products come up and as the products grow in sophistication, the messages become more complex. When this happens, consumers tend to trust and rely more on the brand they know.

Kim knew that consumers are very smart and loyalty was not something to be taken for granted:

No matter how big you are, no matter how powerful you are, you can't say "well my customer is loyal and therefore I could take it easy" . . . And now especially with the internet one customer with one voice could be amplified throughout the world. And so in that sense the challenge is bigger, the challenge is more difficult.[24]

He was of the view that electronics companies had to continuously leverage their technological advantage and complement that with strong marketing to reach the minds and hearts of consumers if they were to have a chance of gaining acceptance.

There is also a complementary view that supports Kim's position, one that is more strategic in its approach to marketing. This is where the company works on owning "the last inch of glass" between the consumer and the internet. According to digital blogger Heath Row, the whole idea of owning the first inch through the glass—as in reaching from the consumer into the network—can be a powerful marketing approach. Using this approach, he said, Samsung didn't need to be in the content or distribution business. "If the company can continue to create the devices we use to access the Net—be they cell phones, displays, or microwaves—it will do just fine."[25] Identifying this "sweet spot" Samsung had entered its next phase of growth. The question was whether Samsung America would be allowed to continue to lead.

By 2004, Samsung Electronics was experiencing a sense of Samsung fatigue—commentators were finding the continued stress on technology in Samsung to be rather tedious. Samsung had gone into its "DigitAll" campaign in 2001 in the spirit of 1998, but was it wearing out its welcome? Those who were watching Samsung's moves closely felt that a new cell phone launch every two weeks was a bit over the top. And if fans of Samsung could be enamored by sleek new products, they could similarly be turned off by the confidence exuded by Samsung's marketing approach, particularly that of Peter Weedfald, senior vice president of strategic marketing and new media for Samsung Electronics America.

Branding builds market capitalization

By 2005, Samsung had moved up in brand value as measured by Interbrand, but still trailed Sony in revenue terms. The biggest leap was to be found in the value Samsung created as a company. It had not only overtaken Sony in brand value, but had created a higher market capitalization, despite having a lower turnover. The sincerest applause for Eric Kim's branding achievements had come from global investors. By the end of 2004 Samsung's market valuation had risen to US$62 billion. Not only was that higher than Sony's, but observers noted that "it dispelled memories of bleak IMF days when patriotic Koreans were melting down family heirlooms to help ease the currency crisis, and Samsung seemed on the verge of bankruptcy."[26] In 2004, Samsung achieved after-tax profits of US$10 billion—the highest among electronics and hardware companies and second globally only to Microsoft.

Shortly after leaving Samsung Electronics, Kim summed up the special combination of innovation and marketing which allowed Samsung to pull this off. He said that during his career, he had mainly been involved in innovation, in R&D, in technologies, as well as marketing. Marketing and perception are intertwined. It is commonly accepted that businesses need to innovate to succeed. Companies typically make big, long-term commitments in R&D technology innovation as well as in manufacturing process innovation to achieve competitive advantage in delivering better products. However, there is, he believed, a third, and truly critical, angle called "perception innovation." Perception innovation has two parts. The first is the ability to understand customers in the marketplace better than the competition. The second is the ability to place an offering in such as way that the intended customers embrace this offering, and then trust and accept it. These two parts of the process are critical to any innovation process, he said.

He said of the nature of understanding customers: ". . . your understanding is really much more than simply asking customers what is it they want but really be able to project out as to what the customers want, what might their needs be given their lifestyles, given their situation, given the choices that are available."[27]

For Samsung, it boiled down to identifying specific focus areas to achieve substantive differentiation. At that time, the focus area for Samsung was the mobile cellular phone and it concentrated its energy on developing highly innovative and unique designs. It then identified selected markets, such as the US, and worked closely with a target list of carrier partners to achieve market penetration. Kim's genius was his ability to help Samsung position itself for acceptance. "I always tell myself that perception is reality and reality drives perception, and so when one focuses on innovation you also have to really focus on understanding your target and being able to position your innovation in a way that gets acceptance."[28]

While Kim's analysis correctly diagnosed Samsung's unique opportunities in the period 2000–05, there were those who questioned how easily this could be replicated in the home market, especially since Samsung was continuously challenged in many areas of consumer electronics by LG Electronics.

Going the next step

While Samsung Electronics was busy developing its global positioning, at home in Korea it was experimenting with a different kind of branding. In white goods, LG had nearly always taken first place. Samsung Electronics wanted to see whether re-branding would work. It had earlier launched a luxury TV brand, PAVV, and then proceeded to launch a Hauzen brand for white goods, neither of which mentioned the Samsung brand name. LG responded with a white-goods brand, Whisen, which acknowledged its own umbrella brand.

On the face of it, it looked like Samsung's consumer marketing in Korea was going in one direction, while globally it was taking a different tack. The decision to build a separate brand for white goods in Korea was a further exploration of what brands could do for Samsung. The home campaign had no impact on the global campaign, and was merely a further experiment to test one particular market see Table 4.1. This illustrates once again that for Samsung the global giant, and Samsung the Korean company, there were two different agendas and challenges.

There is a final bite to this story. In November 2004, just as Kim was being hailed as Samsung's miracle worker, he returned to his adopted homeland to head up marketing for Intel. The world's leading chipmaker was feeling the squeeze from selling a commodity product in a mature market and from the competition of Samsung. Kim had shown how one commodity-maker could become a consumer-product company and Intel turned to him to restore the kind of profit margins that can only come from favored positioning deep within the consumer psyche. Kim's mission at Intel would be to convince consumers that the company that had been at the heart of the PC revolution could deliver the long-promised "convergence," the seamless melding of the PC with the myriad boxes that had been delivering entertainment: in essence, to do the same thing for Intel that he had done for Samsung. At Intel he immediately pronounced that the brand that Intel held was insufficient to drive it forward. Though the brand had driven the PC revolution

Table 4.1   Samsung domestic market share 2006-08

	2008	2007	2006	Source
Color television	51.4%	51.6%	48.3%	GfK
Refrigerator	44.4%	44.1%	44.1%	GfK
Washing machine	41.9%	45.0%	39.7%	GfK
Air conditioner	40.1%	42.5%	41.0%	GfK
Personal computer	39.8%	38.4%	33.1%	Gartner
Monitor	44.3%	42.7%	39.5%	IDC Korea
Printers	30.5%	27.4%	26.5%	IDC Korea
Cell phones	50.2%	50.0%	49.5%	Samsung Electronics

Source: SEC annual report

and was "in many ways synonymous with PCs," he said, "We think that is not sufficient anymore. We need to link our brand with a strong emotional bond based on delivering against user's needs."[29]

The decision to leave Samsung at the moment of success was an indication that the internal battles in running global marketing had caused considerable stress, and many of Kim's more traditional colleagues must have taken his departure as a vindication that a true Samsung Man would not have left the company.[30] There must also have been a feeling that Kim got much of the credit for something which was really a team effort, not only in Seoul but among his colleagues in Ridgefield Park, New Jersey, Samsung's American headquarters. Kim's departure was a triumph for the Korean voice within the company.

Samsung then turned to a second Korean American, Gregory Lee, a marketing executive with a pedigree that included Johnson & Johnson, Procter & Gamble, and Kellogg. *Forbes* wrote that Lee ". . . will be expected to tug Samsung's brand up those last and most difficult notches."[31]

Samsung also decided that it was not satisfied with FCB, its global advertising agency, and began a search for a replacement to manage its US$1 billion advertising portfolio. While some might have taken this renewal to be consistent with Yun's desire to foster a sense of continual crisis, the truth was there was bad blood between FCB and Samsung's in-house Korean agency, Cheil Communications, which resented both the amount of money FCB was making and the fact that FCB got all the credit for the successful campaigns. Publicly, Samsung let it be known that it believed that better creative work could be obtained elsewhere. In fact what was happening was the re-Koreanization of the marketing department. Greg Lee would inherit the search for a new agency.

Lee had taken a much lower profile than his vocal predecessor, something that was partly attributable to personal character and partly to the fact that hard-nosed engineers had recovered control of the company. From Yun's perspective, the company was already on its new trajectory and the momentum of the Kim initiatives was still pushing the company forward. Thus, it was not until mid-2005 that the new agency, JWT, in association with Berlin, together with Group M (for media), and Wunderman (for direct marketing) received the new contract.[32] While all of three were part of the WPP Group, the split did not fit happily with Samsung or with the three units themselves.

For several months following Kim's departure in September 2004, no PR was issued from Samsung Electronics' marketing department. Perhaps we should see this silence as a period of working out what the role of the chief marketing officer was to be in the company of the future. Finally, in June 2005, Greg Lee was allowed to make a significant statement about Samsung's future goals in marketing. This came as the new WPP campaign was ready to be rolled out. Samsung's company release gave a glimpse of the future:

> Building on its established image as one of the world's leading producers of lifestyle-enhancing products, Samsung Electronics is launching the first phase of a new worldwide advertising campaign, showcasing examples of the many ways that innovative Samsung products can brighten lives wherever people live, work, or play. The new campaign is called Imagine, painting human and amusing stories that highlight what happens when Samsung products come into people's lives. Each advertisement asks consumers to imagine how their worlds can be made more fun, exciting, and productive with the creative spark of Samsung design and technology.

> Highlighting a wide range of Samsung products including mobile phones, flat-panel televisions, portable media players and more, the Imagine campaign will be introduced initially in a series of television spots, later expanding to include print advertisements, outdoor space displays, Internet placements and other experiential marketing channels. The first television commercial was previewed in a limited number of spots in the US starting in late May, and the campaign formally began in June in 35 additional countries.[33]

But by October, the marriage with WPP was over, and Samsung had changed agencies again, to Leo Burnett. Comments from the advertising industry painted an unflattering picture of WPP rather than Samsung Electronics. *Adweek* reported on the breakup this way:

> It was almost doomed from the beginning . . . Sources said WPP did not meet its promise to Samsung of

stellar creative and account service from Berlin and JWT, respectively, with the shops at times tussling over responsibilities and their share of the estimated $20 million revenue. The problem was [WPP] promised what it couldn't deliver.[34]

Comments from within WPP acknowledged that the relationship with Samsung "was strained from the beginning because of compensation" and claimed that the agency was "underpaid and undervalued."[35]

In addition to classic client–management problems and squabbles over money, the Samsung creative assignment, although high profile, turned out to be smaller than the agency expected, particularly in the US, where Cheil Communications, a quasi-Samsung house agency, picked up print assignments. Cheil also functioned as Samsung's right hand, paying agencies and doling out assignments.[36] This unusual dynamic might have contributed to the split, even though Cheil had had a long-standing relation with Samsung which pre-dated that of WPP.

Given the hostility of the Korean voice to what they saw as overpaying FCB, the *prima donna* attitudes being displayed by its successors did not play well in Seoul.

The major beneficiary of this falling out was Leo Burnett, whose first task after clinching the deal was to create a campaign tied to the client's sponsorship of the Winter Olympics in Turin, Italy, in February 2006. The effort, which would include TV, print, and outdoor ads, would run in select markets around the world.

This history of chopping and changing and disputes between internal and external agencies did not do much to raise the status of marketing as a whole within Samsung Electronics. In fact, it served only to strengthen the Korean voice within the company that wanted to talk about products and was only enthusiastic about sports marketing, rather than brand building.

By the end of 2004, it seemed Samsung had not yet reached the stage where its brand could stand on its own. Interbrand's head of brand valuation, Jan Lindemann, was quoted as saying that Samsung is "not yet a brand that can live without the product." An article in *The Economist* in 2005 noted that Samsung had yet to reach the iconic status where consumers would turn to the brand before they looked at what product to buy.[37]

It was obvious Samsung still had branding problems it needed to resolve. Although WPP's creative efforts had helped promote the

Samsung brand, the campaign had not run long enough to bear fruit. In a rare interview, Greg Lee told *BusinessWeek* that although the Samsung brand stood for technology, design, and sensation—human sensation—consumers still thought of the company's product and brand as "cold."

Lee also spoke of the need for the company to raise consumers' awareness about the essence of the Samsung brand:

> Our next round [of communication strategy] is centered around our customers and the benefits we bring to their lives. In the past, our communication was all about the product. There wasn't a real story to it. We are really trying to tell a story about how it fits into consumer lives in our newer communications. When we do our studies, most people see our product and brand as cold—and we are trying to move away from that. We want to be warm. But the most important thing is being relevant. I don't know if BMW is warm, but it's certainly relevant and it's cool, and you want to have it. That is the approach we want to take.[38]

A final irony was that in May 2006, Samsung Electronics America announced it had restructured its product marketing teams for the television and audio/video departments, bringing in former Sony executive John Revie as marketing vice president of the visual display products group. The company also announced Jim Sanduski's promotion to senior marketing vice president of the newly combined digital video and audio products group. So Sony ideas about marketing were to be transferred to Samsung after all.[39]

Weedfald, senior vice president of strategic marketing and new media, was not to lead Samsung Electronics America to the sweet spot he had promised in 2004 either. In July 2006 he resigned to take up a much less stressful and turbulent position at Circuit City, the electronics retailer. Continual crisis has its casualties. The Eric Kim era was over.

A good question to ask is whether Samsung had moved forward or sideways in its branding between 2005 and 2008. What is apparent is its failure to rise continually in the Interbrand charts after 2005. Kim's insight was not merely in marketing but in relating marketing expenses to financial results. As John Quelch put it retrospectively:

Today's boards want chief marketing officers who can talk the language of productivity and return on investment and are willing to be held accountable. In recent years, manufacturing, procurement and logistics have all tightened their belts in the cause of improved productivity. As a result, marketing expenditures account for a larger percentage of many corporate cost structures than ever before. Today's boards don't need chief marketing officers who have creative flair but no financial discipline. They need ambidextrous marketers who offer both.[40]

From brand building to sports marketing

In 2006, Greg Lee had begun to unveil to the world Samsung's new storyboard "The Journey to be a Global Brand." It told a different story from that presented by Eric Kim. Lee highlighted Samsung's transformation from follower to global leader in the consumer-electronics business. During its transformative period, the company had focused heavily on design and technological innovations in its new products. The 2008 Olympic Games was hence a great lever for Samsung in its effort to establish itself as a premium global brand. Samsung used advertisements based on the Olympics themes in many markets around the world because, Lee said, the company considered the Olympics to be a global brand.

It was clear that Samsung Electronics had set its sights on sports marketing. This was pursued further in 2006 when Samsung made the move to be the kit sponsor of Manchester United Football Club, which had signed a popular Korean player from the 2002 World Cup. Samsung eventually sponsored another English football club. Under purely Korean management, Samsung's 2008 Beijing Olympics sponsorship meant that Samsung had truly moved away from the idea of demonstrating the value of marketing through brand building, and had moved into an untried form of brand marketing whereby considerable cost is attached to one-off marketing.

Sports marketing is a late entrant into the brand manager's portfolio. It was not until Coca-Cola spent over US$30 million supporting the 1984 Olympics that sports organizers and marketers saw this as a major way to project the brand across the world as a background to the event itself. It was not until the late 1990s that much serious research on sports marketing was undertaken.

The *Sports Marketing Quarterly* was only founded in 1993. The Koreans had developed a special affinity with sports marketing and it was no surprise then to find that a Korean, Kwon Gyeh-yun, was appointed vice president of Samsung Electronics in charge of world-wide sports marketing.

The genesis for Samsung's Olympic marketing journey began in 1988 when it became a local sponsor for the Seoul 1988 Olympic Games. Then it became what is known officially as the TOP (The Olympic Partners) sponsor in the wireless telecommu-nications-equipment category for every Olympic Games—Summer and Winter—from Nagano 1998 through to Beijing 2008. Samsung was prepared to pay the huge amount for corporate sponsorship because it believed in the vital importance of sports marketing on the company's bottom line.

Samsung Electronics believes that the Olympic sponsorship plan helped Samsung increase its brand awareness and enhance its market position considerably. Surveys held before and after the Sydney Olympic Games showed that the number of consumers who became aware that Samsung Electronics was one of the nine spon-sors of the Games almost tripled. However, unaided awareness of Samsung's Olympic sponsorship was 6 percent. This still placed Samsung second after Coca-Cola in the awareness ranking.[41]

With the sponsorship of the Beijing 2008 Olympic torch relay, Samsung was committed to sponsoring this one-of-a-kind relay that was the longest, most extensive and most inclusive in the Olympic history. At the signing ceremony, Kwon said:

> Samsung is thrilled to be the Presenting Partner of the Beijing Olympic Torch Relay. We are extremely proud of the diverse group that will have the honor of carrying the Olympic flame at this historic event. The torchbearers reflect what is best in all of us and also Samsung's corporate values of harmony and shared humanity. In particular, the Torch Relay in China will enhance the understanding and friendship between Samsung and the Chinese people.[42]

But herein lies a dilemma: the deeper Samsung gets into the sports marketing trail, the further it moves away from its earlier goals of building brand value. While the hard-nosed engineers appreciate the appeal of sports marketing, from a marketing standpoint there is a disconnect between building brand awareness through sports marketing, and the positioning of the brand itself. In the Olympics endeavor, as a sponsor, the name is divorced from the product, unless the product is a loved and household name like Coca-Cola. Samsung could easily be a soft drinks or a car company for all the communication which the Olympics brings to Samsung's products. Its Olympics sponsorship therefore took the company away from the goals envisioned by Eric Kim and Yun Jong-yong in 2002.

As exciting as Samsung's sports marketing programs were, this strategy has done little to kickstart Samsung's global brand value. As the presenting partner of the Olympic torch relay, Samsung had the rights to select 1,500 torchbearers, use torch relay logos, and hold torch relay-related marketing events. (It had been involved in similar relays in the Athens 2004 and the Torino 2006 Games.) It was to host a series of public events in cities along the route, with a variety of programs and promotional events surrounding its wireless telecommunication products. Concurrently, it planned to stage a formal launching of the Olympic marketing campaigns throughout China. In June 2007, it kicked off its Beijing Olympic Campaign with a public concert.

The company's view is that through its sponsorship of the Olympic torch relays, Samsung Electronics has made its presence known in all corners of the world. Torch relay sponsorship, together with the Wireless Olympics Works (WOW) and the Samsung OR@S, are viewed as the best marketing approaches that fully capture the Olympics theme. Samsung's Olympic sponsorship certainly increased its brand awareness and promoted sales in China. For the rest of the world, however, the main memory of the torch relays was of the pro-Tibetan protestors—which serves as a reminder that sponsorship has its perils as well as benefits.

Samsung PR would have us believe that Samsung Electronics has increased its brand value through sponsoring Olympic torch relays. If this is indeed the case, why then did the Interbrand valuation rise by only 4 percent during the Turin 2006 Winter Olympics? The truth is that the sports marketing technique has its greatest value in raising the morale of the Samsung Electronics workers rather than, by itself, raising the global brand value. By embarking on the sports marketing route, Samsung was seeing the onset of diminishing returns.

When Samsung was first involved in the Olympics, it was a little-known brand. By 2006 it had become well known and the

Olympics could not raise it much further. Moreover, brand awareness without any communication of the brand's position is not going
to get Samsung Electronics to the point where consumers look to
Samsung purely for its brand, regardless of the product.

Although Greg Lee's message was that Samsung's brand
essence was technology, design and sensation—human sensation—
the Olympics marketing efforts did little to convey this essence. It
was not too late to build the bridges between the two streams, but
to do so Samsung Electronics needed to recreate the kind of team it
had had in the years 2001 to 2005. As a case study of the Samsung
Electronics sponsorship of the Bangkok Asian Games nicely put it:

> Although Samsung's sponsorship in the 13th Asian
> Games has been successful through leveraging and inte-
> grated marketing as a branding platform, the win-win
> partnership will continue to accelerate more sponsor-
> ship opportunities for the ASIAD. However, there will
> be no winner in the relationship, if the positive emo-
> tional tie that customers have with sport is missing.[43]

The writers of this case study concluded that Samsung had
indeed done a good job in its extensive creating of ancillary events
around the arena—from a concert by the Suwon Philharmonic
Orchestra to sponsored runs and communication centers. The
study concluded:

> To summarize, the key to a successful sport spon-
> sorship depends on the creativity and [how the]
> marriage-style partnership is perceived and managed
> by the leaders in sport and corporations in the new
> millennium. Through their creative marketing pro-
> grams and a close cooperation with the Games orga-
> nizers, Samsung was able to fully utilize the benefits of
> the Games. In addition, the Games were able to ben-
> efit from Samsung's financial contribution to provide
> participants and spectators with a successful event.[44]

The authors also warned, however, that sports marketing
alone cannot work for the millions who do not make that positive
emotional tie between the sport and the product.

The future of the Samsung brand

When the mid-2007 crisis of confidence hit Samsung, marketing had no obvious answer. The Kim–Yun initiative had run its course and been under-supported since 2005. Company executives turned to new products with a sub-theme of innovative design rather than to marketers to provide new growth. Greg Lee hit the spot in 2005 with his analysis that Samsung needed to work on its brand strategy. Despite Samsung's aggressive sports marketing pursuits, Interbrand's 2007 survey showed that its brand ranking had slipped one place (to twenty-first); while its total brand value rose only 4 percent. Clearly, the campaign was a costly exercise in brand management. In 2008, Samsung Electronics remained in twenty-first position, while its new catch-up targets, Nokia, stood in sixth position, and Intel, marketed by Eric Kim, in eighth. Sony had moved back to twenty-fifth.[45] Interbrand's estimate of brand value is not everything, but it is the yardstick Samsung chose to be measured by.

Endnotes

1 John Quelch (ed.), HarvardBusiness.org Search—Case Studies Samsung Electronics Commercials, Video Supplement, July 1, 2004, at: harvard businessonline.hbsp.harvard.edu/relay.jhtml.

2 *BusinessWeek*, August 1, 2005, Special Report—The Best Global Brands/ Online Extra, "Samsung's Goal: Be Like BMW," http://www.businessweek. com/magazine/content/05_31/b3945107.htm; accessed June 4, 2007.

3 "Eric B. Kim, Marketing's Miracle Man," by George Tang, Goldsea: *Asian American Business*, at: http://business.goldsea.com/Kime/kime.html; undated 2004.

4 "Why a Marketing Strategy Should be Ambidextrous," by John A. Quelch, *The Wall Street Journal Online*, October 12, 2005.

5 Ibid.

6 http://www.principalvoices.com/beijing.html, May 16, 2005; accessed April 4, 2007.

7 "Samsung Electronics Corp.: Eric Kim interview," video by John A. Quelch. at harvardbusinessonline.hbsp.harvard.edu/relay.jhtml

8 http://www.principalvoices.com, op. cit.

9 Quelch, op. cit.

10 "Look Out, Sony," Heidi Brown, *Forbes*, June 11, 2001, at: http://www.forbes. com/forbes/2001/0611/096.html

11 Samsung Electronics Co. Ltd., press release, May 16, 2002.

12 "Companies, People, Ideas: Samsung's Next Act," by Heidi Brown and Justin Doebele, *Forbes*, July 26, 2004.

13   Brown, op. cit.
14   Brown and Doebele, op. cit.
15   "Samsung in Bloom," by B. J. Lee, Bill Richards, and Joan Raymond, *Newsweek*, July 15, 2002.
16   Ibid.
17   http://www.principalvoices.com, op. cit.
18   Ibid.
19   Ibid.
20   The best summary may be found in the *Wikipedia* article on "Moore's Law" which also discusses what Moore did and did not say, at: http://en.wikipedia. org/wiki/Moore's_law; accessed June 30, 2009. http://www.eia.org/news/ pressreleases/2005–04–27.217.phtml
21   Ibid.
22   FN CNET/news
23   "Sony Chief's Plans Disappoint," *Financial Times*, September 23, 2005, http:// blog.hjenglish.com/ambercindy/archive/2005/10/21/155260.html
24   http://www.principalvoices.com/beijing.html, op. cit.
25   "Digital Darwinism," *Heath Row*, May 26, 2004.
26   http://www.principalvoices.com, op. cit.
27   Ibid.
28   Ibid.
29   Tang, op. cit.
30   This stress comes out in Samsung Electronics Corp.: Eric Kim interview, op. cit.
31   "Follow-Through," by Heidi Brown, Stephane Fitch, and Brett Nelson, *Forbes*, October 10, 2004.
32   "Tense From the Start," by Andrew McMains and Kathleen Sampey, *Adweek*, October 31, 2005.
33   Samsung Electronics, press release, June 9, 2005.
34   "Samsung Fires WPP,"*Adweek*, October 2005.
35   Ibid.
36   McMains and Sampey, op. cit.
37   "Brand New; Consumer Electronics," *The Economist (US)*, January 15, 2005.
38   *Businessweek* 2005, op. cit.
39   "Samsung Changes Marketing Team, Promoting Sanduski, Hiring Revie," by Greg Tarr, *TWICE*, January 5, 2006, at: http://www.twice.com/article/260882- Samsung_Changes_Marketing_Team_Promoting_Sanduski_Hiring_Revie.php
40   Quelch, op. cit.
41   www.samsung.com
42   "Samsung Sponsors Beijing 2008 Olympic Torch Relay," *Samsung*, April 26, 2007, at: http://www.samsung.com/my/news/newsRead/do?news_seq=2&page=1.
43   "Analysis of Samsung Electronics' Bangkok Asian Games: Sponsorship," by Philip Cheng, *Cyber Journal of Sports Marketing*, at: http://fulltext.ausport.gov. au/fulltext/2000/cjsm/v4n2-3/chen42.htm
44   Ibid.
45   *Businessweek*, "The Top 100 Brands," at http://images.businessweek.com/ ss/08/09/0918_best_brands.htm; accessed May 20, 2009.

5

Making the "Samsung Man"[1]

One unsatisfactory point is that we have not invested enough for the future, particularly in terms of developing human capital.

Lee Kun-hee[2]

Putting human development first

Many multinationals claim to set great store by their human-resources development process. Jack Welch claims that Crotonville, GE's education campus, is at the core of GE's success; Louis Gerstner, too, claimed that IBM's emphasis on human-resource development is an important part of its turnaround.[3] Samsung's Youngin campus is no different. In a country in which a culture of human values is central to everything, no Korean *chaebol* places as much emphasis on human development as Samsung. Within the Samsung Group, Samsung Electronics stands out. But a company's training needs evolve with its life cycle. Lee Kun-hee's 1999 statement quoted above would have surprised his late father as well as many in Samsung's HR department who surely thought that Samsung had invested heavily enough.

A more recent statement of the aims of the HR department represents a marked evolution both from where Samsung was 10 years ago, and from the traditional concept of creating the quintessential "Samsung Man" which preceded it. Lee's statement and the extensive training-course structure illustrated the scale of resources which Samsung Electronics was willing to devote to its staff development. There can be no doubt that Samsung's HR statement of its mission (see below) is spot on for Samsung's needs at the end of the first decade of the twenty-first century. The question is whether other aspects of Korean culture work against this program so that Samsung men are not getting the full message.

The Samsung Electronics' HR department's mission for training and development in 2007 read:

> Samsung Electronics believes that educating employees is the core of the company's success. Thus, the company invests heavily on employee training and development. With such efforts, Samsung plans to secure bright and innovative human resources who will lead the digital era. In order to become [a] technology- and marketing-oriented company, Samsung is training people to become leaders who will act as agents of change. It also has systematic training programs to cultivate experts in marketing and technology.

> In order to successfully carry out the aforementioned mission, HR departments, training departments and the rest of the organization are working closely to plan and execute the best HR development. The programs are both developed in-house and outsourced, utilizing local and overseas universities. Samsung also has the Local Expert program, which enables employees to better understand the international business environment. Samsung's training programs are designed to link directly with the company's performance.

> They are learner-oriented, on-site-oriented and task-oriented. In addition, training departments are divided according to their functions and some of the business sites have their own training programs.[4]

Subsequent iterations of the philosophy were more compact, but echoed the same theme:

> The work culture at Samsung is based on the fundamental belief that employees are its most important asset. Respect and genuine concern for each employee in the

organization is the basic principle on which the organization functions. We believe that by giving mutual respect, recognition, trust, open communication, transparency and opportunities for growth, employees will perform to their fullest potential and will be sincere, dedicated and committed to their jobs.[5]

The framework of induction for new employees lasts between six and 12 months as set out in Figure 5.1. "Through this training, new employees gain understanding into Samsung's corporate culture and is able to set his or her vision."

The shift in emphasis which this type of training represents and its necessity is best understood by considering traditional training in Korean companies, and how Samsung Electronics needed to escape from traditional Korean values if it were to pass through adolescence into the prime stage of its life cycle. Intensive training may both accelerate and retard life-cycle changes depending on what is addressed at different stages of the cycle. In later chapters, we shall see why there is mounting evidence to show that Samsung's culture, despite this emphasis in the training, has not, in fact, escaped from aspects of traditional values. This then underlies the degree to which the training content is wrapped in the Confucian message in spite of the seemingly contemporary content of the current

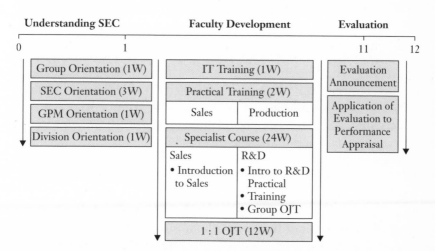

Figure 5.1   Course structure for new employees

programs and emphasizes why in 2009 the corporate stress on the need for creativity is—if anything—increased. To understand where these needs come from, we need to return to the starting point.

Korean corporate values

Samsung Electronics has its corporate HR roots in the traditional HR training which Koreans working at the major *chaebol* received in the 1960s, 1970s, and 1980s. Samsung Electronics' culture is entrenched in the core Samsung values of the past. But the company has been driven in a characteristically progressive direction. What remains unanswered is whether the company has pushed cultural change far enough.

How much of Samsung's HR practice is uniquely Samsung? And how much of it is based on Korea's culture? In 1998, Song Young-hack and Christopher B. Meek tried to assess the impact of national culture on management practices. They outlined several important aspects of Korean culture and then examined their impact on management values and beliefs. In their analysis, management values and beliefs can be traced back to two organizational symbols: the company's motto (*sahoon*) and the company song (*saga*).[6]

Their paper concluded that the core Korean cultural values of harmony, unity, and vertical social relations strongly influenced Korean firms, and that these management values and beliefs played a profound role in shaping human-resource practices in the major companies.[7]

Korea is not unique in this respect. Like most organizations, Korean companies go through their corporate life cycles. They also thrive on a set of organizational values which are heavily influenced by the culture of the place. In his observation of different Japanese and American organizations in their early stages, Adizes notes: "Every organization has a personality and a pattern of behavior or style; in western organizations, this tends to be mechanistic and in oriental organizations this tends to be organic."[8]

One of the four core balancing characteristics of an organization in Adizes' formulation is the "I" or integration role. He illustrates this with the example of a chair and a hand. If a leg of a chair breaks, it cannot be fixed without outside intervention. "Why doesn't one of the other legs move to the center of the chair and create a stool so the function of the chair can be continued?" he asks.[9]

In the case of a hand, if one of the fingers is broken, the hand does its best to function with four fingers because, unlike the chair, it is organic.

In the life-cycle model, this integrative function is supposed to help raise long-term efficiency. But what if it does the reverse, and each time there is an attempt at external change by the chairman or senior managing group, the culture of the company pulls the organization back into its old shape? This is the Korean and Japanese dilemma because the culture of the organization can become too dominant and work against change, be it in Samsung or in Sony.

Song and Meek's study accurately describes the 1960s to 1980s departure point for Samsung Electronics' advanced human-resource development. Consequently, while the new culture described in this chapter was fermenting lower in the company, this change was not happening higher up in the company, where older executives instinctively resisted the globalization of Samsung Electronics. This in turn led to high-level conflicts with the banner-bearers of the new culture, such as Eric Kim, whose role in creating the Samsung brand is discussed in greater detail later. In resolving this dilemma, vice chairman Yun Jong-yong's "continual crisis" mantra should have acted as a constraint on the traditional and Korean elements, and as a release to the new and the global. The evidence of the final two chapters of this book suggests that while this was achieved between 1999 and 2005, weeds began to strangle the flowers in 2006, leading chairman Lee to demand a new change to creative leadership in 2007, but it also led to Yun's departure in 2008.

The following discussion is important because it allows an assessment of the degree to which Samsung Electronics still shares Korean values. These values have become the catalyst for change and, at the same time, a bond preventing change.

As CEO, Yun did much to destroy what many see as traditional Korean values in his effort to push Samsung into a higher level of development from the late 1990s onwards. His revolution led Samsung Electronics to draw on the ideas of a new generation of Koreans, different in many ways from those who drove Korea in the 1960s, 1970s and 1980s. It was his change program that also helped the company incorporate a new generation of foreigners into a quintessential Korean company and put Samsung on track to become a multinational organization.

Naturally this was not to the liking of conservatives within the company. But Yun's drive had the support of chairman Lee. Drawing on the sense of continual crisis, Yun also managed to build round him a sufficient number of progressive managers to drive the company forward. As we shall see, the concept of a Samsung Man contained not only sufficient seeds for ongoing development but new seeds for organic growth. The chair could fix itself.

Capturing the culture of the company

The majority of Korean firms have a *sahoon* or motto, itself modeled on the family motto or *kahoon* which most *yangban* (traditional Korean upper-class) families had.[10] The *kahoon* is a set of simple guidelines for family members and their descendants with respect to proper mental attitudes, correct governance of homes, and distinguishing good from bad to ensure appropriate conduct. The *kahoon* has many different forms. It may be composed of one letter, one word, one or several phrases, or, in extreme cases, a whole book. Although the practice was first started in the early Three Kingdoms period (0–668 AD), it became popular among the *yangban* class in the Chosun period (1392–1910).[11]

From the 1930s to 1997, traditional thinking in Korea shaped the definition of the company as an extended family, with the chairman as the father figure, and all employees as members of his family. Korean companies then developed *sahoon* (company mottos) and *sap-oong* (literally, "company traditions") to match. Company mottos may not always accurately reflect company culture in actual daily practices. This is because a *sahoon* can only indicate the ideal beliefs desired by the founder of the company.[12]

Just as the patriarch provided a *kahoon* to teach his family members and descendants, so the company founder makes a *sahoon* to guide the company and those who work in it. In Western terms, it can be regarded as the company mission statement in compressed Korean format, or management ideology. The *sahoon* have been compared to the core values, beliefs, or commitments of American companies such as Watson's tenets for IBM and Marriott's "15 guideposts."[13] However, they are better compared with contemporary mission statements such as that of Hewlett Packard or other successful companies.

The company *sahoon* generally reflects the values of the remarkable generation of founders of the Korean *chaebol*, most of whom born in the first two decades of the twentieth century. Of these, of course, Lee Byung-chul was one of the most remarkable. In its full extent in the 1980s, Samsung's *sahoon* was unique in setting out those values as shown below. It should be noted that as long as the founder was alive, there was no special culture for Samsung Electronics beyond that of the Samsung Group itself.

Samsung's 1980 sahoon

"The company's philosophy promotes the idea that the individual will grow to be a Samsung man by:

1. Acquiring the capability and the courage for empowerment.
2. Growing an internationally oriented mind.
3. Making use of team spirit and solidarity.
4. Reminding the employee of the sovereignty of his existence as the leader, making history for his time.
5. Thinking in terms of effectiveness, not to be inhibited by past practices and attitudes.
6. Cultivating the pioneering attitude."[14]

If the *sahoon* functions as a general guideline or guiding spirit for the company and its people, Lee Byung-chul had given Samsung a unique approach. In all companies the *sahoon* becomes an important instrument in the process of building character and formulating the correct attitude during the socialization of new employees in training programs, and throughout their career within the organization. The extent to which this philosophy imbued all employees at the time struck Ira Magaziner with great force when he talked to two young Samsung Electronics workers in the early 1980s:

> The subject the two women are most enthusiastic about is product quality. Miss Hwang is convinced no workers in the world pay as close attention to products as those at Samsung. She herself checks her own work a final time even after an inspector double-checks it. Her specific function is to attach serial numbers and name-brand labels to microwave ovens . . . They admit it's the same simple function, hour after hour, but neither thinks the days are dull. They see their jobs as a challenge to

personal discipline, even integrity. Doing their work perfectly each time is a way of teaching themselves excellence. They feel their work should reflect their vision of themselves as people of quality. "I put my spirit, put my soul into this product," explains Miss Hwang.[15]

This devotion to the product helped build Samsung Electronics (and many other Korean companies) to the level of preferred sub-contractor. But the difference was that each Samsung worker was trained to recognize that he or she was building a new Korea at the same time. A Samsung Group corporate advertisement of the same period reflects this. In the advertisement, a Korean school child is looking at a blackboard on which the names and country origin of the inventors of the steam engine, light bulb, telephone, TV and other items are written. "Why has nothing been invented in Korea?" the child asks. "We at Samsung are working to change that," the advertisement declares.[16]

The *sahoon* also tells the public which values and beliefs the company adheres to by hanging it on the walls of every office, plant, conference room, and training center with beautifully crafted calligraphy. It also appears on company brochures, operating manuals, training texts, diaries, and magazines. Thus, the *sahoon* is an official statement which expresses the organization's most important values and beliefs or, at least, the values and beliefs it would like to be known for throughout the nation.[17] Table 5.1 shows some of the core elements of the *sahoon* leading Korean companies in the 1990s.

Company training for new college graduates in all Korean firms focused on instilling management values and beliefs to transform them into a "man" (for example, a "Samsung Man" or a "Hyundai Man"). This is in contrast to American companies, which tend to focus on practical and technical aspects of the job (such as orientation on employee benefits, company policies and rules, disciplinary regulations, and job duties).

The values most strongly and frequently stressed in company mottos are harmony and unity, sincerity and diligence, and creativity and development.[18] According to Song and Meek: "It is important to point out that of the values most frequently stressed 'sincerity' (*songshil*) is also integrally related to the most emphasized value 'harmony and unity.' Both the *shin* and *song* of the word *songshil* which corresponds to sincerity are from Chinese characters."[19] In order

Table 5.1   Comparison of core elements of *chaebol sahoon* in the mid-1990s

Samsung	Respect for individual, pursuit of technology, and empowerment
Hyundai	Diligence, thriftiness, trust, and affection
LG	Creativity, respect for individual, and harmony
Daewoo	Creativity, challenge, and sacrifice
SK	Humanism, rationalism, realism, vitality, and "supex"* pursuit
Ssangyong	Trust, credibility, innovativeness, and unity
Hanjin	Service, credibility, and progressiveness
Hanwha	Truthfulness, self-discretion, and best effort
Lotte	Honesty, integrity, service, and passion
Daelim	Creativity, cooperation, and responsibility

Source: Chung, Lee, and Jung, 1997; Ungson, Steers, and Park, 1997.

*"Supex" is the SK philosophy of using more of the brain than the normal 5 percent which is said to be actually used at any one time.

to maintain good human relationships and build satisfactory social interactions, obtaining "trust" (*shin*) is essential. *Song* is the character meaning "to speak." The character "sincerity" or "integrity" means "to realize that which is spoken" or "being true to one's nature."[20] The *sahoon* is complemented by the company song or *saga*, which is for lower employees.[21]

It is important to understand that until the twenty-first century, nearly all male recruitment within the Samsung Group was graduate recruitment. With compulsory military service in Korea, this meant having graduates as old as 28. In principle, these young men who were recruited by the Samsung Group were starting their first job and required training to become Samsung Men. Samsung Electronics was no different. The women employed by the Samsung Group followed a different recruitment track. Their roles were traditionally limited to temporary employment, as women tend to leave upon marriage.[22]

At Samsung today, the employee induction process takes from six to 12 months. In the 1980s and 1990s, new recruits could expect a two-year induction process. During this period of instruction, between one-quarter and one-third of the annual intake may leave, realizing that Samsung was not their life mission. Once committed to Samsung, the engagement was theoretically for life. However, Samsung recognized that around the age of 40–45 many executives would not rise to higher positions, either because of a lack of ability, or they had too much ability for the Samsung internal environment. As in a Japanese company, many of those who left would join companies, or even start companies, which had a close relationship with Samsung, often as suppliers and distributors. This was seen as beneficial to Samsung as it helped spread Samsung culture further among its partners.

In the case of the Samsung Group, great emphasis was placed on instilling its management values and beliefs to prepare the individual for a long-term career with its firms. In this, it was doing no more than other *chaebol*. The Ssangyong Group, a leading *chaebol* which collapsed in the IMF crisis, also put the highest emphasis on inculcating its management values and beliefs and the sense of belonging to the organization.[23] Similarly, SK Group, one of the top-four *chaebol* survivors, also placed great emphasis on teaching its management values and beliefs, believing that success or failure is determined by how the firm manages its human resources. Thus, it developed the 79-page "SK Management System" which it published as a company document for all employees. In the 1990s SK went further, developing both a relationship with the Chicago Business School and founding its own business school at the Korea Advanced Institute of Science and Technology (KAIST). SK instilled its management values and beliefs, called "SK-Manship," into new employees. Samsung already had relationships with the oldest university in Korea, Sungkyonwhan, the original Confucian Academy created in Kaesong more than a thousand years ago.

Ideally, in traditional Korean thinking, employees are influenced by a deeper understanding of the *sahoon* to the point where, eventually, their attitudes, values, and general personality characteristics fit the firm so well that they are actually seen as a "Samsung Man." Thus, the *sahoon* and the training program function to increase the identification of the new employees with their organizations.[24]

The inculcation of the Samsung culture described above would naturally serve to discourage dissent within the organization and would work against any change of direction which did not integrate these corporate values. It can be seen that what is a binding force in one age can become a powerful brake on change in the next.

From Confucianism to technological leadership

From a sociological point of view, the *sahoon* represents the Confucian concept of training. If a man has a perfect character and is grounded in the basic philosophy of behavior he will make perfect decisions, whether as a management executive, a government official or a family head. But this did not prepare executives for most of the dimensions of a technology company, and for dealing with those who were neither Koreans nor perfect *kunja* (gentlemen trained in the Confucian classics). The Samsung system described above might still work well in some other large Samsung subsidiaries such as Samsung Life or Samsung Corporation but not so well in Samsung Electronics.

The traditional system bred highly loyal Samsung men committed to the company's way of doing things, which would mark them apart from other company men. But Yun needed Samsung Electronics to be in overdrive mode to overtake Sony. Here he was helped by the founder's philosophy. Samsung is the only *chaebol* that has a technology portion in its *sahoon*.

The current Samsung management philosophy statement is: "We will devote our human resources and technology to create superior products and services, thereby contributing to a better global society." Samsung is also committed to "excellence in people, digital technologies which enhance standards of living, and to the mutual prosperity of people all over the world."

Further, Samsung has also raised the bar for the future. Lee and Yun's vision was to become a world-leading company or *choillyu* (literally, "ahead of the best"). In the early 2000s, Samsung also had the ambition to be the most admired company in the world by 2010. If this was to be achieved, Samsung—and particularly Samsung Electronics—needed to recruit the best people.

In 1999, as Yun was preparing Samsung Electronics for its prime performance, chairman Lee was reflecting on the need to recruit special people for this job. He told *Asiaweek* in 1999:

> I am looking for people with unusual talents. Samsung has bred many managers with [typical kinds of skills]. But I am now more interested in the unusual talents of a special few. My observation is that out of 1,000 people there might be one person who is very good

intellectually and has another talent like the ability to sing or has an unusual hobby or special ability. I would like to have these special few people in the Samsung group. To make sure I get them, I am looking at students who are in their third year of high school. If a student only studies and becomes number one in the class, he is no good. But if the same guy is a good rock singer and at the same time is good at class, for example, then he is the candidate for us.[25]

From this came a new concept—Samsung Electronics should open its door to non-Koreans and that it should no longer hire only recent graduates, but should also consider older and experienced people. By the time Yun and Lee, and others, had finished the discussion, the ruling went out that one-third of new hires in the twenty-first century should be people who were more experienced than fresh graduates. The company also adopted an active policy of encouraging foreigners to work for Samsung Electronics. This was made easier by the presence of Samsung Electronics factories and sales and marketing organizations around the world from which talent could be drawn.

In Samsung's definition, a world-leading company is one that creates industry-leading business and products, maintains top competitiveness by continuous innovation, provides new value to the customer, and enjoys strong loyalty and trust from its customers. But the phrase "world-leading" meant both a leading world company, and a company which would lead the world towards a better future. Thus, what the Samsung Group had set out to do, not unsuccessfully, for Korea, Samsung Electronics would now do for the world.

To accelerate efforts towards becoming the world leader, at the company's 2004 strategic meeting Yun Jong-yong outlined the following factors and qualities (which became widely known as "7 DNA") that would help Samsung achieve its goal:

1. Dream, vision and goal
2. Insight and good sense
3. Trust and credibility
4. Creativity and challenge
5. Technology and information
6. Speed and velocity
7. Change and innovation.[26]

These qualities, supported by the company's corporate values ("Samsung's 8 Action Values"), were to serve as uniting principles to link all global employees, each with his personal values. Samsung Electronics had now moved from a Confucian-based *sahoon* culture of the pre-1997 crisis to a company with a global culture. Its global culture, however, has a Confucian flavor which has strong respect for values. Neither were the founder's precepts forgotten. The values were intended to serve as a magnet, connecting each employee to a common platform of beliefs, while at the same time respecting local diversity. This was to be the basis which would connect Samsung employees regardless of nationality or location. This was also to be the tool to manage global diversity. These values are so striking that they deserve to be repeated in full. However, it will be noted that many of the words and phrases in bold in the company documents of the mid-2000s, represent characteristics of the 1980s *sahoon*.

> Firstly, Samsung encourages **creativity** in people and attracts and rewards creative-thinking individuals who strive to develop market-leading products and introduce new ideas. To encourage creativity, Samsung fosters an open environment that supports the diversity of its people, where new and different ideas may be considered and accepted.
>
> • Creating new plans and ideas when situations change
> • Entertaining wide-ranging possibilities to come up with new solutions and approaches
> • Using a variety of communication materials and methods to gain support for new ideas
> • Being good in brainstorming processes
> • Thinking outside given parameters to see if there's a better way.
>
> Secondly, Samsung actively seeks out **challenges** in order to create market-leading products and solutions. The company seeks challenges daily, whether it be finding processes to improve, discovering winning technologies, or learning new skills outside their comfort zone. Individuals who embrace risks are encouraged

to have the confidence to tackle the greatest challenges. Samsung claims to reward those who embody this spirit and to not penalize them for making a mistake in the name of progress. On the individual level, the challenge is recognized as:

- Seizing opportunities as they arise and acts to capitalize on those opportunities
- The will to challenge the status quo, play offense
- Self-confidence and enthusiasm to take risks
- Winning-orientation.

Thirdly, Samsung **strategically selects** the best port-folio of products to develop, processes to implement, and skills to develop. This is based upon rigorous and regular analysis of our markets, our customers and our capabilities. Once selected, they focus and concentrate on creating best-of-breed products, services or systems that will maximize their investment. To choose the best strategies, Samsung strives to create an inclusive environment that draws upon their collective global knowledge and customer insight. Strategic focus requires that Samsung creates flexible and creative solutions in its quest to develop the best end result for its customers, employees, and ultimately its sharehold-ers. In practice, strategic focus requires each Samsung Electronics employee to:

- Understand [the] total business environment
- Make plans according to [the] company's vision and strategy
- Communicate and align [the] shared vision into achievable strategic objectives
- Consider implications, dynamics and demands of organization.

The next corporate value in Samsung is **speed**. Speed should never come at the cost of quality. Speed in operations and decision-making enables [the] company to achieve its common objectives. Samsung applies the speed principle to all processes in manufacturing, marketing, sales and communications in order to improve SCM [supply-chain management], time-to-market, inventory management, cash-flow management, marketing knowledge, sales results, interpersonal interactions and more. As a result, the company looks for quick-minded individuals who can execute quickly and meet deadlines superbly—in other words, the individuals who:

- Make competent and effective decisions in a timely manner
- Respond rapidly in situations requiring quick turnaround
- Deliver results through quick action
- Spend time on what is important by quickly zeroing in on the critical and putting the trivial aside
- Do not "over think" problems or tasks.

Furthermore, **simplicity** is required to make the management processes faster and more efficient. Simpler processes also allow the company to be more customer-focused. Samsung applies simplicity to its management structure and communication channels to enable faster, seamless and more transparent interaction between employees and partners around the world. To benefit from simplicity, obstacles such as hierarchical structures and cultural confusion must be addressed by encouraging greater dialogue and exchange between all employees, of all nationalities, at all levels. On the employee level, simplicity is reflected in:

- Conveying information in an organized and easy-to-understand manner
- Identifying complex situations and proposing solutions to reduce miscommunication and process disconnects
- Being approachable and encouraging direct and open dialogue
- Seeking simplicity in accomplishing daily tasks
- Creating policy, procedures and practices that are streamlined and easy to understand.

Samsung also values **self-control** and **empowerment** which is facilitating results through action and creative thinking. Samsung Electronics' divisions and employees are expected to be free to come up with new ideas and to think creatively, to develop better solutions for the customers. With empowerment comes the responsibility to make decisions and the ability to take action and capitalize on immediate opportunities. On the individual level, the empowerment translates into:

- Feeling personally accountable
- Making decisions within boundaries effectively
- Putting in whatever effort and hours are needed to get the job done right
- Taking the initiative: when something needs to be done, to do it without waiting to be told.

Customer focus drives Samsung's business. The company aims to think of the market and act for the customer with every decision, in every activity. Embracing this value ensures that employees incorporate customer feedback into their processes, plans and activities. Each Samsung Electronics employee must consider how his/her daily work affects both the internal and external customers, whether while building a new product, developing a strategic business partnership, or supporting fellow employees in their endeavors. In practice, a customer-focused employee:

- Is dedicated to meeting and surpassing expectations and requirements of internal and external customers
- Ensures that commitments to customers are met
- Anticipates and responds to customers' current and future needs
- Gets first-hand customer information and uses it for improvement.

Samsung must always operate with a sense of **crisis awareness**, the knowledge that the company is in global competition with the best. To grow stronger, the company must regularly analyze its strengths and weaknesses, as well as potential opportunities and threats. Thinking with a crisis-awareness mentality requires one to be flexible, open to change, and nimble. One must be prepared for changes in the market and global environment. With crisis awareness, one can always look for ways to reduce waste or process time, thereby reducing costs and freeing up resources to work on value-added activities. Crisis awareness is important to financial management; however, short-term concerns should never paralyze long-term activities. Weigh investment decisions against overall rewards, and follow up projects with detailed results to quantify the pay-off. In the end, Samsung expects that each employee:

- Anticipates problems, roadblocks and major obstructions, and reacts accordingly
- Is willing to act regardless of limited information and uncertainty
- Has a sense of urgency
- Involves others in decision-making to minimize potential crisis situations
- Has the ability to respond to rapid or unexpected change.

Finally, all Samsung employees must pursue **continuous innovation** and improvement in their daily work—looking ahead to improve current systems and processes in order to enhance communication, collaboration and efficiency. Samsung encourages its talented employees to bring in fresh ideas which will inspire management and all leaders to innovate themselves. As a result, Samsung looks for individuals who:

- Look for and make continuous improvements in key processes, techniques and procedures
- Motivate others to find new ways of using and looking at technology and systems
- Actively contribute to the development of other team members.[27]

This 2004 program has been repeated here in full because it gives a sense of the quality of thinking about culture at the center of Samsung Electronics. It mixes a sense of traditional Korean values, with the culture of speed which evolved from the 1960s. *"Balli balli"* is one of the first phrases a foreigner learns in Korean. It means "quickly, quickly" (or "hurry up") and is one of the cornerstones of success in that Korea can out-produce competitors through speed to market, even where price competitiveness may be fading.

In some ways, the list of values given above reads like a mix between the new economics jargon of the late 1990s and some of the enthusiasm of Jack Welch. But when it is put into action by a company of the size and velocity of Samsung Electronics—even where the message is not perfectly understood globally—it should make a difference.[28] However, by 2007, these bold slogans had been partially sidetracked by middle management in Samsung just as similar programs were usually sidetracked by middle and senior management in foreign-owned companies in Korea. In a young company, such values would energize the workforce; but in a middle-aged company whose managers had been brought up and indoctrinated with the old Samsung culture and were steeped in old Korean hierarchical principles, the arteries that should be feeding fresh new blood to the brain were clogged.

The way to get new blood was to recruit from outside the company. Samsung Electronics' HR department was showcasing the diversity of its employees by 2005.

The six profiles outlined in Table 5.2 have been selected to give a sense of the international flavor of the emerging culture and of the core attractions of working at Samsung Electronics in 2005. They portray the excitement of working in Samsung Electronics and serve to underline the strength of the existing culture and the potential future strength of the company as these employees and others like them begin to deliver results in product development.

The training of new employees has now shifted to much more empirical subjects than the old *sahoon* guidelines. Through this training, new employees gain an understanding of Samsung's corporate culture and are able to set their own vision. The training also provides the basic knowledge and skills needed to launch their careers at Samsung.

Through on-site practical training, new employees understand the total process and have the opportunity to think about how their individual performances contribute to the company. This is followed by on-the-job training (OJT) which enables new employees to develop functional skills. OJT programs are managed by each site's training department.[29]

Table 5.2   Six Samsung employee profiles

Name: Kei Takeuchi Nationality: Japanese Area: Digital Solution Network Position: Assistant Manager [FAE in DRAM]	
1. What do you do at Samsung?	I joined Samsung about two years ago. And I've been working in the Device Solution Business as an assistant manager in charge of FAE in DRAM products. My main responsibilities include: For customers: a. Introducing our DRAM roadmap b. Technical support in DRAM products c. Trace DRAM's qualification status in their system. For sales: a. Education in DRAM skills
2. What are some of the benefits of working for a company that is growing so fast?	In Samsung I can learn "The Business with Speed." It's very important for me to introduce products in advance of competitors. It's useless if excellent products are shown to customers after their engineering is finalized. Another benefit is to meet many engineers who start a new project using DRAM. Furthermore, it is my joy to participate in the challenge to compete to be the No. 1 in semiconductors.

(Continued)

Table 5.2   Six Samsung employee profiles *(Continued)*

Name: James Cassidy
Nationality: American
Area: Device Solution Network
Position: Senior Manager [HR of System LSI]

1. What are some of the benefits of working for a company that is growing so fast?	A static environment can promote complacency and limit opportunities and perspective in forwarding one's career. In many ways Samsung's growth mirrors the continuing growth in Asian markets—especially China's. It is exciting to participate in a company that is expanding so quickly and is leading in so many product areas.
2. Are there any traits or characteristics that seem to be shared by Samsung employees?	Pride, loyalty, and sense of purpose I feel are the values most shared by Samsung employees. It is important for foreign employees to understand the significance that Samsung management and employees place on these traits in order to fully contribute to achieving our work objectives.
3. What is your work environment like?	The change at Samsung during the last 8–9 years has been remarkable. The work environment here is much more relaxed and even senior management can easily be approached. The present division where I work, System LSI, is probably one of the most progressive divisions at Samsung in this regard.

Name: Mohammed Boussarhane
Nationality: Moroccan
Area: Digital Appliance Network
Position: Assistant Manager
[Overseas Management & Strategic Marketing Team]

1. What gives you most satisfaction about what you are doing?	In Samsung, I am enjoying working with professionals in an environment that has been set up to achieve all the intended goals and targets. And as part of the team, I am part of the success.

2. In your opinion, what is the future for Samsung?	With the growth and speed of Samsung Electronics, I believe that Samsung, along with its strong brands, outstanding reputation, and its superior products and services, will be the market leader in the electronics business.
3. How would you describe the work environment at Samsung?	The corporate culture at Samsung helps its employees to feel personally rewarded, and enables them to perform to their best and realize their unlimited potential. You can also enjoy the corporate life style while having a personal one too. The people that I work with are very helpful and friendly. I enjoy working in an environment where people look out for one another.

Name: Wesley Park
Nationality: Korean American
Area: Digital Solution Center
Position: Manager [Business Planning]

1. What is the most interesting project you have been involved with at Samsung?	I am currently working on a project that involves monitoring people's health anywhere, anytime. Not only does this work involve learning about cutting-edge technology, but my work will also play an important role in relieving people's health concerns. Our team also wants our future business to play an important role in improving people's quality of life while reducing some of their healthcare costs. This work excites me the most.
2. Is life at Samsung "all work and no play"?	Everyone at Samsung works extremely hard. They are all very dedicated to the work at hand and do whatever it takes to finish their work. My co-workers spend a lot of time discussing each other's ideas to help each other develop them further. At the same time, when work ends, we are all

(Continued)

Table 5.2   Six Samsung employee profiles *(Continued)*

	good friends and we spend time looking for new restaurants and bars, watching movies, and exercising.
3. Why did you choose to work at Samsung?	Samsung is one of the fastest-growing companies in the world, and the company focuses very much on innovation. Samsung takes very calculated risks and once the company makes a decision to go into a new business, it is fully committed. While I was working as a management consultant I found Samsung employees asking the right questions and challenging me like no other company employees had.

Name: Mi Yoo
Nationality: Korean
Area: Digital Media Network
Position: Assistant Manager [Digital Video System]

1. Do you feel that you can develop your career within Samsung?	Absolutely. It is a great challenge to keep up with this fast-paced work environment here at the Digital Video System Division; but then again, it gives me a great opportunity to see and interact with so many diverse job functions and people, from R&D, production operation, subsidiaries and channel partners from all over the world!
2. Are there any traits or characteristics that seem to be shared by Samsung employees?	Yes, I describe them as "3Ps." First, "Proactive" where we all try to be one step ahead of others. Second "P" stands for "Professional" where everyone thinks and acts with expertise and professionalism. Last but not least, people at Samsung are also "Progressive." We welcome change, challenge, and we try our best to be pioneers in the area and field we are engaged in.

3. Why did you choose to work at Samsung?	I was attracted by its global network and various products that make people's lives so convenient and entertaining. Especially to be involved in the marketing of Digital Products was my goal when I decided to shift from the service industry to an IT industry.

Name: Park Chan-kyung
Nationality: Korean
Area: Domestic Sales and Marketing
Position: Manager [Marketing Communication]

1. Is life at Samsung "all work and no play"?	My friends and family often ask me how I manage a tough life at Samsung—if it is only work and no play. This is a common understanding about the Samsung Man's life among people outside the company. Yes, people work very hard and plan the day down to the minutes. But on the other hand, I found my colleagues putting much value on their social life and trying hard to maintain the balance between the two. Furthermore, the company provides quite a few programs to help this: Samsung's 8 to 5 work system, instead of 9 to 6 of most other companies in Korea, offers me relatively longer after-work hours so I can spend enough time with my six-month-old daughter.
2. Do you feel that you can develop your career within Samsung?	A lot of talented people continue to join Samsung, as the company puts its first priority on human resources. I believe this is what drives Samsung to success, and that I can develop my career among this competition. My career has spanned three business segments and many operating units. This has provided valuable diversity in my work experiences and a broad perspective that continues to enrich my competencies.

| 3. Do you receive training throughout your career at Samsung? | There seem countless opportunities to receive training throughout your career with Samsung. The company has diverse sponsoring programs which provide employees with re-education and self-development opportunities. |

How deeply embedded are the Samsung values?

Some of the key qualities of Samsung employees around the globe have been described above. These qualities come from the understanding of the "9 Shared Values"—creativity, challenge, strategic focus (selection and concentration), speed, simplicity, self-control (empowerment), customer focus, crisis awareness and continuous innovation. All these qualities, or competencies, constitute the ideal Samsung employee—that is the "Samsung Man-to-be"—and the unique culture, behavior and traits nurtured within the company.

But how successfully have these values been transmitted? The future success of Samsung Electronics partly depends on this. The following section draws on the research of one of my MBA students. The purpose of his research was to verify the portrait of the "Samsung Man" and to discuss different aspects of the "Samsung Man" in the context of Samsung Electronics' shared values between 2004 and 2005.

In a survey conducted between 2004 and 2005 on the reality of this new Samsung Man one researcher looked for:

- Associations, definitions and general understanding of the Samsung Man
- Tools and means for shaping the Samsung Man
- Strengths and weaknesses of the Samsung Man
- The impact of the Samsung Man's characteristics on organizational performance and Samsung's future.

According to this research, 80 percent of the respondents working for Samsung said they often hear about the "Samsung Man" and have a sense of familiarity with this term. However, 14 percent said they have a low understanding of what the term means although they have heard it. When asked what came to mind when they thought about the Samsung Man, most of the respondents pointed out a

Korean male with neat and smart looks, sharp appearance, wearing a well-ironed black or blue suit (not luxurious, simple, and humble); a pale shirt and a non-descript tie, belt, and black leather shoes. The other attributes were short hair, clean and trimmed fingernails, and glasses with no other accessories except maybe a Samsung pin.

This is very different from the creative and continuously innovating Samsung Man that the HR department was promoting. The stereotype described by the respondents—all Samsung employees—was of the traditional worker of the 1980s–90s, not yet the new Samsung Man. The Samsung Man of the survey would be very well-educated, and does not have much time for leisure and family activities as work eats up most of his time. His wife often does not work, taking care of several kids while living in Bundang, a fashionable new town between Seoul and the Samsung base of Suwon. Occasional "lucky Sundays" are spent with kids at Caribbean Bay, Everland, and other Samsung-owned recreational facilities which offer good deals to Samsung employees. Perhaps, thanks to that work-centric lifestyle, many Samsung men are enjoying *soju* (Korea's national white liquor) and smoking their life away. From time to time they could afford some time for trendy sports such as golf, skiing or tennis, though it is often part of their business activity and not their private lives. Samsung men are considered elite representatives and are respected by society because of Samsung's significant contribution to Korea's economic growth.

The Samsung Man is often described as having good manners, always serious about everything but enthusiastic, polite, gentle, friendly, sincere, and warm-hearted. Many, however, see this aspect of the Samsung Man as superficial. They also see the Samsung Man as a rather selfish, arrogant, rational, emotionless, cold-blooded, frustrated, and conservative. Furthermore, the Samsung Man is often perceived as quick and hot-tempered, but at the same time he is said to be very careful, thoughtful, and thorough. He is self-confident, success-oriented, and takes pride in his company.

At his workplace, the Samsung Man is associated with perfectionism, loyalty, goal- and detail-orientation, punctuality, and diligence. Observing manners and etiquette, which are still based on seniority, the Samsung Man does his best in his work, diligently committing all his connections and resources. His management style is rather military—top-down, orders given, no push-back. His corporate culture is a bit dry. Everybody is so busy and engrossed in his work that there is very little time for interaction. Work is the number-one priority in times of economic uncertainties in Korea and was still the case in 2004. Super-motivation comes when there are no other real choices for employment.[30]

In general, the qualities most attributed to the Samsung Man are loyalty (82 percent), execution with determination (61 percent) and responsibility (57 percent). Less frequently, respondents cited effectiveness, aggressiveness, and integrity (39–43 percent). Despite creativity being one of the nine core corporate values of Samsung Electronics, only 12 percent identified it as a quality related to the Samsung Man. In the view of Samsung Electronics employees, the spirit of the Samsung Man is best represented by Samsung Electronics (81 percent) or by Samsung Corporation (25 percent) and the Chairman's Office. Interestingly, 29 percent of respondents did not associate themselves with the Samsung Man. But 34 percent agreed that they have changed their attitude towards being more like the Samsung Man.

Respondents highlighted colleagues and seniors as the key factors shaping the Samsung Man. Corporate training appeared not to have much influence, and came last among the influences. The general Korean culture and social expectations were considered more important factors influencing the behavior of the Samsung Man. One might conclude that the picture painted by the respondents in 2004 appears closer to that of the old pre-1997 Samsung culture, and not the new Samsung Electronics which has been described above. There was no reference to foreigners. There was also little creativity generated within the system. What this seems to represent is the fact that while new employees may have been imbibing the new Samsung Electronics culture, the old employees were resisting change.

Only 27 percent of the respondents believed that the Samsung Man's characteristics were changing. This change was, however, related to the forces of globalization and diversity—changes that the company and the society were going through—rather than through corporate programs intended to create this effect. Younger interviewees viewed creativity, innovation, and flexibility along with a sense of humor as the key traits of the future Samsung Man. The new breed of Samsung Men appeared to care more about their health and family. As the wife might also need to work to pay for that Bundang apartment and skyrocketing university fees, the Samsung

Man would need to take on more parental responsibilities. Work would no longer be the only priority in his life.

There would also be changes in attitude towards loyalty and mobility. In 2004, the respondents felt that it was hard to walk away from a good, well-paying job, but there were some people who were willing to do it. In this survey, the changes that were coming from within through the HR department were rated as less important than the changes which were affecting Korean society as a whole. Diversity in the workplace, however, was having an effect.

When the survey participants were asked what factors, in order of importance, influenced the growth of Samsung, the ranking was as follows:

1. People
2. Products
3. Brand
4. Business model.

According to the survey results, the key factors which would produce productivity growth in Samsung were ranked as follows:

1. Leadership
2. Values and culture
3. Selection and recruitment
4. Human-resource development.

This conclusion suggests that the leadership coming from both the chairman's office and, in particular, vice chairman Yun, had begun to override and guide the work of Samsung Electronics' human-resource development system. As the previous chapters and the coming chapters emphasize, perhaps little of Samsung Electronics' success could have been achieved without the vision of CEO Yun. But this 2004 survey may have been a premature measure to gauge the results of the efforts to change Samsung Electronics' DNA.

The new values adopted were abstract and needed a considerable degree of indoctrination to mould the workforce. Here lies a major problem, in that Koreans normally imbibe, but do not ingest, a great deal of what is fed to them as indoctrination. The values come more from family upbringing than company lectures, and from those leaders whom Koreans assess to be role models.

Jack Welch began reforming General Electric in the early 1980s and was still at it in 2001 when he retired. Yun was given only 12 years. Change in a large, successful Korean company is never easy. The happy Silicon Valley (almost dot.com) image which Samsung HR policy sought to imbue in the mid-2000s was not one that appealed to the older Korean generation. There was inevitably a clash of cultures. In 2007 Shin Tae-gyun, the managing director of the consulting and leadership team at Samsung Human Resources Development Center, was asked the question "Can a truly entrepreneurial culture dedicated to innovation co-exist with Samsung's Korean roots?" His answer was perhaps less affirmative than might have been expected:

> Ever since its foundation in 1938, Samsung has maintained a talent-based management philosophy using the slogan "A company is its people." This people-first philosophy served as the growth engine of Samsung and made Samsung into what it is today. What is particularly noteworthy is that other global leading companies such as GE, DuPont, and Johnson & Johnson also have a talent-focused company culture. In this sense, Samsung's people-first philosophy is part of a global trend shared by many of the world's leading global companies.[31]

He explained that in 2007 this drive was being accentuated in the management plan:

> The only way to become a world leader in this creativity-based society is to pioneer new ways of doing business and producing better products, so we have to break past the unknown to become a first mover. Creative management can be realized through new technologies, products, and markets, which means that we need imagination and creativity from our leaders and top talents. Finding and developing the core of creative talent within Samsung is our biggest challenge today.[32]

In late 2007, CEO Yun was moving further in this direction by praising the values of Google as being appropriate for

Samsung in the future, but his time at Samsung was running out. The company was moving into crisis mode as the old growth engines seemed to be slowing. While creativity was still the slogan, the tendency for the company was to revert to older values, as some had predicted it would.[33] His legacy and the flowering of the seeds of change which he sought to create are considered in the final chapter.

But as we shall see in the next chapter, the tensions between the new and largely foreign or Korean American movers and shapers who took Samsung past Sony were far from muted, and the voice of the new generation of Samsung Electronics was not loud enough to prevent the team that produced such success in the 2000–2004 period from drifting away between 2004 and 2008. The implications of this are considered in later chapters.

Endnotes

1   The early part of this chapter relies heavily on the article "The Impact of Culture on the Management Values and Beliefs of Korean Firms" by Song Young-hack and Christopher B. Meek, which appeared in the June 1998 issue of *Journal of Comparative International Management*; the research of an MBA student at KDI, Sergei Kondratiev; and on contributions by other Korean executives taking part in KDI's evening MBA program.

2   Quoted in *Asiaweek*, November 12, 1999.

3   Tichy, Noel M. and Sherman, Stratford 2005, *Control Your Destiny or Someone Else Will*, New York: HarperCollins Publishers Inc.; Gerstner, Louis V., Jr. 2002, *Who Says Elephants Can't Dance? Inside IBM's Historic Turnaround*, New York: HarperCollins Publishers Inc.

4   http://www.samsung.com/AboutSAMSUNG/ELECTRONICSGLOBAL/Careers/WhySAMSUNG/Training/traning_06.htm; accessed September 3, 2007. This part of the Samsung website ceased to be accessible to non-employees in its restructure of the Samsung website in 2008, when the AboutSAMSUNG/ELECTRONICSGLOBAL page of the site was remodeled so that the website www.samsung.com invites the viewer to indicate their country of interest and no longer presents a global view.

5   http://www.samsung.com/in/aboutsamsung/careers/Careers_WhySAMSUNG.html; accessed July 10, 2009.

6   Song and Meek, op. cit.

7   Ibid.

8   Adizes, Ichak 1988, *Corporate Lifecycles*, Paramus, NJ: Prentice Hall: 126.

9   Ibid.

10 Song and Meek, op. cit.

11 Ibid.

12 Bar-Tal, D. 1990, *Group Beliefs: A Conception for Analyzing Group Structure, Processes, and Behavior*, New York: Springer-Verlag.

13 Collins, J. C. and Porras, J. I. 1991, "Organizational Vision and Visionary Organizations," *California Management Review* 34: 30–52.
14 Private communication, translated by Suh Hyo-yong.
15 Magaziner, I. and Patinkin, M. 1989, *The Silent War*, New York: Vintage Books: 34–5.
16 Korea Federation of Industry, *Company Yearbook 1980*, endpaper.
17 Lee, H. J. 1989, "Managerial Characteristics of Korean Firms," in Chung K. H. and Lee, H. C. (eds), *Korean Managerial Dynamics*, New York: Praeger: 147–62.
18 Ibid.
19 Song and Meek, op. cit.
20 Hall, D. L. and Ames, R. T. 1987, *Thinking through Confucius*, State University of New York Press, Albany: 58; Korea Chamber of Commerce and Industry (KCCI) 1984, *Sashi/Sahoon jib* [Company Policy/Slogan Collection], Seoul: KCCI: 76.
21 Song and Meek, op. cit.
22 Magaziner and Patinkin, op.cit.: 33–4.
23 Sunkyong Chairman's Office in Management & Planning 1989, *Sunkyong Management System*, Seoul: Sunkyong Chairman's Office in Management & Planning.
24 Bar-Tal, op. cit.
25 "The Hard Road Ahead: Interview with Lee Kun-hee,"*Asiaweek*, November 12, 1999.
26 Samsung Electronics, *Annual Report 2004*; Yun Jong-yong 2005, "Samsung Electronics," in Arnoud de Meyer *et al.* 2005, *Global Future*, Singapore: John Wiley & Sons: 54–62.
27 Sergei Kondratiev, "The Making of the Samsung Man," MBA Thesis, KDI School, 2006.
28 Yun, op. cit.
29 http://www.samsung.com/AboutSAMSUNG/ELECTRONICSGLOBAL/Careers/WhySAMSUNG/Training/traning_06.htm; accessed September 3, 2007.
30 Kondratiev, op. cit.
31 Shin Tae-gyun, "Human Resource Philosophy," at http://www.samsung.com/Features/BrandMagazine/magazinedigitall/2007_spring/interface.htm, accessed July 29, 2009.
32 Ibid.
33 Kim, Seongsu and Briscoe, Dennis R., "Globalization and a New Human Resource Policy in Korea: Transformation to a Performance-based HRM," *Employee Relations* 19(4) 1997: 298–308.

6

Mobile Phones

People pull these out at meetings to show off, which makes them a walking brand advertisement. That's what Sony's Walkman did for them.

Peter Skarzynski[1]

Mobile phones: Samsung's answer to the Walkman

Eric Kim's branding campaign was boosted by the fact that his period of working for Samsung coincided with the rise of the digital phone era, especially in America. Kim's own observation was that Samsung's main thrust boiled down to picking specific areas to achieve key differentiation, the most successful of which was the mobile cellular phone. Samsung then focused on flooding the market with innovative and unique products in target markets such as the US and working with a few partners to penetrate the market.

Yun's vision of digital convergence was to be amply repaid first in the development of its hand-phone business, and then a more extensive telecommunications strategy which by the first quarter of 2009 represented 34 percent of sales, up from 28.7 percent in the first quarter of 2008, and which represented 42 percent of company operating profit in the same period of 2008. In the abnormal world of the first quarter of 2009, the mobile phone division made an operating profit of 1.12 trillion *won* (just under US$1 billion) against 1.10 trillion *won* in the first quarter of 2008. But in 2009 this was 238 percent of the overall operating profit because of losses in other divisions (Samsung's overall operating profit was only US$0.47 billion).[2]

The Sony Walkman of 1979 had created the mobile consumer product category. While Samsung was not the inventor of the mobile phone, the company was able to exploit the coolness of the mobile phones. What helped was Samsung's internal decision to transform itself into a consumer-oriented and digitally-convergent company. "We saw the cell phone was changing from a utility item to a fashion statement," Kim told *Forbes*. "People used to say, 'Why would anyone want to take a photo with a phone?'"[3] By 2002, Samsung had a 12 percent share of the camera-phone market—just one point behind Nokia (but well behind NEC). Samsung's coolness factor got a big boost when one of its futuristic phones was featured in the second and third installments of the sci-fi series The Matrix.[4]

This was a striking vindication of the decision not to abandon the consumer-electronics business in 1997–98, of CEO Yun's belief in the power of digital convergence, and of Eric Kim's ability to coordinate a global marketing campaign which raised the status of Samsung to prestige levels. Thus Korean cell phones became the rave of the world. But the prospects of Samsung being in the mobile phone business at all often seemed doubtful up until 1998. How mobile phones came to make up 18 percent of its sales by 2004 and 23 percent by 2007 rested on a series of choices made by both Samsung and the Korean government from 1988 to 1998.

To understand this significant shift, we need to consider first that in the digital contest in the 1990s, the Koreans and the Europeans diverged from the standard technology path, while the American network companies stuck to their direction, reluctant to abandon their investment in analog phones. European phone companies such as Nokia, Ericsson, and Siemens supported GSM (Global System for Mobile Communications) standards which were built round a form of digitalization known as TDMA (Time Division Multiple Access); while Korea, almost alone, took a different technology known as CDMA (Code Division Multiple Access). Japan produced its own system, a variant of TDMA.

This was a government-led technology choice. CDMA meant that Korean domestic phones would not work anywhere else in the world, which both protected Korean companies in the short term in their domestic market, but also could have isolated them as a single global network grew by the end of the twentieth century. Japanese phone makers had the same protection/isolation situation.

In the end, the fact that CDMA was closer to the 3G (Third Generation) technology allowed the Koreans to make superior GSM phones to capture a sizeable slice of the global market.

The start of the story was much less promising. Between 1983 and 1986 Samsung engineers struggled to reverse-engineer Japanese car phones. The results were so disappointing that there were doubts about continuing the program. But it was not in Samsung's DNA to give up, and Lee Ki-tae, the young head of wireless development, decided to risk buying 10 Motorola phones instead. After a long struggle, in 1988 a phone was launched which could be used in Korea. Samsung's phones did not sell many units despite frequent changes in models. Motorola cornered 60–70 percent of the Korean market and Samsung's share grew to just 10 percent by the early 1990s. The company's disappointing financial results fueled arguments that Samsung should withdraw from all consumer appliances.[5]

From analog to CDMA

In 1992, the Korean government handed to the electronics companies a unique problem when it determined that the new second mobile telecom company would use CDMA technology when it launched in 1996. It needs to be remembered that, at this point, the only GSM system in the world was a test system in Berlin and that the decision to adopt CDMA was therefore less odd-ball than it would have seemed two years later when GSM capturing market after market. The Korean Ministry of Telecommunications (now MIC) had been canvassed by Qualcomm which owned the core CDMA technology, and the excitement of new digital technology and being first in the world made the choice seem plausible.

Samsung was still struggling to match the quality of Motorola's analog phone, and in 1993 began a research process that was to give birth to the Anycall brand. The story that did the rounds was that a Samsung engineer had watched a mountain climber make a successful call with his Motorola, while the engineer's Samsung phone had no connection at the top of a mountain. This started intense research into the antenna and connectivity technology which would make phones work throughout Korea's mountainous topography. Under the chairman's "Frankfurt declaration," the mobile phone division was given the task of producing phones comparable to Motorola by

1994 or Samsung would give up making phones. This analog phone, the SH-700, seemed to match the requirements, but there was no guarantee of quality control. Faulty Samsung phones abounded, which ultimately led to the much-celebrated historic incineration at the Gumi plant in early 1995. In the lead-up to the mass destruction of phones, in 1994 the chairman gave Samsung phones as Christmas or New Year gifts. To everyone's horror some of the phones did not work. The consequences became a legend. Below is one account of the company-turning event.

> Even today, people talk about the "voluntary incinera-tion at Gumi." A drab factory town in South-Central Korea, Gumi is home to one of Samsung's biggest plants. A decade ago, the company was best known for budget air conditioners and low-end TVs. Its leader, Kun-hee Lee, had grander ambitions, but when he sent out Samsung's new wireless phones as his New Year's gift, word came back that they didn't work. So that March he paid a visit to Gumi.

At Lee's command, the factory's 2,000 employees donned headbands labeled *Quality First* and assembled in a courtyard. There they found their entire inventory piled in a heap—cell phones, fax machines, nearly $50 million-worth of equipment. A banner before them read *Quality Is My Pride*. Beneath it sat Lee and his board of directors. Ten workers took the products one by one, smashed them with hammers, and threw them into a bonfire. Before it was over, employees were weeping.

The account continued:

> Ritual purification at the command of a heroic leader is an ancient and powerful tradition in this part of the world. With a few superficial changes, this whole scene could have played in Chinese director Zhang Yimou's costume epic. Certainly it had the desired effect—after Lee's visit to Gumi, shoddiness was no longer an option.[6]

Lee Ki-tae, the Gumi factory manager (who went on to become head of Samsung's mobile telecom division in 2004), later told of how he continued to personally test new models by hurling them against a wall or dropping them from a second-story window. Once, he even ran over a handset with his car. Generally they still worked.

Then there was the connectivity issue. Samsung's research on connectivity was the real secret of success. In October 1994, the SH-770 was launched as the Anycall. Samsung's domestic brand share began to rise, partly with the publicity about damaged phones still doing the rounds, and its mountain-top demonstrations still working their magic. Within a month of the launch, Samsung's sales had reached 25.8 percent of the market. By August 1995, this rose to 51.5 percent, while Motorola fell to 42.1 percent.

Samsung now had both a challenge and an opportunity. Two carriers would start CDMA services in April 1996 using untried technology. Motorola had no CDMA model to offer its customers. Samsung had a model ready, the SCH-100, which was not only light and slim compared with the old analog system, but had perfect voice reception. It was a hit. Mobile phone ownership in Korea rose from 10 percent in May 1998 to 43 percent in August 1999, despite these being the worst months of the Asian financial crisis in which Korean GDP was contracting.

Independent of this, in 1996, Samsung received a lucky break. Although most of the world had adopted GSM, some US networks— also heavily canvassed by Qualcomm—opted for CDMA systems. One of these was Sprint, and Samsung was able to create a US$600-million deal which launched Samsung into the highly profitable US phone business for the first time. Samsung Telecommunications America (STA), established that year in Dallas, pledged to become a top-five phone-maker within five years. It reached this objective in two with the clamshell-shaped 3500 phone, which became America's top-selling cell phone in 2000. In 1997, Samsung was able to sell to CDMA service providers in Hong Kong. The following year, it did the same in Brazil, where it also built a factory, ready to service the Latin American market in the future.

The advanced digital technology of CDMA put Korean phones ahead of all but Japan. But the Korean CDMA system was, for a few years, only really available in the domestic market, just as the Japanese system worked only in Japan. While the Japanese phone companies concentrated on the Japanese market, the Koreans turned their eyes to other markets as well. Again it took the team time to produce a winning model. It wasn't until September 1998 that Samsung was ready to showcase a model which matched European consumers' requirements in GSM.

By now, the phone market and Samsung's share in it was growing fast enough to catch the lift which Eric Kim's "DigitAll" campaign was achieving. This was further supported by the US Winter Olympics of 2002.

Samsung moves upmarket

In 2002, among a rush of other introductions, Samsung started selling the I300, a Palm-based PDA which came with an inbuilt wireless phone. Although there were plenty of combo PDA phones on the market, none sold as well or enjoyed as much acclaim. "People pull these out at meetings to show off, which makes them a walking brand advertisement," said Peter Skarzynski, Samsung Telecommunications America's vice president. "That's what Sony's Walkman did for them."[7]

The style and the premium price of Samsung phones made them attractive to the leading edge and early adopters of cell phones in the American market. Analysts could not write the Samsung story often enough in 2002. A *Time* magazine article noted Samsung's prowess in innovation in the market with its voice-activated phone that could surf the Internet and play MP3 tunes. Next came stylish models that kept calendars in color. Then there were the phones that had always-on text messaging and wireless video that enabled users to play games and watch movie clips.[8] And as the magazine noted, all these came from a company that up until a few years before was a mass-marketer of cheap TVs and VCRs:

> Since 1997, however, Samsung has begun rubbing shoulders with the market leaders in high-end cell phones, DVD players, elegant flat plasma TVs and a wide range of other consumer products. These gadgets are sometimes less expensive than those of Japanese or Finnish competitors but by no means inferior. Which is pretty clear if you've tried to order an I300, the Palm-powered PDA that's really a phone (sorry, sold out), or if you feel embarrassed to answer your Motorola StarTAC in public because it's so . . . yesteryear.[9]

Samsung DigitAll: Everyone's invited

Overall, Samsung's cell phone revenue rose more than fourfold in five years; from US$4 billion in 1999, to US$18 billion in 2004 (by which time its handsets were priced at a 44 percent premium to its rivals).

Samsung's mobile phone success was achieved on design excellence rather than just engineering. Samsung had six design labs, of which five were located outside Korea. In 2004, Chung Kook-hyun, who ran the Samsung design center in Seoul and expanded his staff strength by 50 percent in two years to 450 people, explained: "Five years ago engineers told designers what the products would look like. No more. Now the designers tell the engineers what features they want."

At the design lab in London, Clive Goodwin and his staff of 18 created whimsical designs for the European market—a plasma TV with clear plastic speakers; a phone with a keypad that slid downward. "The way a product interfaces with the user is very important. It's like theater," Goodwin said. The obsession with looks paid off in myriad ways. In the same year, Samsung won five design awards at the IDEA competition, more than any other company. A 2004 survey showed that US customers, when asked to compare a Samsung cell to a car brand, most often cited Lexus. This irked Samsung executives who wanted to be compared with BMW; but this was a compliment nevertheless. Typical of Samsung's new design push was the sleek SGH-E700, a clamshell with two LCD panels and a camera with a digital zoom. Designers told the engineers to eliminate the usual bulky antenna in favor of an internal one, and in less than a year, the E700 became one of the world's best-selling phones, at 10 million units.

Product cycles were shortened, costs dropped and employees felt motivated to keep up. It used to take 14 months for Samsung to roll out a product; but by 2004 it needed only five: "Consensus is important here, but the speed of implementation and empowerment of employees is equally important," the head of Samsung's North American memory sales and marketing division at the time, told a reporter. Samsung America had created the kind of "global" Samsung that chairman Lee had dreamed of in 1993, when he first put design forward as the core for the future, and in 1999, when he started recruiting the talent pool to achieve this.[10]

Hot on the heels on the success of its mobile phones, Samsung was hoping the cell phone glamour could spill over to its consumer electronics line, the one laggard in the Samsung stable. In 2002, the rest of the consumer electronics provided only 5 percent of total profit, down from 10 percent five years before. Yun, who spent a good part of his early career on gadgets and televisions, had been making some headway: Samsung's consumer electronics sales in the first quarter of 2002 were up a modest 16 percent, to US$2 billion. In that year, Samsung ranked fourth in the world in MP3 players, trailing Apple, iRiver (founded by Samsung defectors, as described in Chapter 8), and RCA; its DVD players were number three, trailing Sony and Toshiba.

Samsung didn't sell stereos or laptop computers in the US, putting it at a disadvantage to Sony in placing its brand in front of consumers. So Samsung's US marketing chief, Peter Weedfald, resorted to inventive measures, partnering with Hollywood and the music business. "We want brand infatuation," he said. "I think of Starbucks. Also Nike." In June 2002, Weedfald signed up New Line Cinema to help promote Samsung gadgets. To entice online visitors, Samsung offered viewers the chance to win a camcorder and tickets to the New Line Cinema's movie premieres.

Samsung, known by the cold tagline "DigitAll: Everyone's Invited," switched to a more Intel-style of one-liners in its 2005 campaign. "The Power Within" could have become Samsung's slogan, Weedfald said, though he admitted it was risky. "Will consumers care that our own components are inside our products? Plus, our competitors are our customers."[11]

Samsung had a good grip on the faddish cell-phone market. This was due in part to its control of the manufacturing of tiny screens and potent flash memory used in cell phones. Perhaps this could help Samsung it in its quest to grow its consumer electronics business. "PCs used to drive the semiconductor business; now wireless products [do]," said Skarzynski.[12] But would Samsung consumer electronics be able to ride on this?

Sony Ericsson Mobile Communications: The Japanese fight back

While Samsung took the risks by showcasing its mobile phones, Sony did not feel confident that it had the technical expertise to spread its phones around the world. Despite having invented the mobile appliance category, it was not even number one in the Japanese mobile phone market. It was also slow to win consumers elsewhere. Reverting to its strategy in the movie and music industry, Sony resorted to buying into markets. In 2001, it acquired a 50 percent share in the mobile phone appliance business of the Swedish manufacturer Ericsson. This was a case of sleeping with the (captured) enemy. In October 2001, the Japanese and the Swedes set up a 50–50 joint venture, Sony Ericsson Mobile Communications, which announced it first joint products in March 2002.

The new company's website touted the new venture as a global manufacturer of mobile multimedia consumer products, offering feature-rich phones and accessories, PC cards, and M2M solutions. Its aim was to produce technology-driven products for mobile imaging, communications, and entertainment. Combining Sony's expertise in digital imaging and components with Ericsson's expertise in second- and third-generation communication technologies, the venture jostled with the other makers of mobile phones to offer high-resolution camera phones, including the S700 1.3 megapixel "swivel design" phone.[13]

This reads strangely like the kind of hype which Samsung was putting out around 2002. Initially, most of the Sony Ericsson hype stayed on the website. But in Japan, aggressive PR campaigns were beginning to pay off and Sony Ericsson was beginning to attract votes for its industrial design, too. In 2004, its iconic T610 became the first mobile phone to win a "Good Design Gold Prize" from the Japan Industrial Design Promotion Organization. Sony Ericsson continued to improve on its design, and the S700 and K700i dual-fronted camera phones added to its credibility as a design leader. The company also forged partnerships with software developers and content providers to promote itself as a cutting-edge provider in the applications market.

In 2007, Sony Ericsson employed approximately 5,000 employees worldwide. These staff undertook product research, design and development, marketing, sales, distribution, and customer services. Global management was based in London, while R&D was located in Sweden, Japan, China, the US, and the UK. The management team was headed by its president, Miles Flint, a former senior executive of Sony Europe. Jan Wäreby (a former Ericsson executive) was corporate executive vice president and head of global sales and marketing.

The venture tried to put some steam in the chase for a share of the mobile phone market. If product reviews are any indication, the heat was definitely on. One product review of Sony Ericsson's Z200, for example, had this to say:

> The overall looks, feel and personality of the Z200 make it my personal choice of clamshell, and that is hard to say having been a "Samsung Man" for many years now. It has all of the modern features required from a mobile phone, with some excellent (distinct) ring tones and gaming/internet facilities. It has certainly made me more consumer conscious when picking a phone. I will no longer just look at the Samsung section.[14]

With the push by Japanese manufacturers for a slice of the global mobile phone market, Samsung, which had been tracking leaders in the market, now had to keep its vision on the rearview mirror as well. Through the growth years of Samsung's mobile phones, the "Anycall" years, Samsung and LG Electronics were lucky that Japanese manufacturers were (apart from Sony) deeply absorbed in their own market: "We were thinking only about Japan," Atsutoshi Nishida, president of Toshiba, admitted. "We really missed our chance."[15]

But by late 2005—partly as a result of the Japanese electronics crisis—came the idea that the entire mobile industry of Japan would have a rare second chance to compensate for past mistakes. The Japanese producers (who collectively had about the same market share as Samsung's 13 percent) saw that a switch to 3G phones could atone for the Japanese technology's failings.

Their move to 3G helped level the playing field somewhat. But they still could not match up to Samsung's aggressive pricing. The race was getting serious. Just as Samsung allied itself with Sprint in the early 2000s, Sanyo was also aiming to supply 3G phones to Sprint. Toshiba and Sharp allied themselves with Vodafone, and NEC with Hutchison.

In the price war, Samsung and LG were able to price their similar offerings lower. While this was an acceptable marketing strategy for LG, it flew in the face of Samsung's premium pricing strategy.

Samsung had become involved in a price war with Nokia in 2004, when its fourth-quarter profits were lower than expected, losing out to Finnish rival Nokia. Motorola's newest phones had crept up during the holiday shopping season, taking a lead over Samsung.

Samsung was also suffering from some fatigue and lost favor among telecommunication carriers that constantly demanded a flow of new features to keep consumer interest high. In that fourth quarter alone, Motorola released 20 feature-packed phones worldwide, in an aggressive attempt to capture market share. At the top was the heavily marketed RAZR V3. Analysts said that publicity had helped draw consumers to Motorola's overall portfolio, including more-affordable models such as the V265, which featured a camera, advanced speech recognition, and the ability to download games.

At the same time, analysts noticed Samsung's sluggishness in moving new phones to market. "We think Samsung will be plagued with problems until they get their new phones out," said American Technology Research analyst Albert Lin. "Samsung's problems are going to be something that ultimately helps Motorola and Nokia."[16]

Eric Kim's departure from Samsung eased the pressure in Korea to produce and on the American design team to churn out sexy phones.

Samsung, however, was still ahead in brand-power terms. Motorola's onslaught was no match. When push came to shove, where the differentiation was thin, consumers ultimately chose Samsung. By 2006, Motorola—far from profiting—had merely produced an energy surge which was unsustainable. Motorola's share of the global handset market stood at 13.4 percent at the end of the third quarter of 2006, placing it third worldwide. Nokia, the market leader, had roughly 30.9 percent, while Samsung had 13.8 percent.[17]

Nokia gets one part of the market right

While Samsung was busy chasing the premium market in cell phones, the world's top player, Nokia, had been forced to turn its back on super-fashionable phones as a result of Samsung's triumph and LG Electronics' success. Nokia simply could not compete with the Korean ability to turn out fashionable items in Asia or the US. Being edged out there, Nokia saw opportunities in emerging markets. The demand for lower-priced phones and developing-world phones offered real economies of scale for production.

Samsung had been slow to recognize this market because its eyes were on premium phones, and it was advertising premium brands. Only in late May 2007 did vice chairman Yun acknowledge publicly that Samsung needed to pay more attention to the developing world. By then, though, it was a little too late for Samsung to establish brand leadership in the developing market, because it was facing in quite the opposite direction. Nokia was offering a good functional phone for about half the price of the Samsung model. Millions in the developing world had discovered the joys of simplicity and its name was Nokia.

In China, Samsung and LG could enjoy the coolness which was part of the Korean wave. But in countries which were not so fashion conscious, clunky Nokia was dominating. The response to Nokia was partly to regain cost leadership. This meant that phone production could no longer stay in Korea, for either Nokia or Samsung.[18] By mid-2007, Samsung Electronics announced that it was poised to move its main mobile phone production base to Vietnam, which would allow it to produce cheaper phones. (The Bac Nui factory made its first shipment—to the UAE—in June 2009. This is dealt with in a different context in Chapter 8.) In 2006, Samsung produced a total of 130 million mobile phones, about 80 million (62 percent) at the Gumi plant. The plant in China produced 45 million units, or 35 percent of total production. In 2008, Samsung's domestic production accounted for less than 40 percent of the total output. By 2009, Samsung was producing 200 million units and running down production in Gumi. The company had decided that its domestic plant was no longer a competitive production base because labor costs were over 10 times higher than in Southeast Asia and, to go one stage further and compete with Nokia in developing countries, it needed a low-cost base. Ironically between a quarter and a third of Nokia's phones are produced at its Korea factory in Masan, though they are purely for export.[19]

For Samsung, the mobile phone segment has become a staple and vital to its operations. Apart from TVs, this is the one consumer area where Samsung Electronics has a major market share (compared with its very minor share in computers outside of Korea) and it must fight to retain the market against some very savvy competitors. Also, the mobile phone technology is the fountainhead from which all digital convergence will spring.

From mobile handsets to wireless networks

Part of Samsung's initial success came from its expertise in connectivity. As its handset sales increased in markets where mobile phone networks were not well established, the company's accumulated expertise in connectivity brought it increasingly into the area of network equipment and services and into digital convergence—Yun's original vision. In May 2008, Samsung Electronics reorganized its Telecommunication Networks unit by merging its troubled PC and MP3 player businesses, which had been part of the Digital Media unit. The company announced that:

> The decision will boost our synergy with related businesses to enhance our competitive edge throughout the telecommunications industry. We believe we can create a unique platform by merging the latest mobile technology with core computing technology for the PC business, and by leading the market with the most sophisticated products to embrace technology convergence. Our MP3 business also will be fine-tuned by converging core mobile technologies with our world-leading power efficiency and design capabilities. Our leadership in digital convergence will further bolster our mobile communication brand as the industry takes mobility to the next level.[20]

By May 2008, Samsung was aiming to become the "Leader in Next-Generation Telecommunications Technology." In 2006 the company developed the world's first Mobile WiMAX (mobile broadband internet) technology, a next-generation telecommunications technology, and began to commercialize this among Korean service providers the following year. The Mobile WiMAX technology was adopted as the 3G global standard at the International Telecommunications Union (ITU) conference in October 2007, paving the way for increased market penetration worldwide. "Banking on a Mobile WiMAX total solution, including chipset, terminal and system, we provided a commercial package to the US, Japan and Brazil, solidifying our leadership in the field," the company told investors in May 2008.

Table 6.1   Handset-makers' market share 2008-09

	Nokia	Samsung	LG	Motorola	Sony Ericsson	Others
2008 1Q	39.7	16	8.4	9.2	7.3	19.4
2008 2Q	40.4	15.2	9.2	9.2	7.5	18.5
2008 3Q	38.6	17	7.5	7.6	8.1	21.2
2008 4Q	38.9	17.6	8.9	6.1	8	20.5
2009 1Q	38.6	19	9.4	5.2	5.1	22.7
2009 2Q	38	19.2	11	5.1	5	21.7
2009 3Q	38	21	11	4.9	5	20.1

Source: IDC

Samsung's new attention to lower-priced models while continuing the search for top-end models paid off in the global financial crisis of 2008-09. Table 6.1 shows how Samsung's market share rose from 16 percent to 21 percent during the crisis, while it took market share from Nokia, and Sony Ericsson and heavily from Motorola. The only major producer to match this growth was LG, which rose from 8.4 percent to 11 percent in the same period. However, Samsung made big gains in the third quarter of 2009 while LG remained static.

Sales of networks and systems also performed well although no separate data are available. But Samsung was also beginning to tackle the issue of being a content provider with a new generation of smartphones.[21]

And though mobile phones were a major driving force for Samsung in 2009, the company has yet to generate a serious buzz when it comes to smartphones, which provide larger margins than conventional handsets. Although Samsung now controlled about 21 percent of the global handset market and had every prospect of increasing its market share, its share in the smartphone market was less than 4 percent, and none of its premium handsets so far have shown a real ability to compete with either the iPhone or Blackberry despite favorable reviews of Samsung's OMNIA II smartphone, launched in the US in December 2009.[22]

Samsung was looking to make a splash by launching a slew of data-enabled handsets powered by the Google-backed Android operating system in 2010, although Google's political problems in

China delayed the launch of this model in January 2010.[23] However, the old foe, Motorola, which had slipped to number five in the global handset hierarchy, was gaining a lot of publicity with positive reviews over its recently released smartphone, Droid, which contains the same operating system.[24]

The company had finally escaped from the semiconductor conundrum of the 1990s. The Telecommunication division would produce 34 percent of Samsung's sales in the first quarter of 2009, and 238 percent of Samsung Electronics' operating profit in that same period.[25] Yun and Kim's belief in digital convergence which, as we shall see in Chapter 8 was under question in 2007, had been abundantly validated in 2009.

Endnotes

1   Samsung Telecommunications America's vice president; quoted in "Samsung Moves Upmarket," by Frank Gibney Jr., Cathy Booth Thomas, Daren Fonda, Donald Macintyre, and Jennifer L. Schenker, *Time Magazine*, March 25, 2002.
2   Samsung Electronics, at http://www.samsung.com/us/aboutsamsung/ir/ irevent-presentations/earningsrelease/downloads/2008/20090424_conference_ eng.pdf; accessed May 19, 2009. I have also drawn extensively on Lee Boon-young and Lee Seung-Joo, "Case Study of Samsung's Mobile Phone Business," KDI School Working Paper 04–11, May 2004.
3   "Samsung's Next Act," by Heidi Brown and Justin Doebele, *Forbes*, July 26, 2004; accessed July 7, 2007.
4   Ibid.
5   Ibid.; see also Lee and Lee, op. cit.
6   "Seoul Machine: Cell Phones. Memory Chips. Plasma TVs. How Samsung Made Korea a Consumer Electronics Superpower," by Frank Rose, May 13, 2005, at http://www.frankrose.com/seoul_machine_71281.htm. This journalistic account may not be quite correct. The incineration of defective products was held on a monthly basis. Lee and Lee op. cit.: 6.
7   Gibney *et al.*, op. cit.
8   Ibid.
9   Ibid.
10 Brown and Doebele, op. cit.
11 Ibid.
12 Ibid.
13 http://www.sonyericsson.com/cws; accessed May 28, 2007.
14 http://www.ciao.co.uk/Sony_Ericsson_Z200__Review_5489541; accessed May 28, 2007.
15 "Japan Gets a 2nd Chance at Global Phone Market," by Martin Fackler, *International Herald Tribune*, November 17, 2005.
16 Ibid.

17 Ibid. (citing Reuters).
18 Although Nokia has no domestic sales organization, it produces a very high volume of its phones in Korea and Nokia TMC is Korea's seventh-largest foreign company.
19 Tony Michell, "Successful Foreign Firms in Korea;" presentation to the Korea Business Forum, February 2009.
20 Samsung Electronics 2007, Annual Report, at: http://www.samsung.com/us/ aboutsamsung/ir/financialinformation/annualreport/downloads/2007/00_ SEC_07AR_E_Full.pdf; accessed May 18, 2009.
21 "Samsung Executives Meet Murdoch Over Digital Content," by Kim Tong-hyun, *Korea Times*, October 7, 2009, at: www.koreatimes.co.kr/www/news/ biz/2009/10/123_53098.html, accessed January 24, 2010.
22 "Samsung Electronics Expects Record Sales, Earnings for 2009 2010," by Kim Tong-hyun, *Korea Times*, January 7, 2010: http://www.koreatimes.co.kr/www/ news/biz/2010/01/123_58631.html; accessed January 24, 2010.
23 "Google Delays Launch of Two Android Handsets in China" by Kathrin Hille, *Financial Times*, January 20, 2010, at: http://www.ft.com/cms/s/0/189ec730-0575-11df-a85e-00144feabdc0.html; accessed January 24, 2010.
24 See note 22.
25 Samsung Electronics, Investor Briefing, at: http://www.samsung.com/us/aboutsa-msung/ir/ireventpresentations/earningsrelease/downloads/2008/20090424_ conference_eng.pdf.

7

Sleeping with the Enemy: S-LCD[1]

Those companies are very important customers and, at the same time, we compete against them.

Eric Kim, 2004

Rivals in consumer products, partners in components

While Eric Kim and his team had been concentrating on consumers, much of Samsung's energy continued to be concentrated on further technological improvements. Despite both chairman Lee and Eric Kim's emphasis on design, one-quarter of Samsung's workforce was working in technological R&D. Samsung's edge over Sony was that it was producing leading-edge components, of which Sony was a consumer. Sony had greatly reduced its own production of components and increased its outsourcing, despite the prejudice of the Sony engineers. It was a continuation of the stable strategy where outward ventures had seemed to offer senior management more of a hope than inward investment. In mobile phones, Sony had turned to Ericsson. In 2004, for LCDs it turned to Samsung.

Samsung had made its major global consumer breakthrough in televisions, and cathode ray tube (CRT) production remained an important component in its portfolio, even though with the introduction of flat screens in the early years of the new century the writing was on the wall for the traditional TV. By this time Korea, Taiwan, and Japan (and potentially China) were locked in a rivalry over LCD technology which would drive the next generation of consumer (and many industrial) products. Samsung had to be a major player in producing LCD components, and Samsung's well-established joint venture with Corning was part of this equation. Around the world, Samsung and Sony's TVs were in head-to-head competition.

But in making seventh-generation LCD screens, Sony turned to Samsung for a marriage, which was consummated in March 2004. In creating this 50–50 JV, Sony showed how different its strategy was compared to Samsung. Even so, skeptics raised questions about the wisdom of such a joint venture.

For Samsung, the partnership had a lot to do with securing a stable source of demand for a component that required heavy capital investment. For Sony, the carrot was in the technological advantage offered by Samsung, as well as a secure source of supply in a volatile market. Samsung's position was amplified by the following statement by Eric Kim:

> Most of our core components—about 50 percent of that capacity—get sold on an open-market basis. The other half is consumed by our vertical integrated businesses. We're one of the top suppliers to Nokia, Motorola, Sony—you name it and we're there. Those companies are very important customers and, at the same time, we compete against them. It's a classic case of competition.[2]

The Sony–Samsung venture was in many ways not a match made in heaven, unlike the others seen in the market. But there were market pressures to go down this track. Samsung had the clout and position in the LCD market, while Sony was a major player in the television market and a main user of the product. The LCD business soaked up much of Samsung's capital and Sony's involvement was a deal worth going along with.

The flat screens rely on the ability of the factory to cut plate glass into screens. Each "generation" allowed larger sheets of glass to be cut into large screens. The technology essentially belonged to the glass manufacturers and not the electronics companies. Success relied on the presence of glass manufacturers as well as the LCD plants. So Korea's success depended on Asahi Glass, NEC, Merck,

Hoya, and the Korean joint ventures Optical High Tech Korea and Youchang Optical.

Table 7.1 shows the state of play of different companies in LCD technology in late 2005, in which only four consortia were investing in seventh-generation production capacity.

Three Japanese companies, Hitachi, Matsushita, and Toshiba, had already formed a collaborative venture, AU Optronics. Sony and Samsung's venture did not make natural sense in the way that it did for three Japanese companies to cooperate. There was also a question of national pride over who had the casting vote. In the end the vote went to Samsung, which had one more share than Sony. Sony needed Samsung's total devotion to the project and therefore ceded most of the management control. To demonstrate Samsung's dedication to the project, Lee Kun-hee's son and heir, Lee Jae-yong, became the president of the JV company. Together, the two companies invested US$1.8 billion to make the seventh-generation product. Technology was moving so fast that the eighth-generation would be available soon (by 2007, a company could decide to skip the ninth-generation product and go straight to the tenth).

Many observers felt that, ultimately, Samsung would not allow this JV to continue. They believed that Samsung's culture would ultimately be intolerant of joint ventures, as had proved to be the

Table 7.1   Key LCD market players (late-2005)

Company	Generation	Production Capacity	Date of Operation
Samsung Electronics	Seventh	60,000	2005 1Q
Samsung Electronics	Seventh	60,000	2006 2Q
LG Philips LCD	Sixth	90,000	2004 3Q
LG Philips LCD	Seventh	90,000	2006 2Q
Sharp	Sixth	45,000	2004 1Q
Sharp	Eighth	30,000	2006 3Q
IPS Alpha Technology	Seventh	60,000	2006 2Q
AU Optronics	Sixth	90,000	2005 1Q
AU Optronics	Seventh	30,000	2006 4Q
Chi Mei Optoelectronics	Seventh	30,000	2007 2Q
Chungwha Picture Tubes	Sixth	90,000	2005 2Q
HanStar Display	Sixth	30,000	2006 4Q
Quanta Display	Sixth	60,000	2005 4Q

case in alliances such as the Samsung–Hewlett Packard venture in the past. But the demands of the twenty-first century had begun to require more strategic alliances.

The venture's promoters were vindicated, as was demonstrated in 2006 when analysts had predicted a considerable loss for the Samsung division making LCD and PDP screens—which is what had happened to LG Philips, Samsung's major competitor. Instead, as Yun wrote to shareholders:

> In LCD, our continuous early investment despite fierce competition was finally paid back by successful results. Unlike our competitors, who suffered from the steep decline of panel prices, our company recorded outstanding profitability with No.1 market share of 60 percent in the large TV panel market over 40-inch, which is our target segment.
>
> In TV, for the first time, we were ranked first in flat TV including LCD and PDP, and successfully took the largest overall TV market share. Our LCD TV business enabled us to strengthen our top position as the global premium brand with the great success of Bordeaux TV, our global hit product.[3]

What he did not say, however, was that the strategy of sleeping with the enemy was partly responsible. LG Philips had to sell on the world market, but Samsung had a secure partner who took half of its production. From Sony's perspective, the situation was not nearly so satisfactory. Samsung had beaten them in their strongest field, with a product whose basic component was jointly produced. In February 2008, it seemed that the marriage was over. Sony announced that it would enter a new JV with Sharp for the next generation of LCD glass.[4] *Forbes* noted that:

> While the Japanese media have been at pains to portray Sony's decision to switch to a domestic partner as one based on pure economic cost considerations and capacity constraints at the S-LCD facility, Korean critics apparently interpreted things differently. The *Chosun Ilbo* newspaper attributed the move partly to the resurfacing of

long-standing enmity between corporate Japan and Korea. Ban Dong-wook, a researcher at Daishin Securities, was quoted as saying, "Sony may have an antipathy toward Samsung as it has recently been overtaken by Samsung in its main business lines, such as TVs."[5]

But the Japanese media were right and the Korean commentators wrong; within a month Sony announced that it was also reinvesting with Samsung in an eighth-generation plant. This would entail the expenditure of US$1.93 billion.[6] The new plant began operation in June 2009.[7] But this episode exposed the problems of sleeping with the enemy. The new Sony–Sharp alliance played on all the fears of those in Samsung who feared alliances. Samsung was exposed to losing a key client for the company's glass-panel production. An emergency unit was reportedly established within Samsung's strategic planning office to reflect on the implications of Sony's move.[8]

Samsung was also aware that Sony had expressed the need to widen its glass-panel sourcing channels beyond Samsung, including manufacturers in Taiwan, to meet the growing demand. Sony president Ryoji Chubachi identified a reliable supply of glass panels as critical to fulfilling the company's ambition to reclaim from Samsung its former position as the world's largest TV maker.[9] The new plant opened on time in 2009, and CEO Won-kie Chang claimed that the new production line would secure S-LCD's position as a prime global vendor of larger-LCD panels, and "enable Samsung and Sony to overcome the current economic crisis."[10]

A world of alliances

Samsung's leading position in the early years of the decade remained in the components market. The mix of being the leading component supplier and an "also-ran" in all but a few end-user markets is a position Samsung and a small group of Japanese electronics companies occupied. In most of the rest of the world, there were few examples of companies that were hybrids of component and end-user suppliers. The industry leaders were either Intel, Samsung's Korean competitor Hynix—the second-largest DRAM manufacturer in the world—or many Taiwanese companies that make only components go inside the computer, or like Dell, which does not manufacture any components itself. But the Japanese and Samsung position has merit. This is what Hamel and Prahalad termed the core products market: "Many companies seek to sell core products to other companies, even to competitors, on an original equipment manufacturer (OEM) basis, as a way of capturing virtual market share."[11] Leverage here comes from "borrowing" the distribution channels and brands of downstream partners. This virtual market share, and the revenues and experience it brings, allows the company to accelerate its core competence-building efforts.[12] At the same time, those who believed that a national semiconductor company could be created in Europe failed to understand the nature of the business. Some writers have spoken about technology leverage: using bought-in know-how as the basis for new industries: "At first sight, the choice of an industry as fast-moving and technically demanding as semiconductors seems odd, but in fact this sector, with its short product cycles and rapid turnover of technologies, has provided greater opportunities for new entrants than, say, cars or chemicals."[13] This view highlights the constant fear among the followers of Samsung. Those who hold this view also misunderstand the Japanese business model and how the Koreans and Taiwanese have modified the business.

We return then to the tensions that are created when a company undertakes to be a producer of core products as well as of consumer products. In this case, the tension is between the hardcore engineers and the marketers. The trick then is finding the balance. In Sony's case, the balance was lost. In Samsung, the question in 2004 was whether the pendulum would swing too far the other way.

Within Samsung, Eric Kim's point was that companies with direct influence over their component manufacturing have an advantage over those who don't. He was of the view that components have been critical to consumer electronics as the market demands more intelligence devices that require more memory, more processing and more connectivity. While Samsung invests heavily to achieve its global leadership in memory, companies such as Dell—with no position in core components and not focused on R&D—function basically as a distribution company. Kim also noted how consumers have moved up the demand scale: "It used to be that someone would be quite happy with 24K of memory. Nowadays, half a gigabyte is barely enough. Also, we're the world leader in displays. Flat panel is the standard; nobody wants CRTs anymore."[14]

The experience of the 1995–96 period had been traumatic in that there was this fear, particularly among those who did not follow the markets closely, that core products equaled commodities. This view misunderstood the position of a maker of core products when a company was number one, and not an also-ran. In Samsung's case, the price cycle was predictable, but the core product was not a commodity, and being the leader meant that, each year, Samsung got better at producing DRAMs and the number of competitors fell by the wayside. Companies for whom DRAMs were only a part of the portfolio baulked at the next round of expenditure. These included Hitachi, NEC and, earlier, TI and other US manufacturers. One continuing key competitor to Samsung is the Korean company Hynix (a forced late-1990s merger of the old Hyundai Electronics and LG Semiconductor) which, having stripped off everything else of value, is now purely a chip manufacturer.

In the area of LCDs, the DRAM drama was being replayed, except there were many more competitors. The positive side was that demand was still growing. Business planners could see that there would come a time when global demand for LCDs would begin to decline. Indeed, by 2007, at the lower end of the market, supply and demand were matching, and in the global recession that began in 2008, LCD sales began to fall faster than chip set prices. Samsung's semiconductor sales in the first quarter of 2009 were US$5.22 billion, compared with US$5.32 billion in the first quarter of 2008, but LCD sales fell to US$4.11 billion from US$5.15 billion.[15] These numbers show that the new industry of LCDs was rivaling Samsung's traditional core product area of semiconductors, even though the semiconductor product mix had shifted substantially towards NAND and lessened dependence on DRAMs.

As investments became expensive and markets more complex, strategic alliances were being pursued with vigor. For some, peaceful coexistence was better than cut-throat competition. Yun was among these: "Companies such as Intel, Sony, Nokia, Philips: these are Samsung's business partners. We sell things to them and have strategic ties. So there is no need to engage in excessive competition. We want peaceful coexistence."[16] But not everyone in Samsung Electronics shared this view, including Hwang Chang-gyu, head of the semiconductor division.

Samsung's pursuit of strategic alliances (see Table 7.2) was a necessary strategy to keep its core products division healthy. Nevertheless, the company did not create any new alliances after July 2005.

Table 7.2   Samsung's Alliances 2001–2006[17]

Partners	Time	Key Agenda
Avaya USA	Feb 2006	Joint delivery enterprise IP telephony solutions
Salvarani, Italy	July 2005	Development of new built-in products combining household electronics and furniture
Sun Microsystems	July 2005	Cooperation in solution business and next-generation business computing system
Covad	July 2005	Supply agreement on access gateways
Lowe's	July 2005	Supply of household electronics to 1,100 Lowe's stores
VDL, France	Feb 2005	Cooperation in commercialization of terrestrial DMB
Charter	Jan 2005	Joint development of cable broadcasting receiver and set-top box for digital TV Full-Duplex service
KDDI, Japan	Jan 2005	Supply of CDMA2000 1xEV-DO network equipment in East Japan
Sanyo	Dec 2004	Development of high-efficiency, multi-inverter air conditioner (heating and cooling)
Bang & Olufsen	Nov 2004	Partnership of home cinema business
Kent State University	Oct 2004	Joint development of display technologies
Qualcomm	July 2004	Technology cooperation in MDDI (mobile display data interface)
Toshiba (TSST)	Apr 2004	Product development and marketing of optical storage devices
Sony (S_LCD)	Mar 2004	Joint venture for production of seventh-generation LCD (1870 × 2200 mm)
IBM	Mar 2004	Joint development of nano-logic process technologies
Maytag	Feb 2004	Strategic alliance in production and sales of premium front-loading washers

Sanyo	Feb 2004	Joint development of "World's Best" inverter air conditioners (heating and cooling)
Dell	Jan 2004	Supply of multi-functional laser printers
HP	Sept 2003	Technical tie-up for ink-jet printers
Disney	Sept 2003	Supply of "Movie Beam" set-top box for VOD
Napster	Sept 2003	Joint development and marketing for Samsung–Napster player
Sony	Aug 2003	Expansion and consolidation in memory stick business
NEC	July 2003	High-end business computer system
Sanyo	Apr 2003	Joint development of strategic household air conditioner models
Matsushita	Jan 2003	Technology standardization, joint production and joint marketing of DVD recorders
Best Buy	July 2002	Sales of side-by-side refrigerators through more than 500 retailer channels
Mitsubishi	May 2002	Mutual cooperation of washing machine business
Microsoft	Nov 2001	Joint development of digital household electronics

NAND—the next core product and the bewildering range of technical solutions

By 2007, chipmakers were presenting a dizzying array of next-generation or "universal memory" technologies, many of which were claimed to be the successors to DRAM and flash. The battle-field was also dominated by the fight to showcase the next non-volatile memory chip (and its supporting technologies). There were four basic candidates: NAND, or flash technology; FeRAM; MRAM; and so-called phase-change technologies.

Samsung appears to be ahead in NAND and phase-change technologies. MRAM and FeRAM have been introduced to the market by other companies, but they are likely to remain niche-oriented and applied as SRAM replacement parts for the foreseeable future, according to Frankie Roohparvar, vice president of NAND development at Micron Technology Inc.[18]

Samsung surpassed Intel in the flash business—a US$2.2 billion-a-year business (in 2002) that grew out of DRAM production. Samsung's 20 percent market share was the biggest overall. The flash component came in two forms: the first identified by allusions to on-off logic called NOR (the older entry, dominated by Intel); and the second, NAND (the newer, used in memory sticks). Samsung had established supremacy in NAND, where it controlled 65 percent of the world market by 2007. Both approaches are popular in wireless devices, but many analysts believed correctly in 2006–07 that NAND would win. "NOR is faster now, but NAND has more storage space. Give it five years," said Peter Nori, who covered global hardware for Franklin Templeton Investments, which owns US$1 billion in Samsung shares.

Samsung was bent on accelerating its innovation in NAND. Samsung was also able to alleviate market swings in chip prices through customization—its chips already fetched a 17-percent premium on the market average, thanks to special orders from companies like Nokia, Dell, and Microsoft. Dr. Hwang Chang-gyu, head of semiconductors at Samsung, was quoted as saying that Samsung—which was locking horns with Intel for supremacy in multi-chip packages, bundled memory and processors that increasingly run cell phones—could overtake Intel (which was in the lead).[19]

Picking the correct technology to back was critical to Samsung's success in the semiconductor manufacturing business. Hwang was correct in his assessment that demand for chips that could contain more memory would be a growth area. As early as 2004 he argued that:

> As we enter the nanotechnology era, a big shift in paradigm comes to the semiconductor industry. The traditional computer industry for dynamic RAM is expected to mature its memory-bit consumption with a relatively low growth rate. Meanwhile, memory consumption and high-density memory usage in mobile handsets and digital consumer applications will grow very fast. For these new applications, NAND flash memory will be the key enabling technology, and its easy scaling and multi-bit cell capabilities require a

new memory growth model. The well-known Moore's law still holds for most cases after the quarter-century history of the integrated circuit industry. However, the paradigm shift in the memory industry requires a new memory growth model: a twofold increase per year in memory density.[20]

Samsung was able to produce innovative products within a short time-span in the chips arena. In September 2006, its semiconductor business team rolled out its seventh-generation "Charge Trap Flash" (CTF) technology used in semiconductors and WiBro (wireless broadband technology). Three months after rolling out the world's first 8 GB NAND flash chips, Samsung announced the development of the industry's first 40 nanometer (nm) memory device. This was a 32 GB NAND flash chip, also hailed as the first to apply CTF technology. Samsung expected to use the 32 GB NAND flash chips in memory cards with capacities of up to 64 GB. This meant that devices would be able to carry 64 hours of DVD movies, and about 1,340 hours of MP3 audio.

Announcing this new move, Samsung described the innovation as a "revolutionary new approach" to further increasing manufacturing efficiency while greatly improving performance. The new CTF-based NAND flash memory increased the reliability of the memory by sharply reducing inter-cell noise levels. Hwang called this development a "surprisingly simple structure" that enables higher scalability, which will eventually improve manufacturing process technology from 40nm to 30nm and even 20nm, ever increasing the density and reducing the size of the chip.[21] In each 32GB device, the control gate in the CTF is only one-fifth of the size of a conventional control gate in a typical floating-gate structure. With CTF, there is no floating gate. Instead, the data is temporarily placed in a "holding chamber" of the nonconductive layer of the flash memory composed of silicon nitride (SiN). This results in a higher level of reliability and better control of the storage current.

The chip technology will undoubtedly be incorporated in consumer-based devices. However, the uptake of wireless broadband—which it is intended to serve—was not growing as the digital gurus had predicted. Insufficient thought had gone into who would want such high-speed devices. By May 2007, young Koreans, who should have been in the vanguard, were surrendering their advanced phones, believing that the features were not used and the rental charge too high.[22] The greatest demand would come from wifi connections, which began to pick up rapidly about the same time. Nokia's post-2005 vision (discussed earlier) of where the immediate growth lay (in the developing markets) seemed to be more accurate than the Samsung endless-upgrade model. Herein lies the lesson: While Samsung is better placed than Sony to survive bad technology predictions, it is, nevertheless, still sitting in the same danger quadrant.

A further question was whether Samsung would be correct in betting on the NAND technology. Would NAND be at the center of the stage? The world was in a frantic search for the next-generation memory technology. There were concerns that DRAM and flash parts would no longer scale in the near future. The complexity of semiconductor design compared with simple DRAMs is illustrated in Figure 7.1.

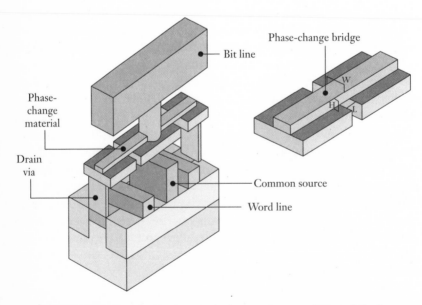

Figure 7.1   Phase-change memory, faster than traditional flash

Source: EE Times Asia (http://www.eetasia.com/ARTICLES/2007FEB/A/EEOL_2007FEB01_STOR_NT.jpg)

Simply put, the next-generation memory market was up for grabs. It is still unclear which technology will win the potentially huge universal-memory business, one that could reach US$75 billion by 2019, according to iSuppli Corp.[23] Cost and manufacturing issues will keep most of the also-rans from mainstream applications.

By 2007, there were obstacles to presenting continued technological improvements. At Samsung, the latest DRAMs and NAND flash parts were built around 50nm and 40nm processes, respectively. But current DRAM and flash technologies faced various scaling roadblocks in the dreaded "deep nanoscale" era, which would fall at the 20nm node and beyond. Hwang of Samsung put it this way:

> There is a growing concern about whether semiconductor technology can continue to keep pace with demand when silicon technology enters the deep nanoscale era. There are ultimate limits to transistor scaling, and narrowing margins in manufacturing due to ever-increasing fabrication costs. Though most experts believe silicon technology will maintain its leadership down to 20nm, beyond this node, a number of fundamental and application-specific obstacles will prevent further shrinkage.[24]

By 2007, the need to solve this was urgent. Memory devices were hitting the wall to some degree. For example, DRAM vendors, in tandem with their logic counterparts, had attempted to double the density of their products every 18 months. Vendors had announced parts based on 50nm processes. "Beyond 50nm, we may need another breakthrough for array transistors in DRAM," Hwang noted.[25] Samsung was working on a system known as "a body-tied, fin-shaped FET, or FinFET," that could take the DRAM down to 30nm. There were similar issues in flash, especially NAND. But, in fact, NAND vendors are moving faster than Moore's law by doubling their product densities every year. This has created a major disconnect between NAND vendors and their lithography tool suppliers, especially for production at the 50nm "half-pitch" node and beyond. "We are ready to go to the market, but the equipment suppliers are not ready to supply us," Frankie Roohparvar, vice president of NAND development at Samsung's rival Micron, observed in 2007.[26]

Equipment makers ASML Holding NV and Nikon Corp. have separately shipped 193nm immersion lithography tools, which promise to process chips at geometries down to 40nm. But in 2007–08, chipmakers were still scrambling—if not struggling—to get these newfangled and costly scanners into production.

Since this technology will partly decide the future growth trajectory of Samsung, it is worth looking more closely at what is involved. Scaling remained the biggest challenge for flash vendors. The floating-gate structure is the key component of traditional NOR and NAND devices, but many in 2007 wondered just how long the technology would scale before economics and technology prevented further measures. Woo Been-jon, director of flash-technology integration at Intel Corp., has suggested that the floating-gate structure will extend at least to the end of this decade. "After that, we will have to make some major changes," he said.[27] But Samsung was ahead of Intel in this game.

In September 2006, Samsung introduced a 32 GB NAND chip made on 40nm process technology that eliminated the floating-gate structure. Instead, it sported a proprietary oxide-nitride-oxide layer that the company called "charge trap flash." Samsung claimed this technique would allow it to scale NAND down to the 20nm node more easily.

Taking another approach, Hitachi Ltd. and Renesas Technology Corp. reported a refinement in their ongoing efforts to develop a phase-change memory technology. The novelty of the design lay in its use of an interfacial layer of tantalum pentoxide between the plug that connects to a MOS (metal oxide semiconductor) transistor and the phase-change film, which is a standard germanium antimony tellurium chalcogenide alloy. According to these firms, the technology will lead to a new class of advanced MCUs (microcontroller unit) by the end of the decade.

In February 2007, Samsung presented more details on another type of phase-change memory, dubbed "phase-change RAM" (PRAM). Samsung said it had developed a working 512Mbit PRAM based on a 90nm process. Geared as an eventual replacement for the NOR flash, a PRAM is similar to the technology used in CDs and CD drives. In a PRAM, an electrical current heats a chalcogenide film to either a crystalline or an amorphous state, each with very different electrical resistivity.

Samsung also moved in a completely different direction by combining today's NAND technology with 3D stacking techniques.

The company has demonstrated an ultra-dense flash-memory device by stacking 32 GB NAND cell arrays, or structures, on top of each other with 63nm dimensions. This is done by implementing a single-crystal-layer stacking technology. The NAND cell arrays are formed on the interlayer dielectric, thereby doubling the density without increasing the chip size. The technology is said to scale beyond the 30nm node. Samsung is highly dedicated to finding the right technology, including looking at solutions in 3D technologies as well as non-silicon technologies on a molecular scale.

The 2007 semiconductor conference confirmed the opinion of many at a previous conference that, at the end, only two semiconductor companies will be competing in this area—Samsung and Intel. Because the full cost of a new line was now more than US$3 billion, many of the bigger chip-design companies could no longer justify their own investment.

On the demand side, the market was still strong, as shown in the case of Apple, where applications for iPod and iPhone helped underpin the demand. In 2005, Apple booked 40 percent of Samsung's NAND production for its iPod and a similar situation lined up for the iPhone. The Apple–Samsung relationship also well illustrates the "sleeping with the enemy" dilemma. Samsung had limited interest in iPods because its main success escaped as iRiver, as will be related in the next chapter. The iPhone is a direct challenge to Samsung's core mobile product. Apple's mobile phone venture will be powered by Samsung technology but will cannibalize part of Samsung's core market, first in the US and then, if successful, the rest of the world. Samsung as a telecommunications company will have to fight tooth and nail against Samsung as a semiconductor company.

Either way, if Samsung Semiconductors wins, Samsung as a telecommunications company loses and *vice versa*. But the group is riding on a tiger's back—getting off in any direction may be dangerous. The situation is quite different for Samsung's rival Hynix, whose plant is located just 30 kilometers away from that of Samsung. Unlike Samsung's dilemma, Hynix can only win from Apple's success.

Samsung is firmly on top of several of the new technologies which, like DRAM, will become household words in the near future, but no one is sure of the scale of future development. As for Sony, even though its R&D could play with this technology, it seems unlikely it would make a US$1 billion bet on a production line of its own.

At the time of its alliance with Avaya in February 2006, Samsung Electronics described itself as one of the fastest-growing global brands.[28] This ceased to be true by 2007. By succeeding as a leader in the electronics market, it had climbed to the top of a slippery pole. Its challenge is to stay on top.

As at 2005 Samsung could claim to have the perfect balance of core products and consumer products recognition. It could describe itself as being composed of five main business units: digital appliance business, digital media business, LCD business, semiconductor business, and telecommunications network business. Recognized as one of the fastest-growing global brands, Samsung Electronics was a leading producer of digital TVs, memory chips, mobile phones, and TFT-LCDs.

But in an industry in which technology changes every three months, did Samsung retain the nimbleness to exploit this lead? Was its rise to success a combination of good strategy, good management, good technological portfolio choice and good luck? If that was the case, all these needed to continue. If the world markets were about to go into recession, how could a company which relied on other companies to sell to end-users support its own business?

Endnotes

1   I am indebted to Jang Gyeong-deok, J. H. Shin and Ferdinand B. Ventura, my 2005 students at KDI School, for assistance in this chapter and, in particular, in formulating the title.
2   "The Next Electronics Giant?" by Charles Cooper, *Cnet News*, November 5, 2003, at: http://news.cnet.com/The-next-electronics-giant/2008-1041_3-5102413.html
3   SEC, *Annual Report 2007*.
4   "Sony Jilts Samsung for Sharp in LCD Panel Production," by Shu-Ching Jean Chen, *Forbes*, February 26, 2008.
5   Ibid.
6   "Sony, Samsung Strengthen Their LCD Panel Venture," Market Scan, Forbes. com, March 4, 2008.
7   "Sony Samsung Joint Venture Opens Giant LCD Line, Will Produce 70,000 Substrates Monthly," HCC News Team, June 2, 2009: http://www.homecinemachoice.com/blogs/team+hcc/sony+samsung+joint+venture+opens +giant+lcd+line+will+produce+70000+substrates+monthly.
8   See note 6.
9   Ibid.
10 See note 7.

11   Hamel, Gary and Prahalad, C. K. 1994, *Competing for the Future*, Cambridge, MT: Harvard Business School Press: 215.

12   Ibid.

13   Mathews, John A. and Cho, Dong-Sung 2000, *Tiger Technology: The Creation of a Semiconductor Industry in East Asia*, Cambridge University Press: 389.

14   Cooper, op. cit.

15   Samsung Electronics, Investor Briefing 2009, at: http://www.samsung.com/us/aboutsamsung/ir/ireventpresentations/earningsrelease/downloads/2008/20090424_conference_eng.pdf; accessed May 20, 2008.

16   "South Korea Company: Reign of the 'Chaos-Maker,'" by Andrew Ward, *Financial Times*, March 13, 2003. http://www.eiu.com/index.asp?layout=VWArticleVW3&article_id=1525979352&country_id=1590000159&channel_id=180004018&category_id=280004028&refm=vwCat&page_title=Article&rf=0

17   http://www.samsung.com/us/aboutsamsung/companyprofile/majorstrategicalliances/CompanyProfile_MajorStrategicAlliances.html; accessed July 2007 plus later additions.

18   "Next-gen Memory in the Limelight,"*EE Times India*, February 2, 2007, at: http://www.eetindia.co.in/ART_8800451715_1800009_NT_59998f26.HTM; accessed June 6, 2007.

19   "Companies, People, Ideas: Samsung's Next Act," by Heidi Brown and Justin Doebele, *Forbes*, July 26, 2004.

20   Dr. Hwang Chang-gyu, "The Role of Semiconductors in the Next IT Era," talk presented at the Massachusetts Room of the Mullins Center, University of Massachusetts, Amherst, April 14, 2004; at: http://www.ecs.umass.edu/tang/tangseries5.html

21   The nanometer is the most common unit to describe the wavelength of light, with visible light falling in the region of 400nm–700nm, and the industry standard measurement for semiconductors.

22   KT, 2007 May.

23   "Universal Memory Market to hit $75 Billion in 2019 Says iSuppli," by Peter Clarke, *EETimes*, July 27, 2005.

24   Brown and Doebele, op. cit.

25   Ibid.

26   See note 18 and "Memory Quest Goes 'Universal': With Market up for Grabs, Next-Gen Contenders Vie for Spotlight at IEDM," by Mark LaPedus, *EE Times*, December 18, 2006.

27   Ibid.

28   See http://www.avaya.com/gcm/master-usa/en-us/corporate/pressroom/press-releases/2006/pr-060228.htm

8

Retaining Creativity and Avoiding Bureaucracy

As we are fully aware that remaining satisfied with the current achievement will only set us back, we will renew our sense of crisis by returning to the basics and strengthening the fundamentals, as we did so with drastic restructuring efforts post the financial crisis of 1997.

Yun Jong-yong[1]

Inadvertently slipping into aristocracy

According to Adizes' life-cycle theory, companies that are successful and long-established but are in the stable (that is, the early aging) phase, have a tendency to slip into aristocracy. This is particularly true in a company where the management has been running the business for a long time and is in need of fresh blood. This is not evident to the company, because it is still outstandingly successful financially. Within the ranks, there is a group of senior managers who think they have "earned" their right to be in the positions they hold, and they resent newcomers and outsiders. After this aristocratic phase comes ossification and early bureaucracy.[2] In the Korean setting, there is a greater inclination to fall into the trap of aristocracy and bureaucracy—bureaucracy and hierarchy are, after all, written into Korean corporate DNA, and some of the core behavioral code which Adizes describes as "aristocratic" is present even in very young companies.

While American companies are heirs to a frontier ethos, Korean companies have inherited 1,000 years of bureaucracy. Traditionally, in Korean history and culture, bureaucracy and aristocracy were intertwined.[3] The Confucian system encourages an aristocracy of the old. Korean companies, in short, are bureaucracy-prone. In describing Samsung Electronics as a product of Korean resourcefulness in outrunning these tendencies, there is also a corollary that if the company stops running, the bureaucracy will take over.

Yun had always been aware of the dangers of complacency. Having transformed Samsung Electronics during a time of crisis in a way that would not have been possible in times of economic stability, he is acutely aware that at any moment bureaucracy rather than creativity might begin to dominate, especially following the extraordinary success of the company in recent years. This is why he instituted his culture of "continual crisis" to prevent this possibility. His 2007 message to shareholders repeated the need to get back to basics:

> We are now standing near the top with an ambitious goal and vision to be a world premier company. As we are fully aware that remaining satisfied with the current achievement will only set us back, we will renew our sense of crisis by returning to the basics and strengthening the fundamentals, as we did so with drastic restructuring efforts post the financial crisis of 1997.[4]

When Jack Welch became the head of General Electric, he formulated a policy to "nuke the bureaucracy." The "Neutron Jack" era lasted six years as Welch struggled to remove the bureaucratic tendencies that beset American companies in the 1980s. Leaders found that the only way to control bureaucracy was to be eternally vigilant. Yun found that he could counter open bureaucratic tendencies in the senior management directly through argument, through demonstrating success, through employing outsiders like Eric Kim, and by globalizing the operation. He could also influence the lower levels of the company by employing young people of considerable creativity. In this he had the full backing of his chairman, Lee Kunhee. But neither he nor Lee could control the counter-indoctrination of young recruits, or the minds of middle managers, or the secret challenges to his ideas among his senior management. Despite his belief that an inbred cultural ability to deal with crises can indeed become a competitive edge over companies that are less agile in dealing with disaster, this was not a philosophy shared by everyone in the company.[5] As Samsung Electronics became more global there were many older Koreans who resented the new prominence given to voices from outside Korea.

Korean voice versus global voice

By the 1990s, there was a generation gap in every Korean company and this was the source of problems. In 1999, Lee Kun-hee acknowledged that "in an organization as big as Samsung, some friction is bound to exist," but that was much less than a year earlier because "throughout the downsizing process, a significant part of the older generation has left the company."[6] Lee and Yun's solution to the difficulties was not to argue with the older generation but to persuade them to leave the company.

From the moment that Yun became CEO in 1996, there were arguments about what was appropriate for Samsung Electronics. During the period of downsizing and in 1997–98 reform, the dissenting voices were muted. Older, conservative Koreans felt that they were being held responsible for the crisis which had descended unforeseen on the Korean system. But as the reforms progressed and the global (American and American–Korean) voice increased, the Korean voice also became more pronounced. Even in marketing where the global voice predominated, the Korean voice was represented by Cheil Keweik, the Samsung agency which liaised with FCB, the international agency appointed by the company. In particular, the large fees earned by FCB were regarded jealously.

By 2007, the sources of disagreement had shifted somewhat. The generational differences were still there but the increasing number of foreigners working for Samsung stirred things a little more. At first, the introduction of foreign engineers did not appear to greatly disturb Samsung's Korean executives. Recruiting the brightest and best from global business schools at high salaries for a year did not matter too much. But hiring Korean–Americans and challenging the core of the Korean corporation's DNA did. Letting Samsung America dictate marketing policy also irked Koreans. It is always a mistake to underestimate the power of the old system in any Korean company, even those which are foreign-managed and owned.

At the end of May 2007, an internet letter, entitled "The reason I quit (the) Samsung that I love," posted on the Samsung Corporation bulletin board highlighted the problem. A young Samsung man had resigned after a year of working for the company. His reason: the enormous strength of conservative forces resisting change, despite Samsung companies having the pick of the best Koreans in the country as its employees.[7] In his post, he likened the company's failure to take the necessary decisive action to deal with its problems to the metaphorical frog in the boiling pot, where the frog tries to compensate for the heat by swimming around the pot, rather than jumping out.

Retaining creativity

In his 2007 message to shareholders, Yun set out his third goal for Samsung as focusing on creativity. He talked about Samsung's need for new values, its need to develop a corporate culture of innovation and self-development in its quest to be a world-class company. This, he said, could be achieved by "creative management."[8]

What is creative management in the Samsung context? "Creative management is really a big shift from the past, where we were very Korean and very focused on efficiency through uniformity," vice president Chu Woo-sik told the *Financial Times (FT)* in August 2007.[9] Former Samsung employees also told the *FT* that the company's culture was its biggest enemy, describing a strict Confucian culture which emphasized discipline and hierarchy at the expense of encouraging creativity. One was quoted as saying: "There's no deviation allowed in any form, and there is no free talk."[10]

This is a far cry from the creation of the "Samsung Man" described in Chapter 5. In reality, what Samsung needed was a culture that was supported by both middle and senior management, so that creativity and competency would not get pushed out by those who resisted change.

Knowledge management and the escape of knowledge

Samsung's Suwon campus is a fortress into which mobile phones, memory sticks, floppy disks, and notebooks are not allowed. Nor are staff allowed to access the internet-based email services or withdraw papers from the company. English teachers arriving to polish the English of Samsung executives are not permitted to carry any textbooks or printed material into the Samsung grounds, nor can files be sent to or from Samsung language students. This may seem like paranoia but at the heart of this policy is the need to protect the company's intellectual property from seeping out.

What Samsung cannot do, however, is stop its employees from leaving the company and taking with them essential know-how. Eric Kim took invaluable ideas on marketing when he moved to Intel. Another good example of the problems that can arise is to be found in ReignCom Ltd., founded by a group of ex-Samsung employees— Yang Duk-jun, Lee Rae-hwan, and five others who left Samsung Electronics in 2000. ReignCom was originally set up as a semiconductor distributor, with Yang as CEO, but later decided to capitalize on the growing market for MP3 players. Yang had worked for Samsung Electronics for 20 years but was frustrated by its culture.

The group decided to depart from the Korean obsession with owning a factory and outsourced its manufacturing to AV Chaseway, located in Shenzhen, China. While keeping its R&D in-house, it contracted product design to INNO Design, an industrial-design company in Palo Alto, California.[11] Using the old route of producing for other OEMs, ReignCom started its own brand, iRiver, which became one of the best-known brands among young people and became the most popular MP3 player in the US before the launch of iPod. iRiver still had more than 50 percent of the Korean market in 2008.

In losing two talented employees, Yang and Lee, and their business ideas, Samsung also lost the opportunity to add a potential US$500 million to its revenues. The company gained some form of revenge, though, when it supplied flash memory for Apple's iPod, which destroyed iRiver's dominance in the US. A glance at iRiver's website shows the dedication to creativity and designing "products with the ability to change and enrich the life of an individual. To this end, the day-to-day lives of each and every one of our customers have served as the engine powering our creativity."[12]

Yang and Lee were not the only ones leaving Samsung. In contrast to the devoted workers described in Chapter 6, by 2003 Samsung was finding it difficult to find Koreans at the factory level, however highly paid, who had the same outlook as those who helped start the company 20 years earlier.

In March every year, Samsung's blue-collar female technicians resign in large numbers to attend college. In 2003, 285 out of 3,500 female workers at the Chonan semiconductor plant resigned, despite having received record year-end bonuses of between 5–10 million *won* (approximately US$5,000–10,000). The head of HR for the factory told *The Chosun Ilbo*: "There was a time in the mid-1990s when Samsung asked technical schools to send it students whose grades come in the top 30 percent, but now, we are just grateful if the schools send us any students."[13] Koreans no longer wanted to work in factories, nor give their jobs the devotion that a previous generation had given them.

The generation gap was also evident in work attitudes: between what the company expects from an employee, and what Samsung's younger generation want out of their work. Experienced employees resigned for a job which offers a lower salary but a better work-life balance. Workers were no longer prepared to feel guilty when they want to take time off at the weekend instead of working. In the R&D center at Suwon, work from 8am to 10pm was still common in 2007, including every Saturday and one or two Sundays per month. It was also common for staff not to go home at all, but to sleep near the company campus. In general, the present generation of Koreans does not expect to work this hard. If they do, they expect either overtime pay, or year-end bonuses related to their own perceptions of their individual performance. Their seniors see this as a kind of disloyalty to the company and to their elders who worked with far fewer complaints. The demand for talent is, however, creating a problem for Samsung Electronics. These talented people can easily leave and find work elsewhere. There is no high unemployment in Korea or a sense of obligation to stay with one employer for life. Koreans no longer seem to share the attitude expressed in the 1980s by a Samsung Electronics engineer on learning that Americans worked only eight hours a day, five days a week: "He smiles. He is envious of that. So why is it worth working so much harder, for less money? 'Because you don't measure your success against Americans,' he says, 'you measure it against the last generation of Koreans . . . If our generation doesn't work hard . . . the next generation will suffer.'"[14]

Younger Koreans are also rapidly disconnecting from the values of the older generation. Increasingly, Koreans are comparing themselves to Americans and Europeans, and they do not feel the need to sacrifice their life for their work: the concept of a

68-hour work week has lost its appeal. In 2007 *The Korea Times* cited a report by a recruitment firm that showed that the average tenure of a Samsung Electronics worker was only 6.4 years, compared to an 11.8-year average among 100 Korean firms surveyed. Hyundai Motors had an average of 14.9 years and POSCO 19 years. Perhaps a better peer comparison would be the 7.4 years seen at LG Electronics, indicating a higher number of job opportunities for electronics workers.[15]

For Samsung—a company which has invested so much time creating the Samsung Man culture—this is a disastrous record. Employees stated that they were also disenchanted by the lack of a union to voice their views.

The emergence of a generation gap is not exclusive to Samsung, but a growing trend in Korea. In most companies adjustments are taking place. The change is a bit more difficult at Samsung Electronics because of its strong and conservative culture. The younger generation is often pitched against managers in their 40s or 50s who are used to the stoicism of working long hours.

Samsung's HR communication on its core values is lost on the older generation. It was still very much an uphill battle creating an open culture (where seniors and juniors are encouraged to act based on mutual respect and trust). The aspiration for change and innovation to pursue Samsung's vision is also lost on many of the workers. One way the company dealt with the need for talent renewal was to remove older workers. In 2007, the company took the bold move of announcing the option for older workers to retire. One media report in August 2007 said that Samsung Electronics was taking applications for early retirement from a number of mid-level staffers, based on lists of target employees selected by each division.[16]

This was the first reduction of its kind since 2,000 section chiefs and upper-level employees were laid off in 2003. The company's workforce was reported as being agitated because they knew that layoffs are usually followed by personnel reshuffles.

Samsung Electronics' Suwon Complex (the company's R&D center) alone was reported to have received about 400 applications for early retirement in three stages from May to July 2007, based on a list of targeted employees. In addition to severance pay, Samsung was said to have paid each early retiree one year's salary and a bonus of between 10 million to 20 million Korean *won* (US$1 = 923 *won*). Several more rounds of early retirement were held in 2007.

A worker at the Suwon Complex told *The Chosun Ilbo*: "Unlike in the past, the company is taking applications for early retirement without giving us opportunities to work at subsidiary or affiliate companies. So those subject to this measure are all the more upset."[17] Unlike in the past, during 2007–08, the company quietly slashed personnel from its business divisions (semiconductors, telecommunications networks, and digital media) in several stages for an extended period. Samsung Group's corporate restructuring office said there was no uniform restructuring plan (such as a 10 percent layoff) for the group's subsidiaries. "We are reviewing ways to enhance each subsidiary's competitiveness according to their circumstances," the office said.[18] In 1998, the year after the country was placed on the IMF bailout program, Samsung Electronics had instigated about 1,500 early retirements.[19]

Now was the time to create task forces which would shake up the culture and add business value to each business and Samsung insiders said subsidiaries were now operating taskforces to develop a future growth engine and adjust investment according to the added value yielded by each. To enhance its competitive edge, Samsung was also pushing to improve its corporate culture, including swifter decision-making, nurturing creative talent, and revitalizing the organization.[20] Yun was pushing for this restructuring to try to renovate the company, not realizing that his own performance was under review and that resistance to this continuous reform was also reaching a head among the "aristocracy." The growth model that he had adopted, they muttered, was flawed, and it was running out of steam.

Moving abroad

One way Samsung Electronics dealt with the shackles of its cultural problems was to move abroad. Indeed, it had been one of the first Korean companies to establish a venture abroad—a joint venture television factory in Portugal in the 1970s. During the first half of 2007, Lee Kun-hee twice issued a warning that Korea faced a critical future sandwiched between low-cost China and hi-tech Japan. In his view, Korea's industrial might would be decimated by the twin effects brought on by China and Japan. He gave no specific reason for issuing his warnings, but one must see them as a consequence of the pressures Samsung had been experiencing in recent years.

The "Republic of Samsung," as it is often described in the Korean press, has one advantage over the Republic of Korea. In the last decade it had become a truly global organization and does not need to stay on the peninsula. In an article on Korea's dying industries in 2003, *The Chosun Ilbo* had cited Samsung among many Korean companies building their next-generation plant in China or closing down their factories in Korea:

> Samsung Electronics has over 80 percent of its production facilities abroad. Almost 60 percent of Samsung's refrigerators, air conditioners, and other household goods are made outside of Korea. The basis of production for high-tech manufactured goods is currently being moved to China, as well. Up to 30 percent of the firm's TFT-LCDs was reported to have been transferred to China starting in 2004.[21]

According to *The Chosun Ilbo*'s count, Samsung had 26 factories overseas, five of them completed in 2003; and seven in Korea, with no new plants for over four years. To give Samsung credit, it had tried to invest US$18 billion in a new semiconductor plant in Suwon, but the government had refused permission on environmental/planning grounds. Samsung, which understood the benefits of agglomeration, also knew what this refusal would cost the company. "Korean investors are seeking profits elsewhere, as uncertain policies, restrictions, powerful labor unions, high wages and an anti-corporate culture reign in the country," the newspaper concluded.[22]

Greg Lee, Eric Kim's successor, made this move overseas a core marketing element when he told an audience in Dubai that Samsung, with US$4.5 billion invested in China, was the second-largest investor there. Samsung had production facilities in 19 countries, he said, including China. In 2007, the company's 14 subsidiaries in China produced more than US$20 billion in sales and it was claimed that Samsung was both the largest foreign investor in China and the largest exporter.[23]

As noted in the previous chapter, Samsung Electronics began moving its main mobile phone production base to Vietnam in 2008. The annual sales output of Samsung's cell-phone unit was estimated at 17 trillion Korean *won* in 2007–08. By 2007, Korea's largest phone-maker had already stopped recruiting new staff for its local plant in Gumi, which employed some 700 to 800 people a year. Samsung Electronics' global sourcing system meant abandoning its reliance on the Gumi plant, even for domestic production. As part of the new strategy, Samsung began building its plant in Vietnam in the fourth quarter of 2007 and completed it in late 2008. This will eventually shift the firm's phone production base, already partly based in China, abroad. The Gumi plant maintained a transitional role. In 2006, Samsung produced a total of 130 million mobile phones, about 80 million (62 percent) at the Gumi plant. The plant in China produced 45 million units, or 35 percent of total production.

In 2008, Samsung's domestic production accounted for less than 40 percent. Annual production at the new Vietnam plant at Bac Nui—which was licensed in March 2008 and began operating in mid-2009, earlier than expected—was planned to be 100 million phones. Production in China was also to rise to about 100 million in 2008.[24] A mobile phone industry insider told a Korean newspaper that Samsung had decided that its domestic plant is unattractive as a production base because labor costs are over 10 times higher than in Southeast Asia.

This was not the first time Samsung Electronics had moved production overseas. But the nature of plant transfers has changed. Around the year 2000, when the exodus started, plants that moved overseas were simple assembly lines for electrical home appliances. Despite the high wages, cutting-edge industries, such as cell phones, LCDs, and semiconductors, remained in Korea because of their high profitability and fears of a technology drain. Samsung's latest decision opened up a vista where any production could move abroad. During the 2000–07 period, industrial employment had grown in Korea, despite the rapid build-up of capacity at Korean plants overseas, but this move was taken as a sign that this era of Korea's development was about to come to an end.[25]

Already, Samsung's decision to stop hiring in Gumi meant that 800 jobs effectively disappeared in 2007. Conservative Korean newspapers observed: "When Samsung's plants in China and India are poised to produce 60 million more phones than they do now, another 2,000 to 3,000 jobs will be created overseas instead of Korea."[26]

By 2007, Korean industry analysts realized this was going to become a trend. "Tech-savvy component companies will build their own plants in Vietnam or China following in the footsteps

Operating data of entities classified according to geographic
area as of and for the year ended December 31, 2007

(In millions of Korean won)

	2007 Summary of Business by Geographic Area							
	Korea		Americas	Europe	Asia	China	Elimination	Consolidated
	Domestic	Export						
Gross sales	W 18,962,111	W 57,414,865	W 31,657,811	W 41,703,043	W 23,668,887	W 35,184,906	W(110,083,806)	W 98,507,817
Intersegment sales	(4,788,207)	(50,449,491)	(12,089,350)	(14,751,677)	(7,928,861)	(20,076,220)	110,083,806	-
Net sales	W 14,173,904	W 6,965,374	W 19,568,461	W 26,951,366	W 15,740,026	W 15,108,686	-	W 98,507,817
Operating profit	W 6,819,490		W 206,549	641,551	W 326,685	W 723,686	W 252,325	W 8,973,286
Total assets	W 84,014,706		W 10,458,239	W 10,877,916	W 5,593,774	W 7,798,092	W(25,367,591)	W 93,375,136

Figure 8.1 Consolidated accounts for Samsung Electronics 2007

Note: for further details see Appendix 2.

of Samsung Electronics," said Song Myung-sup, an analyst at CJ Investment & Securities. "Those who don't will be dealt a severe blow."[27] Daishin Securities analyst Kim Gang-oh added: "Domestic companies will also speed up globalization of component production, because they will have to compete with international companies capable of securing cheaper parts." Strategies to advance into growing markets will accelerate the development, he added.[28]

Samsung now gave greater emphasis to its global production by offering a consolidated set of accounts as an appendix to its annual report which gives the following information as shown in Figure 8.1.

The table shows that by 2007 Samsung's exports were mainly not finished products, but components and sub-assemblies which poured into Samsung factories and other companies factories in the rest of the world, and that the final product was sold fairly evenly across the globe, with Europe taking the highest share, followed almost equally by the Americas, Asia, China and the Korean domestic market itself. Samsung's consolidated sales therefore equaled 93.4 trillion *won* (US$98.3 billion, which made Samsung's total global sales about 45 percent larger than Samsung's Korean corporate return which has been used as the basis of comparison with Sony in Chapter 3.

Products versus marketing

During the 2005–08 period, the engineers had tended to shift out the marketers. The team from Samsung America was gone. Compared with Eric Kim, Greg Lee kept a low profile, and sports marketing was all the rage. The engineers inside Samsung were not the only ones to eschew marketing and believe that products were the core of Samsung's success. Cambridge engineers shared the same vision. The story of Samsung's transition from imitator to innovator formed a case study in a recently completed IMF research project which identified that the roots of Samsung's achievements could be traced to strategic, coherent and consistent management in three key areas: R&D, organization and production.

The study concluded that R&D had been central to Samsung's success—but Samsung had pioneered a unique collaborative culture between product and process technology development. "Process technologies are afforded the same significance as product technologies, and development groups work closely together with regular weekly meetings." When research trails ran cold in either product or process technology, they were not abandoned but kept in view, so that they could be incorporated in future developments as opportunities arose. From a production point of view, in particular, Samsung was pioneering not just products but production processes. The study picked out two key features of this process—fluid organization and an integrated approach:

> Organization structure is designed around the rapid dissemination and exploitation of expertise across the company. Individuals move freely between product and process technology groups and the manufacturing group maintains a close watch on expertise and its deployment. This allows the interactions between product-based and process-based technologies to be understood very early in project cycles. Production capability [and] rapid production process development are enhanced by well-structured R&D and integrated organization, but also developed as a specific capability.[29]

The commissioning of new and complex production lines requires many small-scale but critical technology developments and rapid calibration, and balancing of interdependent processes.[30]

The study's findings continued:

> There is, of course, no single reason for business success, but the Samsung example illustrates how

effective integration of product and process development and rapid production ramp-up can contribute
to a devastating strategic position. A position which is
respected by Samsung's major global competitors. It
is interesting to reflect whether Samsung would have
been so successful if it had adopted the current fashion
for outsourcing its production.[31]

There was no doubt that there was innovation and creativity in the product and production process. But the company's core
period of development in marketing creativity was the Eric Kim era
and the trajectory it inspired. By mid-2006 the innovation effect of
the branding and marketing had departed. The problems revealed
by the Interbrand analysis showed in 2007–08 that the momentum
of 2000 to 2006 was over and Samsung did not know what to do.

In 2007, creativity was officially back high on the company's
agenda. Subsidiaries were all putting together taskforces to search
for a future growth engine and to adjust investment according to
the added value each business yielded.[32] This in itself was a reflec-
tion on the way that the restructuring of Samsung Electronics
during 2005–06 to increase the independence of divisions had led
to a waste of resources, exactly as it had in Sony. It was also based
round the idea that growth engines were product-driven and not
marketing-driven. By November 2007, Samsung came up with a list
of new product drivers. "The upcoming possible 'money sources'—
printers, system LSI units, WiBro mobile Internet technologies,
energy and bio technologies, healthcare and robot businesses—
were announced amid stalled growth of its core businesses—chips,
handsets, and LCD TVs—and falling stock prices."[33]

To enhance its competitive edge, Samsung was now once
again pushing improvement of its corporate culture. It should be
noted, though, that the cultural crisis was not confined to Samsung
Electronics alone. It was one that afflicted the entire Samsung Group,
if not Korea itself, since what was true of Samsung was true of many
other large Korean organizations. But Samsung had been able to
hold back time more effectively, and its workplace culture could be
said to have changed less than in most other companies. By May
2008, the company would tell its investors that it would continue its
efforts to "restructure a company respected and admired by people
around the world" and would "systematically implement our new

management structure by emphasizing transparency, compliance and greater sensitivity to customer needs, thereby fulfilling our social responsibilities as a company growing hand-in-hand with shareholders, customers and business partners."[34] What the company did not tell its shareholders, though, was that included in this change was the retirement of its CEO, Yun, who had led the company for 12 years, a month before the report was issued.

Endnotes

1   2007 message to shareholders, Annual Report 2006.
2   Adizes, Ichak 1988, *Corporate Lifecycles*, Paramus, NJ: Prentice Hall: 65–79.
3   Michell, Tony 1986, "Confucianism and Generational Change," Royal Asiatic Society: 97–130.
4   Samsung Electronics, Annual Report 2006 (published May 2007).
5   *Fortune*, September 5, 2005, No. 15.
6   In an interview with Laxmi Nakarmi for *Asiaweek*, November 12, 1999
7   *Korea Times*, June 7, 2007 at: www.koreatimes.co.kr/www/news/include/print. asp?newsIdx=4315
8   2007 message to shareholders, Annual Report 2006.
9   Quoted in "Samsung Searches for 'Killer App,'" by Anna Fifield, *Financial Times*, August 22, 2007.
10 Ibid.
11 www.iriver.com/ceo story, accessed May 20, 2009
12 Ibid.
13 "Job Market Chills in the Second Half," by Song Eui-dal, *Digital Chosun* July 23, 2003.
14 Magaziner, Ira and Patinkin, Mark 1990, *The Silent War*, New York: Vintage Books: 36.
15 *Korea Times*, June 7, 2007.
16 "Samsung Electronics Starts Personnel Reduction," englishnews@chosun. com, August 8, 2007; accessed June 27, 2009.
17 Ibid.
18 Ibid.
19 Ibid.
20 "Samsung Head Urges Execs for More Growth," *Digital Chosun*, July 30, 2007; "Samsung Anguishes Over How to Remain Competitive," by Lee Kang-hoe, July 20, 2007; "Samsung Must Lead Us into the Future," by Rhee Dong-kee, July 18, 2007; accessed August 30, 2007.
21 Song, op. cit.
22 Ibid.
23 Michell, Tony and Lee, Julia 2008, unpublished research on Samsung Electronics in China.
24 "Samsung Ships Cell Phones to UAE," at: http://vietnamnews.vnagency. com.vn/showarticle.php?num=01ECO120609; June 12, 2009, accessed June 27, 2009.

25 Michell, Tony, "Korean Industrial Growth 2000–2007," presentation to the Korea Business Forum in February 2008. The slide in the Korean *won* from April 2008 also slowed down this tendency.

26 englishnews@chosun.com; updated May 15, 2007.

27 "Samsung Electronics to Go Abroad," englishnews@chosun.com; updated May 15, 2007.

28 Ibid.

29 www-mmd.eng.cam.ac.uk/cim/projects_imit_innov

30 Ibid.

31 Ibid.

32 Evidently, vice chairman Yun was not satisfied with these teams and created a new one, with himself as chairman. See "Special Samsung Team to Sniff Out New Ideas," *Digital Chosun*, November 15, 2007.

33 "Samsung Looks to Future With New Drivers," by Kim Yoo-chul, *Korea Times*, November 29, 2007.

34 Samsung Electronics, Annual Report 2007 (published May 2008).

9

The Crisis of Samsung Electronics: The Descent into Bureaucracy

The ideal chief executive must be capable of "flawless planning" and have a strong drive for action, "whether it be forward or retreat."[1]

Waking in the wood: Exchange rates and competitors

The aging of Samsung Electronics and the strength of the aristocracy created the debate on what to do next, described in the previous chapter, when Samsung's growth momentum and profitability had slowed down. The next stage in Adizes' representation of the corporate life cycle is bureaucracy, which is dominated by a search for who to blame for the wrong decisions. The debate centered around whether it was a failure of Samsung Electronics to be nimble enough and to be more global—which was Yun's view and one shared to a large degree by his chairman—or a failure to stick to the knitting and produce better products as the "Korean voice" within Samsung's management insisted. The sacrificial lamb chosen was one of the golden figures in the Samsung Electronics engine room, Dr. Hwang Chang-gyu, head of the memory division (the largest of the four divisions), because the Korean voice could not yet reach Vice Chairman Yun.

The period between 2006 and the first half of 2008 was not as kind to Samsung Electronics as the 2002–05 era. Profits and revenue from semiconductors flagged, reminding the company of its own mortality. Worse, the exchange rate moved strongly against Korean exporters as the Korean *won* strengthened against the US dollar. Likewise, the constant friction between the Republic of Korea and the "Republic of Samsung" continued. Old competitors such as Nokia fought back, using the same forces that had helped Samsung rise so fast, and new competitors gnawed at the company's market. More than that, Samsung was at the frontier of the electronics digital revolution, where the next step might be over the precipice. Within the company, the Korean voice continued to criticize the global voice. The new organizational structure based on product divisions, adopted in 2006, made it more difficult to reach consensus, just as it had plagued Sony in previous years.

Korea had managed to gain a huge competitive advantage when, in December 1997, the Korean *won* was allowed to have a free float against the dollar. In the world money markets, the *won* was almost one-third of its pre-crisis value before recovering to about 60 percent of its former value. However, this did not last forever.

Despite it having an instant current account surplus and falling debt, the world's money market had not pushed Korea's currency far from its 1998 year-end value of 1,206 *won* against the dollar until 2004. During 2005 and 2006, the *won* surged against the dollar and by 2007–08 it was hovering in the 920–930 range, compared to 800 seen during mid-1997 before the crisis. This 15 percent margin was not enough to allow Korean companies to exploit the productivity gains to retain their profit margins, even where they moved offshore. Worse, the cross-rate against the yen had also recovered back to pre-crisis levels.[2]

Samsung wasn't able to benefit from the gentle appreciation of the Chinese *renminbi*—as Chinese exports slowed, so did the Korean components that went into Chinese-made products. Samsung had established itself as the largest or second-largest exporter in China before 2007. Demand from richer Chinese consumers for Korean goods only partly offset the overall fall in demand overseas. Korea's labor-input cost was also rising, further negating any profit margins. Korean blue-collar labor costs were now calculated on an hourly basis close to US levels, and 10 times the rate paid to Chinese production workers. Korean labor law also imposed heavy extra penalties and burdens on the employer, not dissimilar to the burden placed on auto companies in the US.

Despite the challenges, Samsung Electronics' operating profit had reached 7.9 trillion *won* (US$8.3 billion) on 59 trillion *won* in sales in 2006. In areas where competitors saw falling margins on semiconductors and LCD screens, Samsung maintained its profit margins by concentrating on the large-sized LCD sector. The Samsung brand value rose by US$1.1 billion. Compared to its competitors, Samsung seemed to be almost immune to the difficulties of the industry in 2006.

Hence, Yun was able to report to shareholders in May 2007 that Samsung had achieved super results by selecting the right market segments to compete in, by increasing R&D expenditure, and by improving on its technology. Among the company's key achievements in 2006, he reported, were that it had:

- **Received top margins in its semiconductor business**. In this business, the operating profit margin reached an industry-topping level of 26 percent as a result of strong sales of DRAM and lower costs in the production of NAND flash, despite a dramatic fall in prices.
- **Strengthened its global brand position.** Samsung handsets led the ultra-slim trend with the launch of the Ultra series, with high features.
- **Achieved the leading market share in the large LCD market.** Heavy investments paid off for Samsung which recorded outstanding profits and claimed 60 percent of the market share in the large (over 40 inches) TV panel market. Competitors had suffered from the steep decline of panel prices.
- **Ranked first in flat TVs, including LCD and PDP.** For the first time, the company took top ranking for its flat TVs, which took the largest overall TV market share. Its premium product, Bordeaux TV, was a global hit.

After presenting this rosy picture, Yun focused on the need to strengthen Samsung's foundations based on human resources, R&D, and brand value. To be a world-class company, the company had concentrated on building its core competencies by securing competent human resources, innovative technology, and differentiated brand value since it set its sight on being a world premier company in 2004.

One of the most impressive achievements, he felt, must be the company's heavy emphasis on recruiting R&D talent. The company had about 30,000 employees devoted to R&D, with an annual increase of 20 percent. R&D staff made up about 35 percent of the total workforce in Korea. Given this strong focus on R&D, Samsung was able to register more than 2,600 US patents in 2006, moving it into second position in the number of patents registered, up from fifth position in 2005.

Also, based on continuous investment in next-generation core technology, Samsung developed the world's first 50-nano 1 GB DRAM and 40-nano 32 GB NAND flash, and successfully commercialized WiBro, the next-generation wireless-communication technology.

According to the Interbrand/*BusinessWeek* joint survey, in 2006 Samsung's brand value rose to US$16.1 billion, up from US$15 billion the previous year. Yun told investors that this put the Samsung brand in tenth place among global companies, and seventh among global IT companies.

Despite these achievements, the management was worried that Samsung was, like the rest of the electronics industry, now moving into a falling profit cycle. The 2006 profit was against the much higher operating profit of 12.4 trillion *won* (US$12.4 billion) achieved in 2004.

Despite Yun's comments on the company's improved brand-value position, according to the Interbrand ranking, Samsung remained at its 2005 position of 20. Even though it was, according to Interbrand/*BusinessWeek's* commentary, rolling out hot LCD TVs and increasingly powerful memory chips, when it came to low-end handsets it was missing in action, and this was hurting its market share. The 8 percent growth in brand value was under threat.[3]

And for Samsung, now the third-largest electronics company in the world, to rank at only seventh place in global brand rankings of electronics companies seemed lower than its status warranted. The company seemed not only to have missed the market for the lower-end handsets, but to have begun to miss hitting consumers with the right marketing messages.

This became evident when the 2007 Interbrand results were published. The writing was on the wall—Samsung's brand value had risen only 4 percent, to US$16.9 billion, while its ranking had actually fallen one place, to twenty-first.[4] To add insult to injury, Sony's brand value had risen by 10 percent, pushing it up to twenty-fifth position. The Yun miracle appeared to be running out of steam.

The "sandwich" theory and the start of restructuring

By July 2007, the Samsung Group as a whole was feeling a sense of crisis as it was presented with the challenges of operating in a dynamic marketplace in multiple product and service areas. The focus had to be on gearing the company up for the fundamental shifts that were taking place in the global economy while responding to a multitude of competitors, old and new. Hence the initiator of change had to be the chairman, Lee Kun-hee, rather than Yun. As we saw earlier, Lee had mentioned several times in 2007 that South Korea, as well as Samsung, was in danger of being "sandwiched" between hi-tech Japan and cost-efficient China. Yun, with his typical enthusiasm to promote a sense of "continual crisis," leapt wholeheartedly into the chairman's campaign. *The Chosun Ilbo* reported that:

> Samsung Group has embarked on a restructuring drive, improving its management system and revamping its business structure. The group will review investment priorities, seek out new fields that will serve as its main growth engine over the next five to 10 years, create a global supply chain for components and get rid of waste. Samsung Group subsidiaries have already formed restructuring teams, and they have started working. There's even talk that the workforce at some subsidiaries will face major downsizing.[5]

The newspaper raised nationalistic concerns of how Korean Inc. could be outclassed or out-competed by China and Japan. Samsung's restructuring, it noted, could be the tip of greater problems faced by other Korean conglomerates:

> The average profit margin of the Korean electrical and electronics sector is 1.4 percent. That's less than one-third of the average 4.5 percent profit margin of the world's 100 largest businesses. The average profit margin of Korea's automotive, steel and chemicals sectors is also less than half the average of global companies. Declining profit margins are a trend that has been developing since 2000. It's not just a problem

involving the exchange rate or oil prices, but one that
involves the deteriorating competitiveness of our
key industries.[6]

Quoting Samsung Group chairman Lee Kun-hee, the paper
warned that the entire country faced extremely difficult conditions
in the next five or six years if Korea failed to find a new and sustain-
able line of business.

This last comment touched at the heart of the specific crisis
at Samsung Electronics. In departing from the branding strategy
of building a world in which the consumer looked to the Samsung
brand regardless of the product and its current marketing pursuits,
the company was now thrown back into the problem of the 1990s—
how to avoid dependence on a very few items. In the early years of
the new century, digital convergence seemed to be the answer as it
would throw an endless stream of products at the consumer, and the
company that understood digital convergence—Samsung—would
be the natural beneficiary.

If this was not the case, then Samsung Electronics needed a
new engine of growth and rumors came out of the fortress that
a crisis-driven search had begun. In mid-2007, Chu Woo-shik, head
of Samsung's investor relations, told the *Financial Times* that the
company was "still in a good position" but that there was a need to
overcome "some inertia because of our success." The company had,
he said, to "make the next transition . . . To do this we need to find
another business that is as good as components or semiconductors,
or we have to excel within our existing businesses."[7]

Indeed, it was semiconductors which weighed heavily on the
minds of the chairman and vice chairman.

Chairman Lee's warnings about the need for Korea to change
in 2007 could be seen partly as a warning to the nation; partly as
a warning to those within Samsung Group, including Samsung
Electronics, who were supporters of the Korean voice; and mainly
as a warning that Samsung itself was about to become more global.
Samsung Electronics' competitive advantage had to be in being more
global than its competitors. For all its Western competitors, the global
advantage was to be based in Asia (read "China"), as this was where
growth—and production—was happening. For the Koreans, though,
the China moment was already over. In 2005 and 2006, Korea, the

third-largest investor in China and already ahead of the US, switched dramatically to Southeast Asia and India, as shown in Figure 9.1.

The Koreans had calculated that the rise in basic labor in China and the strengthening *renminbi*, made other locations more attractive, particularly Vietnam. Of course, Korea would keep pace with the China market, but global production should now increasingly be in the ASEAN countries. For this reason, moving the mobile phone division to Vietnam was a bellwether for all Korean mobile phones.

In his announcements in 2007, Lee was not spotting a new trend but warning that the government would kill Korean industries if it didn't relax its anti-corporate culture. The media reaction was unsympathetic—the view was expressed that it was not Korea that was sandwiched, but Samsung and the other major-leaguers. On June 7, 2007 *Korea Times* noted: "The job to break this impasse falls on the top managers in these big companies that command the pool of the country's finest human resources."[8] The newspaper was of the view that Samsung had an important role to play in helping to pull the country out of its predicament: "To do so, it must jump out of the boiling pot first. Samsung should not underestimate its capability to change as it has done over the past few decades."[9]

Lee tried to tone down the media's hyperbole. At the end of July, he downplayed the imminence of the crisis that he had talked of in the previous months. "The reason I have kept mentioning 'crisis' is not because we are in a crisis situation now. What I have meant is that we must start preparing for big changes in the next four to five years," he said.[10] Being prepared, he said, would allow Samsung to transform "this potential crisis into an opportunity."

Full-scale restructuring?

Events belied these words. The Samsung Group announced in late July that it was trying to enhance its competitiveness by developing new growth engines and reprioritizing investment. The measures were, in effect, contingency measures to counter the effects of a lackluster semiconductor market. Samsung had made huge profits in semiconductors but this was fading fast in the face of unfavorable external conditions such as oil prices, the strong *won*, and strong competition globally in the DRAM memory-chip business which had

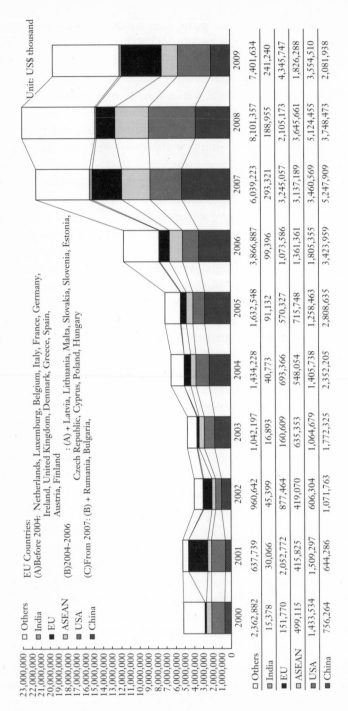

Figure 9.1   Korean overseas investment, 2000–09

Source: Korea Export Import Bank Overseas Economic Research Institute, KOREA

been Samsung's cash cow. Company officials tried to downplay the seriousness of the need for change, with one telling *The Chosun Ilbo*: "Samsung may adjust and rearrange some human resources and businesses, but it does not mean the large-scale layoff that some speculate."[11] The company had meanwhile started campaigns to reduce basic costs, one of which was switching off lights not in use.[12]

In August 2007, the Korean press announced that the Samsung Group was carrying out a group-wide restructuring. Rumors of a real crisis spread in the wake of an unexplained blackout at the Samsung Electronics semiconductor plant in Giheung, which cost the company an estimated US$50-million loss in production. *The Chosun Ilbo* told its readers that Samsung SDI and Samsung Electronics' Telecommunication Network had carried out a management evaluation earlier in the year and that Samsung Electronics' semiconductor business was about to go through the same process. The press noted that it was unusual for Samsung to evaluate its key business units in the same year. Based on the results of the evaluation of the Telecommunication Network, a structural reorganization was to take place. Meanwhile, Samsung Electronics' Suwon complex had sought and approved 400 volunteers for early retirement in a matter of a few months. These moves were more than regular restructuring efforts. Reorganization within the electronics unit was also picking up speed. Projects with greater chances of success were being concentrated within competitive affiliates. A case in point was the appointment of Samsung Electronics Digital Media president Park Jong-woo to oversee the Samsung Techwin (formerly Samsung Camera) digital camera unit, which had aspirations to become the number three in the world.

Along with the evaluations, Samsung businesses were drafting cost-cutting measures. On August 1, 2007 Samsung Electronics activated its crisis mode. These were really penny-pinching measures. At the time, it was hard to judge whether these measures were really needed or merely used to accentuate to employees the need for economy. Dormitory fees at the Hwaseong plant were doubled. The traditional gifts to employees for weddings and funerals was also scrapped. Paid long-service leave was severely cut back; holiday bonuses were scrapped; meal subsidies in the company cafeteria were cut; and restrictions were placed on paid overtime and transport allowances, leading to perceptions that employees were being pressured to finish their work during normal hours.[13]

Executives were feeling the pinch too, with overseas business trips being curtailed and restrictions being placed on the use of corporate credit cards. Of these moves, the Samsung Group said: "We only told the affiliates to cut down on unnecessary costs. Detailed guidelines and action plans are set within each affiliate."[14] This was Yun's "constant crisis" philosophy in action.

Managing the portfolio

In September 2005, Samsung Electronics had announced a dramatic investment plan of US$30 billion for new facilities over the coming years. This was at the time that Sony announced further losses and restructuring moves. The model for success for electronics in the twenty-first century requires concentration on a portfolio that produces profits. Samsung follows this portfolio. In contrast Sony is diversified, and in the wrong sectors. But the dilemma for Samsung is that its loss-making consumer products division provides brand leadership for the company's mobile sector. Its profit, however, lies in the semiconductor and LCD fields.

However, the profit margins of key products, such as mobile phones, semiconductors, and LCDs, were felt to have been declining for several years. Samsung's belief, as described in the previous chapter, was that there should be products which were new growth engines. The search had been going on, without any great urgency, for several years but without finding anything to replace semiconductor chips.

How should the product portfolio be managed? Eric Kim's model (like Sony's) had pushed towards to the endless production of new SKUs (stock keeping units) for consumers. On the other hand, the DRAMs and NAND and LCDs led towards an Intel model of market domination of what could otherwise be purely commodity products driven by price and not brand if not managed with care. But both of these approaches built profits rather than brands. One solution was to divide the company into divisions which would cherish their respective areas, but this was again the Sony model that led to senseless competition and misallocation of resources, especially in a Korean or Japanese context. A second approach—which was more in tune with Yun's views, those of Hwang Chang-gyu, president of the semiconductor division, and probably ultimately of the chairman himself—was to formulate a broad vision of the future that would allow for preemptive investments.

Yun had announced such a vision in 2002 when he spoke of an era of digital convergence. The extension of mobile phones into MP3s had been a dimension of this, and the Koreans believed that 3G phones would take this further, creating a new demand for high-quality semiconductors. Unfortunately, old cool Apple upstaged new cool Samsung. For the other consumer products, the convergence was still not happening and the laptop was becoming, with wifi, a challenge to the mobile phone. But Samsung had stayed out of the US laptop market and in September 2007 it announced it was withdrawing from the Australian market as well. In 2008, it retreated from Sony's home market, not only for laptops but all consumer products.[15]

Hwang Chang-gyu had a more coherent view of the future, though it was filled with continual stress from the endless demand for better memory and display devices. He did not need to know which was the winning consumer product; only that it would be a combination of memory and display, and that Samsung had to get there first. At its roots, this was a highly technological debate about the way to achieve future memory potential, and one which barely involved the individual consumer. Indeed, after the departure of Eric Kim, Samsung re-emphasized its technology rather than the brand. This shifted the direction of the investor relations (IR) discussion with shareholders back towards technology and "hardnosed engineering." Samsung ran technology forums and analyst events to boost the market's confidence in its growth prospects and to help investors understand the company's core competencies and technological trends. This effort paid off when regional media such as *Asia Money* and *Finance Asia* acknowledged the effectiveness of Samsung's investor relations efforts.[16]

Just as Samsung was getting used to going back to the concept of building superior products, chairman Lee reverted to his old theme that it was design and not merely products and technology that would drive Samsung forward. After his return from an unsuccessful bid for the 2014 Winter Olympics to be held in Korea, he began a campaign to emphasize design. After touring a comparative exhibition of advanced products at Suwon, Lee chaired a meeting of subsidiary heads.

Around 20 top executives attended the meeting, including Yun, Hwang, Lee Hak-soo (vice chairman of Samsung's corporate restructuring office) and Choi Gee-sung (president of the telecommunications division).

Amid growing concerns of a crisis at Samsung, Lee repeated his view that "Such concerns imply that we should be bracing for the changes that will come in four or five years, and not that Samsung is having difficulties now."[17] He added that the crisis could be turned into an opportunity through preparation. Lee laid out his creative management cards again as a group catchphrase, warning that the time of "unpredictably rapid changes" would arrive in the electronics industry in a few years. He pointed out that Samsung was still behind its global competitors in its ability to provide useful software and user interface for its hi-tech hardware products.

Lee's message was an encouragement to Samsung Electronics workers, whose morale had taken a hit from declining profits and rumors of restructuring.

Managing the competition

This did not answer the question as to whether Samsung needed a new product engine of growth, or a rebalancing of the portfolio or more effective branding. As Nick Skellon had expressed the dilemma in 2001: "Large businesses such as Samsung Electronics are surrounded by competitors and Samsung did not have the security of being number one or number two in the end-user market."[18] A strong argument for explaining Sony's failure was that it had too many competitors and could not compete against them all. It had also entered a new industry—entertainment—with a quite different product life cycle and financial structure. Samsung had stayed in the same business but it was under constant threat from new competitors, principally the Chinese and sometimes in combination with the Taiwanese. In the prophetic words of Nick Skellon, "Samsung, like Sony, is threatened by death from a thousand competitors."[19] Other competitors, such as Nokia, were also in revival mode; and during the second half of 2007 Samsung had to contend with Sony and, above all, the rebirth of Apple in the US. When Eric Kim said in 2007 that Dell could not move out of the PC industry easily, he had forgotten that other companies could. As Skellon pointed out, the nature of competition in the twenty-first century had changed:

The new policy of collaboration and alliances was not a peace treaty but a cold war. Much of the analysis of business strategy presumes a fixed hierarchy of competitors, or a single competitor. An entire segment of analysis draws an assessment based on military analogies in which there are by definition in conventional warfare only two sides.[20]

While electronics is the industry *par excellence* of the late-twentieth and early twenty-first centuries, we have seen the variety of business models which electronics companies have pursued; from being purely consumer product centric to manufacturing only electronic components. Here, we will contrast the development of Sony as a consumer-products company diversifying into areas such as films and entertainment, with Samsung, where components and consumer products are equally part of the portfolio, but the core areas are narrowly focused. At the same time, the alternative models pursued by Dell, Cisco, and Matsushita are considered and contrasted with Samsung.

Until 2007, according to the old-timers at Samsung Electronics, its real strength lay in being at the leading edge of chip manufacturing. Whatever trends emerge among consumers, whether this device or that device wins out, the secrets will lie in chips and displays. If it can get there first or get there cheaper (but profitably) then Samsung can continue to grow by leaps and bounds. For this it relied on Dr. Hwang Chang-gyu and his team at Samsung Electronics Semiconductor, who were committed to what he termed the "New Memory Growth Model"—double density growth every 12 months. The growth pattern is reminiscent of Moore's Law that the number of transistors that can be placed inexpensively on an integrated circuit has increased exponentially, doubling approximately every two years.

Dr. Hwang had gradually emerged as the key figure, not only in Samsung's lead in semiconductor technology but in the world's advanced chip technology. He began his career with Samsung Electronics in 1989, as general manager in charge of DVC development. A graduate of Seoul National University, he received his PhD in electrical and computer engineering from the University of Massachusetts, Amherst in 1985. Among his many technical accomplishments, he developed the world's first 256MB DRAM, for which he received the Samsung Special Prize Award. His many honors include election as a fellow of the Institute of Electrical and Electronic Engineers; recognition by *BusinessWeek* as one of "25 Stars" in 2003; selection as "CEO of Asia" by *Asia Money* in 2005, and recognition in 2005 as "Technology Leader" by the Electronics Industry Association.

In 2005, he was the recipient of The Electronic Industries Alliance's (EIA) Leadership in Technology and Innovation Award, given for his role in creating groundbreaking technological achievements and in guiding Samsung's ascendancy in advanced semiconductor technology solutions. At the awards presentation, EIA president Dave McCurdy had this to say:

> As the market leader in advanced semiconductor technology such as flash and mobile memory, Samsung has enabled manufacturers to develop higher-performance, multifunctional electronic products, and is poised to create future innovative semiconductor solutions for corporate, mobile and digital consumer communication. We are honored to present this award to Dr. Hwang and are grateful to him for charting a path of innovation for the world to follow.[21]

Green Samsung

Dr. Hwang was also a visionary environmental health and safety (EHS) leader, pioneering the creation of a "Green Samsung." He was the recipient of the prestigious Akira Inoue Award in 2006 for his contributions to decisive and visionary EHS leadership at Samsung Electronics, where he had "demonstrated extraordinary leadership" in developing processes "that consume less resources and the use of environmentally friendly materials in manufacturing, [which] have helped make Samsung one of the most respected semiconductor electronics companies."[22]

The achievements cited by the Award committee in selecting Dr. Hwang included helping reduce carbon dioxide emissions by waste heat recovery, introducing energy-efficient equipment, and wafer-processing optimization; making progress towards helping the semiconductor industry reduce greenhouse gas emissions by 10 percent by 2010 from 1997 baseline levels; reducing greenhouse gases by 57 percent since 1997; and introducing environmentally friendly product alternatives to the six hazardous substances used in electronics products banned by the European Union.

Return of the Samsung Man

Dr. Hwang's work was indeed a credit to Samsung and was its hidden strength; but so were thousands of other Samsung Electronics managers and workers. But in July 2007, he was replaced as head of the memory division by Samsung Electronics vice president Cho Soo-in, and demoted to head the semiconductor division.[23] In the following year he would be moved out of line management and given the title of Chief Technology Officer.[24] (Later a Samsung spokesman was to say apropos of dropping the term "Hwang's law" in 2008; "What's important is to boost production capacity with existing chip technologies rather than holding a kind of show-off event, as time is very crucial in beating out rivals." The bureaucracy did not like showy stars, it wanted solidity and conformity.[25])

The nature of Samsung's structure is such that the chairman plays a very limited role in the group's operations. Founder Lee Byung-chul built a professional structure that enables the company to survive the loss of the chairman, as the *zaibatsu* in Japan survived the loss of their ruling families in the 1940s. Lee, who spent part of every year in Japan, decided to build his group round a set of skills which sharply differentiated a Samsung Man from a Hyundai Man or an LG or Daewoo Man. Samsung was to have a fully professional management team, thoroughly trained in the Samsung principles at its training institute in Suwon.

These principles included building a corps of managers who moved from subsidiary to subsidiary. (Lee Byung-chul was famous for his year-end parties which senior management from the entire group attended, but left with a new appointment, which was as likely to be in another Samsung company as another division of the same company.)

The problem, as in many Korean companies in the early 2000s, was to ensure that middle managers did not discourage new entrants, or delay innovation and change from the top.

This homogenization throughout the company enabled Samsung to become the most professional of companies. Lee Kun-hee rarely took an active role in the company—except at times when leadership and quick decisions were required. A Samsung Group without a dominant Lee would have been more conservative, as the Japanese groups are conservative. Historically, Lee's one big business intervention was the creation of Samsung Motors, and the group could do without that kind of initiative from the top.

But under Yun and his team, there was, as we have seen, a real division of thinking about the future company between the "Korean voice" of traditionalists and the "global voice" of the younger generation.

In October 2007, Yun suggested that Samsung needed to look at Google as a model. "All executives and employees have to get rid of their old habits, and exert themselves to create and implement creative ideas," he said in his monthly speech. "Creativity comes from failure. We should reform our corporate culture to forgive failure if workers did their best."

Samsung is known as a hardcore manufacturing company—both notorious for its long working hours and highly popular for handing out handsome performance-related bonuses. On the other hand, Google is considered an archetype of the Silicon Valley style, with a relaxed corporate culture, epitomized in popular slogans such as "You can be serious without a suit."[26]

Samsung's life cycle and its product cycle had reached the aging phase by the second half of 2007. Its challenge was to rejuvenate itself. Samsung Electronics had enjoyed fantastic growth between 1997 and 2007. Its leader, Yun, was now 63 years old. His leader, Lee, was 66 years old. Behind Yun was a strong team of research-oriented engineers who managed the divisions. Samsung's Achilles heel lay in the age of its team and in the style of the company, which was increasingly out of step with the life style and culture of today's Korea. Things would have to change.

Earlier, at an on-the-spot guidance meeting at Suwon in July 2007, Lee Kun-hee had reflected on the fact that Samsung had to go further in two directions: the actual soft execution of products, and in seeking out new directions. Those present took his remarks as an endorsement for his executives to focus on discovering new growth engines.

Lee's remarks were made on the occasion of the annual review of competing products mentioned earlier. These products were made by the likes of Sony, Panasonic, Sharp, GE, Nokia, and Apple and were selected as representing Samsung's main competitors. The exhibition contrasted 70 Samsung products with about 500 other items made by other firms. Initiated in 1993, the show—which is off-limits to outsiders—is intended to provide Samsung engineers and researchers with a snapshot of the differences between Samsung's products and those of its competitors.[27]

While previous events had been mostly about hardware comparisons, the 2007 exhibition focused on areas of "soft" competitiveness, such as design and interface. Having viewed them, Lee was reported as saying: "It's true that the competitiveness of Samsung products has grown but they still lag behind the world's best in areas such as design, software and finishing touch. Samsung used to have advanced companies that served as lighthouses, but now it must venture into the open seas on its own."[28] In saying this, he stressed the need to further sharpen Samsung's competitiveness and discover new business areas.

In this regard, there are echoes here of Eric Kim's words in 2004, when he said that it was the differentiation that enabled consumers to make choices based on perception that determined whether a product had a chance to succeed:

> When I joined the company in 1999, it was already a very, very big company. It was close to $20 billion in size, they had massive global manufacturing scale, tremendous investments in R&D. It had very strong portfolio of technology, it had many product and yet in the market place it was perceived as a low-end, cheap commodity. Thus despite all that investment it wasn't able to command the kind of price position that would give sufficient profit to continue, and therefore when the Asian financial crisis struck it literally put the entire company in jeopardy. They had to go through some massive restructuring and coming out of that was the really fundamental realization that they had to do more than be just great technologists, great manufacturers. They also had to be a great marketer and so there was a very concerted effort to build brand for the company.[29]

Where Samsung Electronics ventured would depend on its ability to resolve the issues between the "Korean" and the "global" voice. Success would mean embracing both contemporary Korean values and global values (including those which argue for the value of positioning). It would also mean valuing consumer knowledge rather than simply leaving the Suwon R&D department at the helm. And, for Samsung, success also means making the right technology bets.

In the 2003 annual report, Yun Jong-yong had pointed out the reasons for the company's superior performance:

> We emphasize profits rather than sales growth. We drive competitiveness through bringing premium products to global markets. We relentlessly strive to augment the power of our brand and the undying efforts of employees and shareholders. Our people continually move toward aggressive goals with dedication, innovation and high ideals.

For the future Yun picked out six winning features of world-leading companies:

1. Product innovation
2. Technology innovation
3. Market innovation
4. Cost innovation
5. Global management innovation
6. Organizational culture innovation.[30]

As we have seen, Samsung has put great effort into each of these areas. But the strength (and sometimes the weakness) has been the Korean dimension. There was a question still to be answered, though. Samsung was already in a serious state of crisis in late 1997. How would the company face both a global economic crisis (no longer simply a product-cycle downturn) and the loss of both its chairman and its CEO?

Endnotes

1 Lee Byung-chul, quoted in "The Biggest Bosses 35. Lee Byung-chul Samsung A Tough Comeback Artist," by Louis Kraar, *Fortune Magazine*, August 3, 1987, at: http://money.cnn.com/magazines/fortune/fortune_archive/1987/08/03/69354/index.htm
2 Historic exchange rates from http://www.x-rates.com/cgi-bin/hlookup.cgi; accessed May 20, 2009.
3 *BusinessWeek* 2006, Top 100 Brand results.

4   "Best Global Brands: 2007 Rankings" *Interbrand*, 2007, at: http://www.interbrand.com/best_global_brands.aspx?year=2007&langid=1000

5   "A Sense of Crisis at the Samsung Group," *The Chosun Ilbo*, June 29, 2007, at: http://english.chosun.com/w21data/html/news/200706/200706290023.html

6   Ibid.

7   "Is Samsung Strong Enough to Survive?" *LA Times*, September 3, 2007, at: http://www.smartoffice.com.au/Management/Leadership/A2P9E2H5?page=3

8   "Sandwiched Korea, and Samsung," by Cho Jae-hyon, *Korea Times*, June 6, 2007, at: http://www.koreatimes.co.kr/www/news/opinon/2009/11/164_4261.html

9   Ibid.

10 "Samsung's Lee Reignites Creative Management Drive," by Cho Jin-seo, *Korea Times*, July 29, 2007. http://www.koreatimes.co.kr/www/news/biz/2009/08/123_7336.html

11 "Samsung to Tighten its Belt," *The Chosun Ilbo*, June 28, 2007, at: http://english.chosun.com/w21data/html/news/200706/200706280016.html

12 englishnews@chosun.com, August 14, 2007.

13 englishnews@chosun.com, The Korean system pays lowish wages to production workers but pays well for overtime.

14 englishnews@chosun.com

15 Darren Murph, posted November 9, 2007. http://www.engadgethd.com/2007/11/09/samsung-no-longer-selling-flat-panels-other-wares-in-japan/#comments; accessed May 2008.

16 "CG & IR Awards," *Samsung*, 2009, at: http://www.samsung.com/us/about samsung/ir/corporategovernance/cgirawards/IR_CGIRAwards.html

17 "Samsung Head Urges Execs for More Growth," *The Chosun Ilbo*, July 30, 2007. http://english.chosun.com/w21data/html/news/200707/200707300007.html

18 Skellon, Nick 2001, *Corporate Combat: The Art of Market Warfare on the Business Battlefield*, London and Naperville, IL: Nicholas Brealey Publishing.

19 Ibid.

20 Ibid.

21 http://www.eia.org/news/pressreleases/2005-04-27.217.phtml

22 "Chang-Gyu Hwang Receives 2006 Akira Inoue Award for Environmental, Health and Safety Excellence," December 4, 2006, at: http://www.semi.org/en/about/semiglobalupdate/articles/p040274

23 "Samsung Electronics Reshuffles Senior Executives," *Digital Chosun*, July 17, 2007.

24 See Chapter 10.

25 "Hwang's Law Phased Out," by Kim Yoo-chul, *Korea Times*, September 11, 2008.

26 "You Can be Serious Without a Suit—Google," *Salient Marketing*, 2006, at: http://www.salientmarketing.com/seo-resources/search-engine-review/google/lighthearted.html

27 *Korea Times*, July 29, 2007.

28 englishnews@chosun.com, July 30, 2007; *Korea Times*, July 29, 2007 (slightly variant quotations from Chairman Lee).

29 "Beijing Debate Abridged Transcript," *PrincipalVoices.com*, May 2005, at: http://www.principalvoices.com/beijing.html

30 Ibid.

10

Samsung's Crisis and the Global Crisis, 2008–09

> *This year, the instability of the global economy is expected to continue as financial markets absorb the impact of the subprime mortgage crisis, oil prices rise further and the global economy slows down overall. The domestic Korean market has been directly and indirectly influenced by these phenomena. Moreover, our business environment has been beset with various new competitive challenges. Nevertheless, Samsung Electronics will do its best to solidify its status as a top global company through its efforts to succeed in the face of adversity as well as a seasoned understanding of the best ways to turn crisis into opportunity.*
>
> Lee Yoon-woo[1]

Management restructuring and the departure of Yun

A world economic crisis of the proportions of that which has engulfed the world since September 2008 reveals every fundamental flaw and weakness in a national economy, in the operations of corporate and financial institutions, and in every product and service area. What was initially described as instability in the system—and which, up until September 2008, looked essentially containable—broke in full force with the collapse of Lehman Brothers. No bailout could remove these weaknesses; only strong determined restructuring.

At a national level, the degree to which a country can solve its fundamental weaknesses quickly, and not divert resources into cosmetic bailouts, is the measure of how well it will come out of the crisis with its economy stronger. At a corporate level, what in good times could be tolerated weaknesses and phased declines become toxic as the market and liquidity shrink at the same time.

Samsung had two weaknesses in mid-2008. The first was the global glut of chips, especially memory chips, which had depressed prices to the point where most manufacturers were in danger of selling below the cost of production and the sense of strategic crisis that this engendered. The second was the political–legal crisis surrounding the chairman, which was to remove the architects of Samsung Electronics' growth in April–May 2008.

This meant that Samsung had to struggle to find a new generation of leaders and a new core strategy at a time when its basic cash cow was not performing, and when world demand for most consumer electronics was beginning to collapse.

Lee Kun-hee stepped down as chairman of the Samsung Group and resigned all his official posts on April 28, 2008. Lee Haksoo, who headed the group's strategic planning office and was vice chairman of Samsung Electronics, also resigned. Both had been convicted of tax evasion and breach of trust arising from the investigations described earlier. At that time it was announced that Samsung Electronics' three remaining top executives—Yun Jong-yong, vice chairman and CEO; Lee Yoon-woo, also vice chairman; and Choi Doh-seok, executive president and chief financial officer—would continue in office, leaving the two vacancies unfilled until the next annual general meeting.[2]

But on May 14, 2008 it was announced that Yun would also retire. Rumors had been circulating for about 10 months that the chairman was holding Yun and Hwang responsible for the company's slowdown and that they would be made scapegoats for the division's stagnant performance. Despite Yun's nine years' service as Lee's right-hand man, both the Korean voice and the global voice suggested to the chairman that it was time that he should go. When Samsung Electronics' English annual report was published at the end of May 2008, Lee Yoon-woo's name and unfamiliar photograph carried the title of CEO. For the first time since 1996 the letter to shareholders was written and signed by a new name. Lee Yoon-woo, 63, had been a member of the Samsung Electronics board with the title of representative director and vice chairman, but his main role had been Corporate Chief Technology Officer of Global Collaboration, and vice chairman of the Samsung Advanced Institute of Technology of Samsung Electronics Co. Ltd. since 2005. He had established a long record of technological developments since he joined the Samsung group in 1968.

Commentary on this sudden change varied from the cynical view that Mr. Lee was merely a "seat warmer" for the ex-chairman's son and heir, to the following more positive view expressed by Endgadget:

> From 1996 to 2004 he was the President of Semiconductor Business and since then he's been working as Vice Chairman of Corporate CTO. Given Samsung's dominance in the Flash and DRAM memory markets, it's hard to call this a bad move, but Samsung also has appointed Hyung-Kyu Lim to work on new "growth engines" to help Samsung find new ways to make cash as its current strongholds meet stronger and stronger competition. Nice to have you back on your feet Sammy, now let's see some more of those world firsts you're so fond of.[3]

The Samsung Group underwent a further massive management restructuring in January to March 2009. Samsung's founder, Lee Byung-chul, had established a tradition of shuffling senior managers at the end of each year. This restructuring of management throughout the Samsung group was unprecedented, and took three months. Even prior to that, the next generation of Samsung Electronics managers had moved up. In a January 16 announcement, Samsung said it would combine its handset, television, computer, and all other consumer businesses into one group. Choi Gee-sung, who had been running the company's mobile phone business, was to head the newly formed Digital Media & Communications unit.

Industry analysts thought that the bigger role for Choi, 57, improved his chances of succeeding CEO Lee Yoon-woo, who was still seen as only a stopgap leader, mainly playing a coordinating role for Samsung's various groups. Though Lee remained CEO, his operational responsibilities were said to be limited to the struggling electronics-parts businesses, which was being combined into a single division.

In addition to Choi's promotion, Samsung advanced three executive vice presidents, all in their early fifties, to head the LCDs division, its TV and visual-display media division, and the auditing team. Samsung executives told the media informally that the company would soon follow this up with more organizational shuffling deeper within the company. The following week Samsung reassigned lower-ranking executives and more divisional changes, such as streamlining manufacturing units, were expected to follow. "There has been a sense of crisis in the company for more than a year," one senior manager, who asked not to be identified, told Moon Ihlwan of *BusinessWeek*. "Radical change is in store."[4]

Moon, one of Korea's long-term Samsung Electronics-watchers felt that "Choi's rise underscores a break from Samsung's tradition of picking top managers with backgrounds in engineering." After joining Samsung's trading arm in 1977, Choi had a stint as chief design officer and established Samsung's chip business in Europe in the 1980s. Choi was regarded as a marketing expert, and is credited internally with having steered Samsung past Sony to become the world's leading TV brand in 2006. He took over the running of Samsung's mobile phone business in January 2007 and, by September 2008, the company's global market share stood at 17.1 percent—second only to Nokia and up from 14.4 percent in 2007.[5]

Analysts said that the rise of Choi and other non-engineers shows that Samsung, having established its technological credentials, wants to listen more carefully to customers when developing future products. As Kang Shin-woo, chief investment officer at fund manager Korea Investment Trust Management, saw it, "Samsung's benchmark is shifting from Japanese companies to innovators like Apple (AAPL)."[6]

An acquisition fails

At the point in the life cycle (in late 2007) that Samsung had reached, acquisition would be a normal way to expand. The Samsung Group had made few acquisitions outside of Korea (having been prevented by the Korean government from acquiring Fokker Aircraft in the 1980s on the grounds that it would make the Group too powerful).

In September 2008, Samsung Electronics attempted to acquire its first major overseas company, SanDisk, for US$5.8 billion.

The aim was to consolidate the global market for memory chips and deprive Toshiba of an ally. Samsung, Toshiba, and SanDisk together had a 57 percent share of the world memory market and SanDisk had an important memory-card business.[7]

Samsung offered close to double the current market price for SanDisk shares, but this was not enough for the SanDisk board to agree to sell the company, referring to the higher price earlier in the year which had made the 52-week average above Samsung's offer. The offer was withdrawn on October 28 in the wake of the collapse of Lehman Brothers, although the further fall in the value of the Korean *won* was not mentioned as a factor.

In a statement withdrawing the offer, Lee Yoon-woo wrote:

> Your surprise announcements of a quarter-billion dollar operating loss, a hurried renegotiation of your relationship with Toshiba and major job losses across your organization all point to a considerable increase in your risk profile and a material deterioration in value, both on a stand-alone basis as well as to Samsung. As a result of these developments, we are no longer interested in acquiring SanDisk at $26/share.

SanDisk responded to Samsung's statement with one of its own:

> From the start of this process SanDisk's Board has remained open to a transaction that recognizes SanDisk's long-term value and contains the right protections for SanDisk's shareholders. We repeatedly outlined a clear path to hold further discussions, including most recently in our letter on September 15, and Samsung consistently chose to ignore that path and, in fact, never contacted SanDisk regarding their proposal after we delivered our letter. We believe this raises questions about the real motivations behind Samsung's offer.[8]

Boston.com quoted analyst Kim Young-jun from KTB Investment as saying:

Samsung probably has decided that as the memory chip market continues to weaken, the kind of price SanDisk was asking wasn't what they were willing to go along with. The fact that the macroeconomic environment continues to worsen and that the South Korean government has warned against big overseas M&A deals also probably weighed.[9]

Some thought that Samsung was hoping that SanDisk would see the light and, under the pressure of declining stock prices, would be more open to takeover at a lower price. At the same time, SanDisk may have been hoping that Samsung would fear SanDisk's closer ties to Toshiba and pay more to keep its rival from acquiring what it coveted. As the global crisis deepened and Samsung Electronics moved towards its first-ever operating profit loss, interest in acquiring more semiconductor capacity waned. The loss of interest probably reflected division in Samsung between Lee, who continued to look at the semiconductor business he had worked in most of his life, and other senior managers. Others may have merely pointed at how financing a similar deal was weighing down the Doosan Group, which had paid about US$4.7 billion for the Bobcat division of Ingersoll Rand and was now in trouble. Had the SanDisk acquisition proceeded, it would have been the largest M&A deal by a Korean company.

Counting the losses

The biggest task the new leadership faced was to steer the company through the worst global slowdown since the Second World War. Samsung was the only maker of memory chips that remained profitable in the three months that ended in September 2008. However, analysts expected Samsung to report a net loss in the following quarter, largely based on the collapse of memory-chip prices and poor prices for LCDs, two of its three core businesses. In fact, the net loss was, at 22 billion *won* (US$22 million), better than expected (a loss of 256 billion *won* or US$256 million), although the net profit figure required analysis with a fine toothcomb to really see what had happened. The fourth-quarter operating loss (Samsung's first ever) was 96 billion *won* (US$96 million), compared with a third-quarter profit of 1.26 trillion *won* (US$1.26 billion).

At the time of writing, the 2008 Annual Report had yet to be issued, but the first-quarter results for 2009 are available. The results, as set out in Table 10.1, are significant for exemplifying the change in the company, and justifying former CEO Yun's vision of selective specialization in an age of convergence.

With the new presentation of product groupings, the company's business was divided into two global businesses: device solutions—components such as semi-conductors and LCDs; and digital media and communications. In this new way of looking at the company, device solutions (at 2008 depressed global prices) represented about one-third of sales, and digital media and communications about two-thirds. Between first quarter 2008 and first quarter 2009, digital media and communications had grown from 61 percent to 69 percent of Samsung's business. More impressive was the fact that, despite a world slowdown, Samsung had increased sales by 10 percent (although this may turn out to be purely the effect of a lower value for the *won*).

In a complete reversal of the past, the main profit driver was now telecoms, which provided 1.12 trillion *won* (US$1.12 billion) of operating profit, while digital media provided only 0.38 trillion *won*, and semiconductors and LCDs made a loss. Overall, even at the nadir of the world economy, Samsung Electronics was profitable, and its profit was coming from convergence. Net income had fallen to 3 percent of sales, compared with 13 percent the year before, but the company was no longer making a loss.

Table 10.1   Financial Results, First Quarter 2009 (in Trillion *won*, Parent Basis)

Business	Revenue			Operating Profit		
	'09 1Q	'08 4Q	'08 1Q	'09 1Q	'08 4Q	'08 1Q
Digital Components	7.49	8.16	8.76	−0.95	−0.91	1.20
Semiconductor	3.74	3.92	4.39	−0.65	−0.56	0.19
LCD	3.75	4.21	4.34	−0.31	−0.35	1.01
Digital Media	11.08	10.25	8.34	1.10	−0.02	0.97
Telecommunications	8.06	7.73	5.99	0.94	0.16	0.93
Appliances, etc.	2.93	2.41	2.23	0.15	−0.17	0.04

The accounts suggest that a new Samsung Electronics had the potential to rise on the back of the transformation that Yun and his team had created.

The rise of the Northeast Asian consumer

There is a further source of growth which, it could be argued, Samsung Electronics is not pursuing as well as its local competitors. Despite the global recession, China continued to grow at between 6 and 7 percent. For many Korean consumer companies, the rise of the Northeast Asian consumer with common purchasing characteristics was enough. This is a world of 1.5 billion Chinese, Japanese, and Koreans who are developing a new culture that will dominate the world of the 2020s as Americans dominated the world in the latter half of the twentieth century. In this, it will be Korea Inc. helping Samsung, and not the other way round, as the cultural explosion known as *halligyu* (the Korean wave) has swept across Asia.

During the early years of this decade, Korean dramas, pop singers, online games, and other aspects of Korean culture became hot items across Asia. Many Korean companies realized that they could use the popularity of Korean culture across the region to advertise their products. Once again traditional Korean marketing—personality marketing—rose to the fore. The content of promotion and the positioning of the company were secondary to the charm of the model and simple product-related messages. Such marketing worked on a "fashion" basis, but represented a retreat from the ordered themes of the Eric Kim era. This was not brand building but product attention-grabbing in which a Samsung model might have no great advantage against another company's model, and in which the consumer's brand loyalty was not extended to other products.

Samsung had been carried by the Korean wave into the gigantic Chinese market and other Asian communities. Samsung had helped to create the wave through its approach to sports marketing and Olympic sponsorship, but this was a product of the outpouring of creativity from Korea as a whole—an outpouring that was carrying Samsung's local competitor, LG, into the world as well. In 2005 analysts noted that LG Electronics had entered the Interbrand index at number 97. LG was projecting an image of "cool" to millions of Chinese and was somewhat warmer in branding than Samsung. Its Chocolate mobile phone and the associated campaign were tailored to China and not to global markets. But LG's campaign worked its magic just the same. LG dropped off the Interbrand top 100 in 2008, but it continued to increase its sales. In the first quarter of 2009, its global sales were 12.5 trillion *won* (US$12.5 billion), compared with Samsung's 18.57 trillion. Excluding the 7.49 trillion *won* in device solutions—an area in which LG Electronics did not compete—the two companies were almost neck and neck;[10] although, in brand equity terms, Samsung was way ahead. While the two companies claimed almost identical operating profits, caution should be exercised in comparing the two because they use different measures for combining Korean parent sales with overseas subsidiaries. The fact is, though, that LG Electronics, the successor to Goldstar Electronics which Lee Byung-chul had set out to challenge in 1969, was continuing to do well and to harness the energies of Koreans.

LG Electronics, like many Korean companies, had concentrated more heavily on Northeast Asia, and established brand and product presence in the same areas that Samsung claimed as its own: mobile phones and TV devices. In both areas, it was a close challenger to Samsung's market position, and making better use of the Northeast Asia card than Samsung.

Samsung at 40

At the end of May 2009, former Korean President Roh Moo-hyun, who was under investigation for a receiving a small amount of money while in office, committed suicide. On the day of his funeral, which drew massive street demonstrations of affection, the Supreme Court of Korea cleared Samsung Group's former chairman Lee Kyun-hee of the charges that had forced his resignation. Cleared, he could resume control of his group in June 2009, almost 40 years after he and his father had founded Samsung Electronics. On November 1, 2009, Samsung Electronics marked the fortieth anniversary of its founding. It was a relatively low-key birthday party attended by about 400 employees, including previous CEOs and other officials and videoed congratulations from such international celebrities as president of the International Olympic Committee, Jacques Rogge, and former New York City mayor, Rudolph Giuliani.[11] Vice Chairman Lee Yoon-woo's speech contained some resounding 10-year goals, but the actual strategy reflected the outcome of the debate of the previous two years, mentioned above.

The year 2009 had been kind to Samsung. Chairman Lee estimated that the company would earn 130 trillion *won* (US$115.5 billion) in annual revenue—up 3.15 million-fold from the 37 million *won* (US$76,000) in its first year. Operating profits for this year are expected to surpass 10 trillion *won* thanks to a massive turnaround in its key memory chip and LCD panel businesses, and strong demand for its TV and handsets. But as a reminder that the Korean economy is maturing and growing faster than Samsung itself, where five years ago Samsung Electronics had accounted for about 25 percent of the market capitalization of the Korean Stock Market, but in October 2009 it accounted for just 14 percent.

The vice chairman said that by 2020 SEC would achieve sales of US$400 billion, overtaking Hewlett Packard and Siemens, and belong among the top 10 global companies through creative innovation. It would rank fifth in the world in brand value and would transform itself into a top-tier environment-friendly enterprise.[12]

Under the company's new vision—"Inspire the World, Create the Future"—Samsung is determined to produce new technologies, innovative products, and creative solutions, so enhancing people's quality of life and contributing to global prosperity for years to come. If it is to secure a dominant position in the industry by 2020, Lee said, Samsung Electronics should step up its efforts to produce differentiated products and create an advanced value chain. Samsung should actively join the international trend to protect and seek harmony with the natural environment.

Lee laid out six ways Samsung would achieve these goals. Though all of these had been discussed in previous years, there was more of a sense of synergy than in past statements and linkages with the previous vision:

- Foster its number-one position in the memory-chip, LCD, TV and mobile phone markets, while strengthening six other industries, including home appliances, computers, and printers.

- Aggressively enter the new fields of biochips, medical appliances, u-health services, and solar-cell manufacturing in order to meet the expanding needs of customers.
- Strengthen the analysis of customer groups and lifestyles, so facilitating the application of diversified marketing strategies.
- Pursue "open innovation," through which outward assistance is welcomed, R&D partnerships are reinforced, and various collaboration channels with other organizations will be established.
- Build mature symbiotic relationships with its collaborators, strengthen its corporate social responsibility, and pursue environment-friendly business management.
- Cultivate a sound work environment by employing a creative performance evaluation system and advanced personnel management.

The struggle for leadership of the electronics industry is to continue with Samsung Electronics challenging both new competitors and new fields of endeavor. The new vision will take it beyond its present product areas into areas that will challenge companies such as General Electric, Siemens, and Philips in some of their core competencies such as medical equipment. The vision also looks towards the realm of green products which the Copenhagen era will augur, and in which Korean industry looks well equipped to take the lead.

The year 2009 ended on an even more confident note as Samsung announced on January 9 that it had reached 139 trillion *won* (US$123 billion) in sales and 10.9 trillion *won* (US$9.7 billion) in operating profit, a growth of 15 percent on 2008.[13] In *won* terms this would be Samsung's most profitable year and in dollar terms the second-most profitable year. Samsung also became the first Korean company to achieve 100 trillion *won* and 10 trillion *won* in operating profit.

December 2009 was a remarkable month for the whole Korean economy. Exports rose 32.8 percent year on year, and exports to China 93.1 percent.[14] For Samsung, an additional boost came from a rise in memory-chip prices during the final quarter as demand for electronic products recovered. The global prices for DRAM and NAND flash-memory products rose 11 percent and 4 percent, respectively, during the fourth quarter.[15]

It should be stressed that these achievements were made with the products and concepts of the Millennium Vision of 1999, and that the new business areas outlined since CEO Yun's departure had yet to make a significant impact on the sales or profitability of the company. It seems a suitable valediction.

A matter of will

Has Samsung changed?

It is too early to determine whether the changes in management and in business strategy will be effective. In all change management there is a strong chance of failure, which makes the rebirth of giants like IBM all the more remarkable, set against others like GM which could never change enough. Yun was convinced that the Jack Welch approach of continual crisis was the best, but this was never understood by some senior Samsung Electronics executives. It remains to be seen whether the strengths which Samsung have used over the years are relevant to the future Samsung faces and the new strategy it is adopting.

Double-or-quits strategy

No Korean company has ever been afraid of massive investment. An across-the-board range of world-scale investments by Korea Inc., using short-term borrowings, led eventually to the Asia crisis. Game theory, as taught in Western business schools, does not teach the "double or quits" strategy. Fundamental to competitive business psychology, the strategy refers to the simplest gambling ploy of all time. In gambling, double or quits is a second-tier gamble. In some games (poker, for example), the aim is to make the stakes so high that the other player withdraws. Samsung Electronics has steadily employed this technique in both its forms—double the stakes or withdraw. In the SanDisk overture, Samsung chose withdrawal. Indeed, within the company in 2008–09 no one was clear where money should be invested, although consolidation in the memory-chip business was obviously in the interests of the company's traditional business.

Commitment to manufacturing

From the first success of its microwave venture, Samsung has consistently shown its strength of commitment to manufacturing. Samsung's management bet correctly that this dedication was higher than that of General Electric. In the case of DRAMs, Samsung also bet that its dedication to continuing to produce and invest into the next generation would outrun all its competitors. This strategy works well against a US competitor such as General Electric or a modern Japanese company like Sony, but not so well when the competitor is another Korean company. But the balance between "device solutions" and "devices" distinguishes Samsung Electronics from the competition, and the loss of this balance could lead to market mistakes.

Elixir of eternal corporate life

So, has Samsung Electronics discovered the elixir of eternal corporate life? The answer is that it may require a continuation of continual crisis to preserve the elixir. The crisis of 2008–09 has been resolved by not only using the strengths of the past, but removing the weaknesses, especially the retreat from global marketing. We have to divide the elixir into its various components. In Samsung's case, working on all these components will decide whether it can stay immortal.

Management will

As long as the Lee/Yun bond held and their health continued, there could be little doubt that Samsung Electronics had the will to succeed. The succession problem has not been resolved, despite the departure of both figures. The shift towards consumer devices and younger leaders appears positive, but might threaten the balance between "device solutions" and "devices."

Pre-emptive investment

This is a core Korean quality, but it depends on making the right investment choices. In 2008–09, was acquisition a better way to expand than building capacity? On the other hand, the "device solutions" require continued investment, and several competitors may fall behind in the next round, to Samsung's advantage.

Product portfolio choice

The balance when Yun was CEO was almost perfect for the first decade of the twenty-first century. Despite fears that the old products have reached the end of their life cycle and there are no obvious replacements, the actual focus has remained valid. Although Samsung talks about developing the bioengineering, energy and health businesses as new growth engines, taking the wrong decision would be to follow the direction taken by Sony in its wasted Columbia years.

Speed

Speed is undoubtedly a Korean quality that is hard for most non-Korean companies to match. Samsung has to stay on course at full speed. There are signs that it is slowing down and some analysts believe that key reinvestment decisions that should have been made in 2008 were not taken. As one commentator put it: "The problem is that Samsung seems to be complacent in its current status as a giant conglomerate but is ageing rapidly, losing its earlier challenging spirit to make bold investments and take risks."[16] Chang In-whan, chief executive at fund manager KTB Asset Management, expressed the view this way: "It's critical for Samsung that the new leadership keep investing in new technologies and equipment fast enough to increase market share and benefit from the downturn."[17]

Marketing strategy

It has been argued that Samsung's marketing strategy cannot be purely Korean-led and that it must select the global best. A team like that which existed in Samsung during the period 2000–04 would be hard to match, and Samsung Electronics has fallen away from its branding commitment.

Human resources

A Japanese business consultant is believed to have reported that Samsung's success is the result of the "involuntary devotion of its workers."[18] He was commenting on the excessive hours that Samsung staff worked compared with other Korean companies. The key for younger Samsung workers is to work smart rather than work devotedly. The underlying training of Samsung's HR should begin to fire on new cylinders if the old culture is removed.

Conclusion

Put in the right ingredients and Samsung Electronics can recreate the elixir of eternal corporate life to continue its growth trajectory. Will a pragmatic and determined management keep the Samsung legend going? Or will Samsung fall behind due to the ossification of ideas, and the wrong choice of business directions, as in the case of Sony? To extend its corporate longevity, Samsung needs to have regular doses of the elixir. The dose cannot be a one-shot affair, given the complexity of the company's business, its sheer size, and global position. In the CEO's message for the 2008 annual report (in terms which might be a criticism of the Yun era), Lee wrote:

> Strong will and passion may have been enough to become a "world class" company, but becoming a "world premier" company calls for a change in our values and the way we think and work.

> Therefore, we will commit ourselves to create a corporate culture that encourages all employees to freely exercise change and innovation, and develop creative methods and tools that cannot be easily imitated by our rivals.[19]

For Samsung to succeed, it will need to focus more than ever on finding that Korean magic that helped transform the company from an industry newbie into the powerful pacesetter for the global electronics industry.

Endnotes

1   Annual Report 2007 (issued May 2008).
2   englishnews@chosun.com, April 29, 2008. For background, see "Dark Days for the Empire: A Corruption Scandal is Threatening to Take Down the Republic of Samsung, and Reshape Korea Inc.," by B. J. Lee and George Wehrfritz, *Newsweek*, December 10, 2007.
3   http://www.engadget.com/2008/05/14/samsung-electronics-names-yoon-woo-lee-as-vice-chairman-and-ceo/
4   "Samsung Electronics: Same CEO, New Leadership Team: Korea's Biggest Company Hopes a Management Reorganization Will help it Through Tough Times," by Moon Ihlwan, *BusinessWeek*, January 16, 2009.

5 Ibid.

6 Ibid.

7 http://www.cdfreaks.com/news/15046-Samsung-SanDisk-buyout-not-likely.html

8 http://www.insidetech.com/news/articles/3363-samsung-walks-away-from-sandisk-merger-talks

9 Ibid.

10 http://www.fiercewireless.com/press-releases/lg-electronics-exceeds-1q-expectations-amidst-global-contraction

11 "Samsung Electronics Aims at Top 10 Global Company by 2020," by Sam Roe, *Korea Times*, November 4, 2009, at: http://www.koreattimes.com/story/5677/samsung-electronics-aims-top-10-global-company-2020; accessed January 5, 2010.

12 "Samsung to Celebrate 40th Anniversary Samsung Aims to Pass Over Siemens, Hewlett-Packard in Total Revenue," by Kim Yoo-chul, *Korea Times*, October 29, 2009, at: http://www.koreatimes.co.kr/www/news/tech/2009/11/133_54259.html; accessed January 5, 2010.

13 "Samsung Electronics Expects Record Sales, Earnings for 2009 2010" by Kim Tong-hyun, January 7, 2010, at: http://www.koreatimes.co.kr/www/news/biz/2010/01/123_58631.html; accessed January 24, 2010.

14 Korea Customs Service December 2009 export data.

15 Kim, op. cit.

16 Moon, op. cit.

17 Ibid.

18 *Korea Times*, June 7, 2007.

19 Samsung IR, "CEO's message," at: http://www.samsung.com/us/aboutsamsung/ir/ceomessage/IR_CEOMessage.html; accessed June 30, 2009. Despite holding its shareholders' meeting in March, the English-language annual report for 2008 had not been placed on the Samsung website at the time of writing.

Appendix 1: Samsung Group in 2005

Chemicals
Samsung General Chemicals Co., Ltd.
Samsung Fine Chemicals Co., Ltd.
Samsung Petrochemical Co., Ltd.

Electronics
Samsung Electronics Co., Ltd.
Samsung Electro-Mechanics Co., Ltd.
Samsung SDI Co., Ltd.
Samsung SDS Co., Ltd.
Samsung Kwangju Electronics Co., Ltd.
Samsung Electronic Service Co., Ltd.
Samsung Thales
Novita Co., Ltd.
DNS Korea CO., Ltd.
Steco., Ltd
Samsung NEC Mobile Display Co., Ltd.

Trade, Service & Other Business
Samsung Corporation
Cheil Industries Inc.
Samsung Everland Inc.
Shilla Hotels and Resort Co., Ltd.
Cheil Communications Inc.
S1 Corporation
Seoul Communication
  Technology Co., Ltd.
Samsung Economic
  Research Institute
Samsung Lions
Moojin Development
  Co., Ltd. *(Merged)*
Samsung Fire Marine Insurance
  Claim Adjustment
  Service Co., Ltd.
Samsung Motors Inc. *(Liquidated)*
HTH Logistics Co., Ltd.

Machinery & Heavy Industry
Samsung Heavy Industries Co., Ltd.
Samsung Techwin Co., Ltd.
Samsung Engineering Co., Ltd.
Samsung Corning Co., Ltd.
Samsung Corning Precision
  Glass Co., Ltd.
Samsung Commercial Vehicle
  Co., Ltd. *(Liquidated)*
Samsung Corning Micro-Optics
  Company *(Acquired stock)*
Bluetech *(Established)*

Samsung

Finance
Samsung Life Insurance Co., Ltd.
Samsung Fire & Marine
  Insurance Co., Ltd.
Samsung Card Co., Ltd.
Samsung Securities Co., Ltd.
Samsung Capital Co., Ltd.
Samsung Futures Inc.
Samsung Venture Investment Co., Ltd.
Samsung Investment Trust &
  Securities Co., Ltd.
  (Merged into Samsung Securities)
Samsung Investment Trust
  Management Co., Ltd.

Internet
SECUi.com Co., Ltd.
Unitel Co., Ltd.
All at Corp.
Care Camp.com Inc.
CVnet Corporation
e-Samsung
Samsung Aizen
e-Samsung International
Credu Corporation
Open Tide Corporation *(Established)*
Inuca Co., Ltd *(Established)*
Enforever *(Established)*
Gaccinet Co., Ltd. *(Established)*
FnGuide Inc. *(Established)*
Bank Pool Co., Ltd. *(Established)*
e-Niz Co., Ltd. *(Established)*
Insvalley Co., Ltd. *(Established)*
eMFORCE *(Established)*
365 Homecare Co., Ltd. *(Established)*
Korea Electronic Information
  Distribution *(Established)*
Toros Logistics *(Established)*
iMarketKorea Inc *(Established)*
MPEON Co., Ltd. *(Established)*
Global Technology Video
  Co., Ltd. *(Established)*

Source: FTC April 2001/Figure in parentheses is
for July 2000.
Note: Established 16, Acquired stock 1. Liquidated
2. Merged 2.

Appendix 2: Exchange Rates and Consolidated and Unconsolidated Accounts and Sony versus Samsung

Unit:
USD billion
KRW trillion

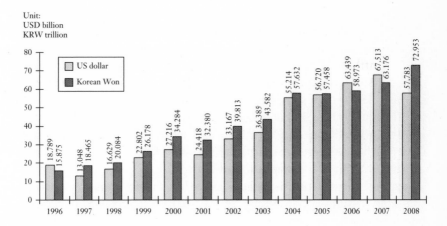

Sony versus Samsung

The comparison between Sony and Samsung given in Chapter 3 contains a number of simplifications. It takes no account of contrary exchange rate movements of the yen and won against the US dollar. It compares SEC's use of the calendar year January–December with Sony's use of the Japanese Financial Year April–March, and it compares Sony's consolidated sales, with SEC's unconsolidated sales. As it is assumed that the reader is only interested in general trends and not down to the bone statistical analysis, these simplifications allow consistency and seemed permissible.

Exchange Rates

Samsung Electronics results quoted in US dollars which remain the basis for international comparisons suffer from the volatility of the won. During the main period under discussion the won shifted first from 800 *won* to the US dollar in 1996 to momentarily touch 2,000 to the US dollar in the last days of December 1997, (but rapidly correcting to 1,350 early in 1998) and then rose to 920 in 2007 before falling again to 1,350 at the end of 2008, and now resuming its rise back past 1,150 in early 2010. Appendix diagram 1 shows the different trajectory of the won and dollar totals.

Consolidated Accounts

Consolidated accounts require the calculation of the additional revenue created by a subsidiary by subtracting any sales from the mother company and between one subsidiary and another. The number is of management and shareholder interest, but in Korea the fiscal requirements only concerned the domestic company and not its overseas affiliates in other tax jurisdictions.

Until the mid-2000s, Korean companies generally did not offer consolidated accounts which included the sales of their overseas subsidiaries. In Samsung's case consolidated accounts merely added the revenue and profit of Samsung Card, which was at the time a wholly owned subsidiary of Samsung Electronics but had no business overlap. All overseas subsidiaries were listed under assets and dividends from the subsidiaries added to the non-operating profit. Therefore throughout the main discussion in this book the unconsolidated results recorded by the Korean Financial Supervisory Service have been used.

In June 2007, Samsung Card was listed on the Seoul Stock Market and Samsung Electronics shareholding in the subsidiary fell to 35 percent. At about the same time, Samsung began to issue consolidated accounts for the entire operation, which greatly boosted the full income of the company. Both the process and the details can be seen in Appendix table 1.

From this date on, Samsung Electronics' consolidated income was a considerably higher figure than SEC Ltd.'s sales figures, which has resulted in conflicting press releases about Samsung Electronics' total sales. The local press tend to report only the Korean company's sales and this is followed by the international press, but some Samsung press releases cite the consolidated sales. As consolidated accounts are issued only once a year, but the accounts of the Korean listed company are released quarterly, two sets of numbers continue to be reported. For further discussion and the on-going evolution please see www.kabcsamung.com.

All figures quoted in the text unless otherwise stated are for unconsolidated accounts.

Index

3P Innovation, 31
3Ps (Proactive, Professional, Progressive), 142
7 DNA, 132
8 Action Values, 133
9 Shared Values, 144

A

Adizes, Ichak, 9, 10, 11, 12, 13, 88, 124, 185, 201
Aibo, 81
American Depositor Receipts (ADRs), 73
American Forces Korea Network (AFKN), 21
Apple, 74, 83, 158, 181, 189, 211, 212, 216, 224
Asia Business Leader Award, 36
Asian financial crisis, 6, 33, 55, 155, 217
Asia's Businessman of the Year, 36

B

Balli balli (quickly quickly), 138
Bankruptcy, 3, 20, 28, 29, 54, 107
Bateman, Graeme, 39
Beijing Olympic Torch Relay, 115
Best Buy, 39, 40, 175
Biochips, 231
Brand equity, 38, 40, 71, 229
Brand strategy, 94, 118
Brand valuation, 41, 112
Brand value, 4, 40, 43, 71, 72, 85, 87, 102, 107, 115, 116, 118, 203, 204, 230

Breach of trust, 66, 67, 222
British government, 21
Buchon, 22
BusinessWeek, 43, 63, 113, 204, 214, 235

C

Canon, 17
Chaebol, 2, 5, 17, 28, 29, 30, 32, 38, 47–50, 52, 54, 55, 56, 58, 62, 63, 65, 66, 67, 68, 94, 121, 124, 126, 129, 130, 131
Charge Trap Flash (CTF), 177
Cheil Communications, 110, 112
Cheil, 18, 50
Cheil Jedang, 50, 53
Chin Dae-je, 103
Christian Science Monitor, 27
Chrysler, 53
Chu Woo-sik, 43, 54, 188, 206
Chun Doo-whan, 23
Circular shareholding, 49, 53
Clinton, Bill, 21
CNBC, 36
Code Division Multiple Access (CDMA), 152, 153–156
Columbia Pictures Entertainment, 75
Commercial Code, 29
Company culture, 126, 148
Company song, 124, 129
Computer World, 39
Concentration on Selective Resources, 31

Consumer marketing, 109
Continual crisis, 35, 44, 110, 113, 125, 126, 186, 205, 232, 233
Continuous innovation, 132, 137, 144
Control Data, 17
Convertible bonds (CB), 49, 67, 68, 87
Corning, 22, 168
Corporate life cycle, 5, 7–16, 34, 124, 201
Creative management, 44, 148, 188, 212
Credit Lyonnais, 80
Crisis awareness, 136, 137, 144

D

Daegu, 18, 50
Daesung Heavy Industry, 52
Daewoo, 30, 32, 52, 129, 215
Daewoo Electronics, 25, 32, 101
Datamonitor summary, 48
Debt ratio, 30, 62
Decentralization, 42, 88, 90
Digit-all, 38
Digital convergence, 35, 36, 99, 151, 152, 162, 163, 165, 206, 211
DigitAll, 99, 100, 107, 156, 157–158
Domestic interest rate, 29
DRAMs, 4, 13, 23, 24, 25, 30, 33, 34–38, 41, 42, 43, 60, 139, 171, 173, 175, 176, 178, 179,

181, 203, 207, 210,
    213, 223, 231, 233
Dun & Bradstreet, 38, 95, 96
DVD players, 36, 100, 104,
    156, 158

E
Economic value added
    (EVA), 60
Everland, 49, 63, 66, 67, 145
Everyone's invited, 95,
    157–158

F
Fairchild Semiconductor, 17
FCB, 95, 98, 103, 110,
    112, 187
Financial crisis, 6, 9, 25, 28,
    29, 33, 34, 44, 49, 55,
    97, 155, 164, 186, 217
FishRound, 63, 64
Five Ills, 37
Five-year plan, 18
Fixed exchange rate, 29
Flash memory, 40, 42, 43,
    158, 176, 177, 189, 231
Foreign exchange, 20, 29, 51
Foreign investment, 24, 87
Fortune Magazine, 36
Frankfurt Manifesto, 54
Free float, 202
Fujitsu, 81

G
GDP, 18, 65, 155
GE, 21, 22, 26, 42, 55, 62,
    121, 148, 216
General Trading License, 52
Global campaigns, 96, 99,
    101, 109
Global Product Manager
    (GPM), 28
Goldstar Electronics, 17, 229
Growth engines, 148, 149,
    192, 197, 205, 207,
    210, 216, 223, 234
Gumi, 154, 162, 194

H
Halligyu, 228
Hanbo, 28

Heavy and Chemical
    Industry Plan, 52
High-speed memory
    chip, 23
Hitachi, 21, 24, 74, 169,
    173, 180
Huhs, 17
Hwang Chang-gyu, 43,
    173, 176, 201, 210,
    211, 213
Hyundai, 12, 30, 32, 48, 52,
    53, 54, 58, 129
Hyundai Electronics, 30,
    32, 173
Hyundai Motor Company,
    41, 52, 53, 58, 191

I
Iacocca, Lee, 53
IBM, 3, 74, 83, 104, 121,
    126, 174, 232
Idei, Nobuyuki, 39, 75,
    76, 79
IMF, 6, 28, 29, 30, 49, 53,
    55–58, 77, 107, 130,
    192, 196
Industrial Management, 26
Integration role, 124
Intellectual property, 189
Interbrand, 39, 40, 41, 71,
    90, 94, 97, 102, 103,
    107, 112, 113, 116,
    118, 197, 204, 229
International Olympic
    Committee, 36, 230
Investor relations, 54,
    206, 211

J
J.P. Morgan, 83
J & R Music, 39
Joong-Ang Mass
    Communications
    Center, 51
JVC, 74

K
KABC, 2
KAIST, 130
Kang Kyong-shik, 28
KCIA (Korea Central
    Intelligence Agency), 23

Kim, Eric, 4, 6, 38, 39, 40,
    41, 71, 76, 87, 94, 95,
    96, 97, 98, 99, 101,
    102, 103, 104, 105,
    106, 107, 108, 109,
    110, 111, 113, 114,
    116, 118, 125, 151,
    152, 156, 161, 165,
    167, 168, 172, 186,
    189, 193, 195, 197,
    210, 211, 212, 217
Kim Dae-jung, 31, 32
Kim Yong-chul, 68. *See also*
    Whistleblower
Koos, 17
Korea Development
    Institute, 67
Korea Fair Trade
    Commission, 54
Korea Institute of
    Electronics Industry
    (KIET), 22
Korea Management
    Association, 27, 33
Korea Semiconductor, 20
Korean War, 18, 47
Korean Wave, The,
    162, 228
Kumi, 22
Kunja, 131
Kyonggi, 20
Kyungsangpukdo, 26

L
LCD, 4, 15, 33, 35, 40, 41,
    42, 43, 60, 84, 100,
    103, 104, 105, 157,
    167, 168, 169, 170,
    171, 173, 174, 182,
    194, 197, 203, 204,
    210, 224, 226, 227, 230
Lee, Greg, 94, 110, 111, 113,
    114, 117, 118, 193, 195
Lee Byung-chul, 4, 5, 17,
    27, 50–54, 65, 127,
    215, 223
Lee Hak-soo, 211, 222
Lee Jae-yong, 49, 66, 67, 169
Lee Kun-hee, 5, 20, 27, 53,
    54–55, 60, 63, 66, 71,
    121, 187, 192, 205,
    206, 215, 216, 222

Lee Yoon-woo, 222, 223,
      225, 230
Leo Burnett, 111, 112
LG, 13, 17, 25, 30, 32,
      48, 52, 56, 94, 101,
      108, 129, 160, 162,
      164, 169, 170, 215,
      228, 229
LG Electronics, 17, 25,
      41, 94, 108, 160, 161,
      191, 229
LG Semiconductor, 30,
      32, 173
Life insurance, 24, 51, 58,
      60, 61, 65, 66
London, Michael, 40
Lost decade, 77
Lucky, 17–18
Lucky Goldstar, 17, 18

M
Magaziner, Ira, 21–22, 127
Management values, 124,
      128, 130
Market capitalization, 40, 86,
      87, 95, 107–108, 230
Market segments, 203
Market share, 10, 14, 15,
      21, 28, 34, 81, 83, 109,
      160, 161, 162, 164,
      170, 172, 176, 203,
      204, 224, 234
Market valuation, 107
Marketing strategy, 43,
      160, 234
MarketWatch, 80
Masan, 50, 162
Matsushita, 4, 17, 74, 81,
      169, 175, 213
McKinsey & Co, 64
Memory-chip, 28, 43, 207,
      226, 230, 231, 232
Microwave, 22, 102,
      107, 232
Millennium Plan, 58–62,
      63, 85
Minister of Finance, 28
Minton, Eric, 26, 45
Mitsubishi, 19, 25, 74, 175
Mobile phones, 4, 33, 35,
      36, 37, 40, 42, 43, 60,

99, 100, 101, 105, 111,
      151–165, 167, 181,
      182, 188, 194, 207,
      210, 211, 229
Mobile WiMAX, 163
Morita, Akio, 3, 39, 72,
      73, 75
Motorola, 17, 43, 153, 155,
      161, 164, 165, 168
MP3, 43, 83, 103, 156, 158,
      163, 177, 189, 211

N
NEC, 19, 24, 74, 81, 160,
      168, 173, 175
Net income, 40, 77, 78, 80,
      84, 85, 227
Net profit, 30, 34, 41, 56,
      64, 65, 83, 87, 226
New Economy, 3, 33, 56,
      59, 63, 75, 76, 99, 100
New Line Cinema, 158
New Memory Growth
      Model, 177, 213
Nintendo, 14, 75, 81
Nissan, 57
Nokia, 43, 118, 152, 160,
      161–162, 164, 168,
      173, 176, 178, 202,
      212, 216, 224
Nomura Securities, 39
North Korea, 18, 47

O
Office of Restructuring, 55
Official Wireless
      Communications
      Equipment Partner, 36
Ohga, Norio, 75, 76, 79
Oil prices, 19, 20, 206, 207
Olympic Games, 35, 36, 96,
      114, 115
Olympics, 96, 112, 114,
      116–117, 156, 211
On-the-job training (OJT),
      123, 139
OPEC, 19
Operating profit, 30, 80,
      151, 165, 195, 203,
      204, 227, 229, 230, 231
Outsourcing, 6, 167, 197

P
Panasonic, 74, 81, 105, 216
Park Chung-hee, 18, 23, 51
PDA, 103, 156
PDP, 170, 203
Planned economic
      growth, 18
Plano, 93
PlayStation, 14, 75, 79, 80,
      81, 82
POSCO, 52, 56, 191
Pre-emptive investment, 5,
      20, 210, 233
Profit margin, 95, 109, 202,
      203, 205, 210
Puchon, 20

R
R & D, 22, 73, 79, 107, 159,
      167, 172, 181, 189,
      190, 191, 196, 203,
      204, 217, 218
RAZR V3, 161
RCA, 21, 158
ReignCom, 189
Renault, 57, 58
Restructuring, 8, 24, 25, 31,
      32, 33, 35, 36, 37, 49,
      55, 56, 57, 64, 65, 66,
      72, 75, 76, 77, 79, 80,
      81, 83, 84, 113, 149,
      186, 192, 197, 205–210,
      212, 217, 221–224
Rhee, Syngman, 23
Roh Tae-woo, 23

S
Saboon, 124, 126, 127–130,
      131, 133, 138
Samsung Capital, 49, 62
Samsung Card, 49, 62,
      65, 240
Samsung Chemicals, 59
Samsung Construction, 94
Samsung Display Devices,
      59, 61, 65
Samsung Electro-Mechanics,
      27, 58, 59, 61, 65
Samsung Electronics, 1–3,
      4, 5, 6, 7, 8, 13, 14, 15,

19, 20, 21, 22, 23, 24,
    25, 26, 27, 28, 30, 31,
    32, 33, 34, 35, 36, 37,
    38, 39, 40, 41, 42, 43,
    44, 48, 49, 53, 55, 56,
    57, 58, 59, 60, 61, 62,
    63, 64, 65, 66, 67, 68,
    71, 83, 85, 87, 90, 93,
    94, 95, 96, 97, 99, 100,
    101, 102, 105, 107,
    108, 109, 111, 112,
    113, 114, 115, 116,
    117, 118, 121, 122,
    123, 124, 125, 127,
    128, 129, 131, 132,
    133, 134, 136, 138,
    141, 144, 146, 147,
    149, 162, 163, 165,
    169, 173, 182, 183,
    186, 187, 189, 190,
    191, 192, 193, 194,
    195, 197, 201, 203,
    206, 209, 210, 212,
    213, 214, 215, 216,
    217, 222, 223, 224,
    226, 227, 228, 229,
    230, 231, 232, 233,
    234, 235, 240
Samsung Electronics
    Corporation (SEC),
    5, 22, 30, 123, 230,
    239, 240
Samsung Fire and Marine
    Insurance, 59, 61
Samsung Heavy Industries,
    52, 59, 61
Samsung Man, 95, 110,
    121–149, 160, 188,
    191, 215
Samsung Motor
    Company, 30
Samsung Trading
    Company, 50
Samsung Watch, 57, 58
SanDisk, 224, 225, 226, 232
Sanduski, Jim, 99, 100, 113
Sanyo, 17, 19, 74, 160,
    174, 175
Sears, 39, 67
Second World War, 18,
    47, 226

Semiconductor transistor, 20
Semiconductors, 20, 21, 22,
    23, 24, 27–28, 36, 37,
    42, 44, 53, 61, 65, 139,
    158, 165, 172, 173,
    176, 177, 178, 179,
    180, 181, 182, 183,
    189, 190, 192, 193,
    194, 202, 203, 206,
    207, 209, 210, 211,
    213, 214, 215, 226, 227
    16MB DRAM, 23
    1MB DRAM, 23
    4MB DRAM, 23
    64MB DRAM, 23
    256K DRAM, 23
    64KB DRAM, 23
Seoul National University,
    26, 213
Shinsaegae, 53
Signetics, 17
SK, 30, 48, 52, 60, 129, 130
Slater, Robert, 26
Solar-cell, 231
Sony, 1, 2, 3, 4, 5, 13, 14,
    15, 16, 17, 25, 33, 35,
    38–41, 42, 48, 71–90,
    96, 97, 101–107, 113,
    118, 125, 131, 149,
    152, 156, 158–161,
    164, 167, 168, 169,
    170, 171, 172, 173,
    174, 175, 178, 181,
    197, 202, 204, 210,
    211, 212, 213, 216,
    224, 233, 234, 235, 239
Sports marketing, 112,
    114–117, 228
Sprint PCS, 35
Stiglitz, Joseph, 31
Stock Keeping Units
    (SKUs), 210
Straits Times, The, 31
Strategic market
    development, 98
Stringer, Howard, 41, 72,
    82, 83, 88
Student revolution, 51
Super- motivation, 146
Supply-chain management
    (SCM), 135

Suwon, 5, 21, 22, 117, 145,
    188, 190, 191, 192, 193,
    209, 211, 215, 216, 218

T
Taiwan, 29, 167, 171
Tantus, 93
Target, 39
Tax evasion, 68, 222
Three Diamonds, 19
Three Stars, 18, 51, 68
Time Division Multiple
    Access (TDMA), 152
Tokyo Declaration, 23,
    53, 54
Toshiba, 17, 74, 158, 160,
    169, 174, 225, 226
Toyota, 19
Trinitron, 83

U
U-health services, 231
Universal Studios, 75

V
Velloor, Ravi, 31, 33
Victor, 17

W
Wal-Mart, 39
Walkman, 14, 73–74, 83,
    151–153, 156
Ward, Andrew, 36
Waseda University, 19, 50
Weedfald, Peter, 99, 107,
    113, 158
Welch, Jack, 1, 3, 6, 8, 9, 11,
    12, 25, 26, 42, 55, 121,
    138, 148, 186, 232
Whistleblower, 68
Wireless communications
    equipment, 35
Wiseview, 93
World Bank, 31

Y
Yepp, 93, 103
Yun Jong-yong, 5, 25, 45,
    55, 116, 125, 132,
    218, 222